THE LIBRARY OF ROBERT HOOKE
The Scientific Book Trade
of
Restoration England

Other Books
By LEONA ROSTENBERG

English Publishers in the Graphic Arts, 1599-1700
Literary, Political, Scientific, Religious & Legal Publishing, Printing &
Bookselling in England, 1551-1700
The Minority Press & The English Crown: A Study in Repression, 1558-
1625
Bibliately: The History of Books on Postage Stamps

By LEONA ROSTENBERG & MADELEINE B. STERN

Between Boards: New Thoughts on Old Books
Bookman's Quintet: Five Catalogues about Books
Old & Rare: Forty Years in the Book Business

THE LIBRARY OF ROBERT HOOKE
The Scientific Book Trade
of
Restoration England

LEONA ROSTENBERG

MODOC PRESS, INC.
SANTA MONICA, CALIFORNIA

For

MADELEINE B. STERN

who makes all good possible

Acknowledgments

Among the rich sources for the social, political, and literary life of Restoration England are the diaries of the solemn aristocrat Sir John Evelyn and the rich journals of the garrulous Samuel Pepys. Their evocation of the period is further enlivened by several published diaries and journals of the "sharp, sagacious" Robert Hooke, their fellow member of the Royal Society and one of the greatest scientists of their own and succeeding generations.

Hooke's diaries are complemented by a work published after his death – the auction catalogue of his library. Because he drew to my attention that slim octavo entitled *Bibliotheca Hookiana.sive Catalogus Diversorum Librorum... Quos Doct. R. Hooke... sibi congessit*, I owe an enormous debt of gratitude to Dr. Dennes Rhodes, former Keeper of Western Books, The British Library. The *Bibliotheca Hookiana*, now reprinted for the first time, revealed another dimension of the great scientist: his manifold interests in the many facets of science, ancient and modern history, cartography, literature, political theory, economics, art and architecture. Through the kindness of A.W. Purvey, Photographic Division, The British Library, a microfilm of the auction catalogue was made and permission for reproduction granted. Through the cooperation of Elizabeth Rothe, former Curator, Department of Prints, The New York Public Library, positive plates were made from the microfilm.

My enthusiasm for Robert Hooke and the London book trade he knew so well resulted in my publication, over the years, of several articles in periodicals. To their publications committees and editors I render thanks for their encouragement as well as for permission to reprint or to publish revised and expanded versions of the originals: the late William A. Jackson, Houghton Library, Harvard University; Jacob L. Chernofsky, editor and publisher, *AB Bookman's Weekly*; Frank Paluka, editor, *Books at Iowa.*

My gratitude to Madeleine B. Stern remains limitless. I thank her as always for being my "severest critic." She survived the ordeal of reading manuscript and proofs, and with my perceptive, enthusiastic publisher William Burgess rejoices that Robert Hooke once again strolls the alleys of London and acquires the books he loved so deeply.

Contents

Preface

For a long time the reputation of Robert Hooke was occluded by the great shadow of Isaac Newton. Among the Newtonians of the eighteenth century, Hooke was thought to be no more than a glorified lens-grinder, and glorified principally by himself. This overshadowing of a great man by a greater dates back to the controversy, fostered by Henry Oldenburg, between Hooke and Newton following Newton's first paper on Light addressed to the Royal Society. But the antipathy between the two men, which prevented Newton from becoming President of the Royal Society until Hooke was dead, was clearly temperamental, and ran deeper than the controversy, a small rift that two men of more equable temperament might have surmounted. But now, following the work of Gunther and Andrade, and Espinasse's admirable biography (1956), Hooke has begun to merge from his shadow, and to achieve his rightful position as a genius whose talents encompassed architecture, physics and mechanics, an inventor of extraordinary fertility, and as a scientific writer: as Keynes puts it, "at least one of his books, the *Micrographia,* is among the most important books ever published in the history of science."

Hooke was, arguably, the prototype or ideal founding member of the Royal Society, and as its "Curator of Experiments" exercised a life-long influence on the Society. His own intellectual development therefore demands study, not just for itself, but for the ideas that he communicated to others. Of all this, the best mirror is the books that he bought and read. Books were more than tools but a source of inspiration to Hooke. Buying books, lending and borrowing books, are constant topics of his *Diary.* These passages have a thoroughly modern ring to them: we feel we recognize an attitude to books exactly like our own. One must beware of this, but Hooke was ahead of his time as a scientist in recognizing the importance of books both as sources of information and stimulus.

Miss Rostenberg has studied Hooke's book-buying, owning, borrowing and lending in considerable detail. She has related this to his principal sources of supply, from John Martyn, the Royal Society's "Printer", to the bookstalls in Duck Lane and Moorfield's that Hooke frequented. She has noted his interest in book auctions, a novelty in his time, and the problems involved in importing books. Finally, she has worked through *Bibliotheca Hookiana,* the catalogue of Hooke's library when it was sold by auction after his death. The list of books thus identified is the raw material for a history of Hooke's reading and intellectual history.

I do not think that more need be said to justify such a study. Hooke's importance is now sufficiently established. To know what books he owned is to possess a window, such as no other source will provide, on his mind and character, complex, withdrawn, yet gregarious and infinitely inventive—in a word (and such a word as his contemporaries would have used) "ingenious."

NICOLAS BARKER

Introduction

A library developed over the years by an astute collector becomes an index to the owner's personality and the age in which he lived. It reflects specialized or multiple interests, curiosity and intellectual attainment. It likewise mirrors the period in which his holdings were assembled, its book people, dealers and associations. The great scientist Robert Hooke—hitherto neglected as a book collector—was one of the outstanding virtuosi of the Restoration, the master of numerous experiments in pure and applied science, medicine and the arts. His period of activity coincides with the florescence of the scientific advances in England which produced other giants, Newton, Boyle, Wren, Wallis and their fellow academicians, members of the recently established Royal Society of which Hooke was a corporate member.

Hooke was a professional scientist, the author of *Micrographia,* an early investigation into microscopy regarded by Sir Geoffrey Keynes as one of the most significant books published in the history of science. He was a notable astronomer and from childhood a devotee of mechanics which he regarded as "his first and last Mistress." Following the disastrous Fire of London, 1666, he was appointed one of the city surveyors and after taking sights and views Robert Hooke indulged his passion for books, dropping in at the shops of those book dealers whose premises had escaped the conflagration. He was Curator of Experiments of the Royal Society; for a brief period its secretary; editor of the *Philosophical Transactions;* Cutlerian Lecturer; Professor of Geometry at Gresham College. In 1691 he was awarded an M.D. degree for his many experiments in physiology and respiration.

Hooke had certainly begun amassing his splendid collection before the Fire. The story of the development of the Library can to a large extent be gleaned from his Diaries which cover the better part of the last quarter of the seventeenth century. From their pages emerges the collector-scientist, ever bent on the purchase of a variety of texts in mathematics, astronomy, mechanics, medicine, art, travel and discovery—his lank, dark hair draped over his shoulders, his clear hazel eyes intent upon an early edition of his favorite author Euclid, a relation of the New World, the first edition of Leonardo da Vinci, *Trattato delle Pitture* or treatises of Galileo and Kepler. These and others filled the book shelves which he constantly "rangd" and rearranged.

Hooke died intestate in March 1702/03.* His library which consisted of 3,380 items at the time, originally certainly larger—some books having been given away, lent, stolen or lost—was purchased by the London bookseller Richard Smith who arranged for its disposal at auction on 29 April 1703 at the Inner Walk in Exeter Exchange in the Strand.

Smith entitled the auction catalogue *Bibliotheca Hookiana* which, corresponding to the prevailing mode, was arranged in different sections according to format. A glance at the *Bibliotheca Hookiana* reveals a dull, pedestrian listing of some extremely rare and desirable items cited according to author, title and imprint. The brief entries—often incorrect—conceal the significance of Hooke's treasures, his remarkable selectivity and taste in books. Smith's catalogue is, however, invested with a new aura, a tremendous excitement when the titles are identified as those books hunted by the Curator of Experiments in the West End, the jammed purlieus of Duck Lane and Moorfields, the shops of small dealers scattered about the city in Fleet Ditch, Bunhill, Fish Street Hill, and Shoo Lane. The *Bibliotheca Hookiana* emerges with a bibliophilic radiance, a glowing testimony to the remarkable mind, the curiosity of this outstanding scientist and collector!

Over half of the Hooke Library consists of scientific texts many of which served the owner's professional needs. Others were purchased to satisfy Hooke's inquisitiveness, his mental agility. In

---

* The date 1702/03 reflects the discrepancy in historical dates due to the adoption of the Gregorian calendar by Great Britain in 1752. Two dates are often given for clarification throughout the following chapters.

addition to *materia scientifica* the Library includes Bibles, patristica, English and foreign belles-lettres and a small collection of philological texts, testimony to Hooke's eagerness to dig and unravel. The Hooke Collection cannot be considered chic or sumptuous in fine bindings such as are associated with the libraries of Evelyn and Pepys.

To the arrangement of his books Hooke applied the latest scientific methodology based upon his readings in the library manuals of Durie, Evelyn, Le Gallois, and Naudé. He owned bibliographies and printing histories. He was a close friend of the master of printing techniques Joseph Moxon and his shelves boasted a copy of his *Mechanic Exercises.* Truly a sophisticated collector, Hooke amassed the catalogues of dealers and auctioneers, realizing the value of such staple material for future comparative shopping.

All libraries reflect the influence of the bookselling media, the dealer in modern firsts or the antiquarian bookseller pursuing those texts of the past, the landmarks which influenced man's thought and behavior. As Robert Hooke scouted London for his books in the sciences a little-known array of book dealers and scouts emerges—agents who assisted the scientist in the growth of his collection. Hooke was no snob collector but there is no doubt that his favorite book dealer was John Martyn of the Bell, St. Paul's Churchyard, "Printer to the Royal Society." It is only natural that Hooke should have sought out the premises of Martyn whose shelves were so well stocked with English and foreign scientific texts—some published by the owner, including two editions of the collector's *Micrographia* and works by members of the Royal Society. Here Hooke browsed, purchased "on approval," returned books, chatted with friends and generally regarded the Bell as his personal rendezvous. He frequently visited the Angel, the quarters of Moses Pitt, who published and sold scientific texts and secured the collector's assistance for the arrangement of his ill-fated *English Atlas.* Among Hooke's most joyous book rambles were his forays into the jumbled shops of Duck Lane and Moorfields. Here he hoped for a sleeper and if not certainly a bargain!

Hooke's numerous visits to the London bookshops provide a broad view of Restoration bookselling: its gamut of dealers, location of shops, patrons, apprentices and assistants, warehouses, the circulation of texts and foreign imports. Books crossed the

Channel and the stormy passage of the North Atlantic through a chain of porters and carriers, the Royal Mail Service, foreign factors, members of the diplomatic corps and travelers. Despite the hazard of elements, the threat of shipwreck, the fear of pirates, books became a strong link between the continent and England cementing the intellectual world through works detailing observation and inquiry.

Entries in Hooke's Diaries afford rich details upon the innovation of the sale of books at public auction: his attendance at the "rooms" of Millington and Hussey, his enthusiasm, the works he obtained, prices. In his crabbed hand the scientist has left a memorandum of auctions held within the city and the outskirts from August 1686 to August 1689. On one day the Curator of Experiments bagged at the Pitt Sale of December 1678 twenty-eight books for £9.19.9. Today's auction catalogue can trace its antecedent to its progenitor of 1676. The Conditions of Sale established by William Cooper, Millington and Hussey have become almost traditional—the terms of today's auction catalogue differing but little. The problems which beset the current auction house are not dissimilar to those which confronted the "quick witted" Millington over 300 years ago.

The Hooke Library resulted largely from the new publication of scientific texts in England and the continent, from the holdings of antiquarian specialists. The Library was achieved through Hooke's intensive buying program, his awareness of new English and foreign books announced in the New Books Section of the *Philosophical Transactions* and through the help of friends, notably Dr. Theodore Diodati, who was a fairly regular visitor to Paris. The Hooke Library covers the major scientific disciplines: mathematics, astronomy, physics, medicine, natural history, botany, exploration, travel. It covers the contributions of contemporary and past greats: Boyle, Descartes, Pascal, Kepler, Kircher, Copernicus, Tycho Brahe, Euclid, Archimedes, Ptolemy. Its books on history and travel extend from the Old World to the New and most distinguished among those from distant New England are *The New Testament*, translated by John Eliot into the Indian language and Eliot's *The Indian Grammar*. Other rarities relate to New France, the Caribbean, and the South Seas.

Robert Hooke was a genuine passionate book collector embodying many of the attributes of the dedicated bibliophile. He retained an undiminished joy in the search of books, a loyalty to his dealers who in turn pampered his bookish whims, his little pleasures, appreciated his vast erudition, his eagerness to buy. The Hooke Library not only reflects its owner's continued joy in books but also revivifies the London book world: its dealers, stocks, foreign associations, the vibrance of the auction "rooms." Throughout the shops in the West End, the stalls and "railes" close to London wall, Robert Hooke "low of stature, pale and lean, of hazel eyes stooping" but of a quick shambling gait stalks his quarry searching and questing. And so he acquired those books which were to form the library of one of the greatest virtuosi of the English Restoration.

PART I

THE SCIENTIFIC BOOK TRADE
OF RESTORATION ENGLAND

THE BACKGROUND

1

Robert Hooke, F.R.S.

On 13 December 1660 Henry Oldenburg, German by birth, resident of London and intimate of a distinguished group of English scientists, wrote to the Amsterdam scholar Adam Boreel: "Dr. Wilkins lingers here in this city; he has been made Dean of York and elected President of the new English Academy very recently founded here under the patronage of the king for the advancement of the sciences. It is comprised of extremely learned men, remarkably well versed in mathematics and experimental science."[1]

This group of "extremely learned men"—the original Fellows of the Royal Society—had met at Oxford transferring their meetings in 1658 to London.

According to the Society's first historian, Bishop Sprat, its purpose was "in short to make faithful Records of all the Works of Nature, or Art, which can come within their Reach: that so the present Age and Posterity, may be able to put a Mark on the Errors which have been strengthened by long Prescription; . . . to restore the Truths, that have been neglected." Men of different countries, professions and faiths were elected to membership and admitted to the meetings at Gresham College, "for they openly profess, not to lay the Foundations of an English, Scotch, Irish, Popish or Protestant philosophy but a Philosophy of Mankind."[2]

The French traveler Samuel Sorbière expressed his amazement at the orderliness of the Society's meetings. At Gresham College they gathered in a "large wainscoated room" with a large table covered with a gray cloth and "two rows of wooden benches to leap on, the first being higher than the other to form an amphitheatre. The President is seated in an armchair placed in the middle of the table, his back to the fireplace, the secretary at his left. Each member had paper and an inkhorn. The Fellows address their Discourse to the President bare-headed, till he makes a Sign for them to put on their Hats. He is never interrupted that speaks and Differences of Opinion cause no Manner of Resentment."[3]

A charter was issued in 1662 by Charles II to the Royal Society which at that time included ninety-eight members among them the foremost names in English science: Robert Boyle, the mathematicians John Wallis and Isaac Barrow, the architect Christopher Wren, Samuel Pepys, Commissioner of the Navy, and Robert Hooke who eclipsed his fellow academicians in versatility and ingenuity.

Sorbière enthusiastically discussed the aims of the Society: "The building of a solid philosophy on basis of observations and experiments made with as great exactness as is possible." The Society was to consist of "the most learned and exact philosophers ... to revise, perform, and record all kinds of experiments."[4]

Sponsoring Martin Lister for membership, Oldenburg outlined to him his responsibilities if elected: "1. to contribute what you can, to ye end of yt institution. 2. to give, for ye defraying of Experiments etc. one shill. per week, or 13sh. a quarter." If elected he was required to pay an "admission money" of 40 shillings.[5]

The ranks of the Society swelled not only with English members but also with distinguished foreign scientists: the Dutch physicist Christian Huygens, the Italian physiologist Marcello Malpighi, the French and German astronomers Adrien Auzout and Johann Hevelius, and many others.

Oldenburg's voluminous correspondence reflects the Society's repute, its proselytizing campaign, and the work of its members as well as the great outpouring of books explaining a multitude of scientific theories and inventions.

Association with the Society was certainly a badge of distinction. Planning to study abroad, Samuel Colepresse of Plymouth, a friend of Boyle, requested from the President and the Council "a line, or two in ye nature of a Lettr Recommendatorie under your Common Seale onlie pro forma wch perchance may gaine me Easier admission in to a forreigne Publicke Librarie."[6]

As Secretary, Oldenburg strove to arouse the enthusiasm of distant scholars. To Richard Norwood in "ye Bermudas" he dispatched a copy of Sprat's *History of the Royal Society* in the hope that "the English Plantations in America and everywhere else, when they shall know ... the work of the Institution ... will emulate the same method everywhere." The good Secretary's hope for the pursuit of physics and mathematics in the wilds of North America was dashed since John Winthrop advised him that "here are few in these colonies worth the Notice of the Royal Society."[7]

John Dodington, English Resident in Venice, was frequently advised of the experiments of the London academicians. Oldenburg requested that he "acquaint the Philosophers you converse with in those parts, that ye R.S. still persists in prosecuting experimentall studyes. You may adde, that severall good books of Mathematicks and Physics have lately been published by divers members of the R.S., viz. the 2nd part of Mr. Boyles usefulnesse of experimental Philosophy, as also the Introduction into the History of particular qualities ... Item ye 2d part of Dr Wallis's work de Motu et Mechanica ... Dr. Barrows Lectiones Geometricae. Item Dr. Lower de Catarrhis."[8]

Oldenburg's desire that the work of the Society be emulated was partially gratified. Although a German society, the Collegium Naturae Curiosum, had predated the Royal Society, it was reorganized in 1670 to vie with the English Society. In a letter of 1 October 1670 Dr. Philipp Jacob Sachs à Loewenhaimb commented that the German scientists had been "stirred by the inimitable sample of the illustrious English Royal Society" and were "endeavouring to follow the same track, though with uncertain steps. We have no doubt that our first efforts to borrowing certain things from the work of the English will be welcome to your illustrious Royal Society, since in that way the fame of the Fellows of that Royal Academy is spread further abroad."[9]

The wish of the Fellows to endorse only the best continental scientific journals is evident in a 1672 inquiry of John Beale questioning whether the Venetian journals were published weekly or monthly. "Are they strong enough in Sweden and Denmarke for a Journall? They would thinke of it in Leyden or Amsterdam, if they were not so much enthralld to their god Mammon. Wt think yu of Portugall? In Spaine the Monckes are too dull, & ye Nobles illiterate."[10]

Henry Oldenburg's domestic and foreign correspondents were familiar with the work of the members in general, and with the manifold scientific investigations of its Curator of Experiments,

3

Robert Hooke, in particular. His comprehension of all branches of science, his inventiveness and curiosity, his accomplishments establish him as one of the greatest of all English scientists.

The versatility of this future Curator of Experiments extended to mathematics, physics, chemistry, medicine, zoology, mechanics, technology, engineering, surveying, art and architecture, astronomy, cartography, and the prevailing abracadabra of his age. Before Newton, Hooke defined the true doctrine of universal gravitation but lacked the final mathematical ability to demonstrate his theory. He offered his concept of evolution; he conceived thirty ways of flying; he designed a practicable system of telegraphy. Among his inventions he produced an odometer and an acousticon, an aid to hearing. His *Micrographia* is one of the foremost treatises on microscopical observation including a description of the invention of the compound telescope. His profusion of inventions and experiments aroused the curiosity and admiration of the monarch Charles II whose propensity for science is well-known. Walking in the park with Sir Christopher Wren, Hooke met the King who, as recorded in his Diary of 6 October 1675, "calld me to him bid me to shew him experiment. Followd him through tennis court garden etc into closet. Shewd the experiment of springs. He was very well pleasd. Recommended to me the business of shipping."[11]

Hooke's Diaries reflect the personality and manifold interests of this man of genius. Although the entries are laconic, seldom indited with rhapsodic prose, they indicate that Hooke was not just a towering scientist bent solely upon research and invention, observation and experiment, but also a man who enjoyed the amenities and diversions of his age: its society, its food, its luminaries. He was a frequent habitué of the London taverns—the Bear, Childs in Exchange Alley, the Crowne, the Grecian coffeehouse, the Queens Head. He dined frequently with Boyle, Wren, Sir John Hoskins, President of the Royal Society. He attended the music house; walked with Lords Sarum and Delamere in St. James's park where he paused to chat with the Duke of York. Although he constantly complained of a variety of ailments, from a gaseous gut to a whirling head, he consumed countless cups of chocolate. He attended the theatre with Wren, paying three shillings for a performance of *The Tempest,* later viewing a production of *Antony and Cleopatra.* He passed part of an afternoon at St. Bartholomew's Fair where he saw "a fellow walk on stilts 12 feet high." He noted that the bells of London rang until 3 A.M. after the coronation of William and Mary. With his fellow academicians he discussed the Northwest Passage, flying, California, and the river Gambia. He attempted to use "a pair of China eating sticks." He punctually attended the Monday meetings of the Royal Society where he faithfully pursued his role as Curator of Experiments. As Surveyor of London, he helped rebuild the fire-stricken metropolis. In his free time this most erudite, gregarious, occasionally cantankerous scientist searched the London book-shops and amassed a most impressive collection which reflects the depth of inquiry, the fertility of his remarkable mind.

Born at Freshwater, a peninsula on the west side of the Isle of Wight, 13 July 1635, young Hooke is described by his future biographer Richard Waller as "very infirm and weakly, very weak to any robust exercise." Left to his own devices, the child developed interests which he was to pursue throughout his lifetime. Applying himself to mechanics which he later described as "his first and last Mistress," he made little mechanical toys "there being nothing he saw done by any Mechanick, but he endeavoured to imitate and in some particulars could exceed."[12]

His future close friend, the antiquary John Aubrey, declared that after the painter John Hoskyns had visited the Hooke home, the boy Robert strove to imitate him "getting his chalke and Ruddle, and coles and grinds them . . . and to worke he went and made a picture." Appreciating his son's talent, his father sent him to London, where he was apprenticed to the artist Sir Peter Lely and the miniaturist Samuel Cooper. He remained with Lely for only a short time. Manifesting early symptoms of his future hypochondria, he complained that the smell of paint made him giddy.[13]

His artistic career cut short, Hooke embarked upon academic pursuits entering Westminster School under the administration of Dr. Richard Busby who introduced him to the delights of mathematics—notably geometry. According to Waller, Hooke mastered the first six books of Euclid within a week. There is little doubt that he venerated the great geometer, since his library included 27 editions of his writings. At the same time Hooke was absorbed in various aspects of "his first and last Mistress Mechanicks."

Hooke's life changed radically when in 1653 he entered Christ Church, Oxford. There he became acquainted with its leading scientists, the mathematician John Wallis, the chemist Thomas Willis, and the Savilian Professor of Astronomy Seth Ward. In time Willis introduced the young scholar to the most eminent English scientist of the day—Robert Boyle—who, shortly thereafter, engaged the twenty-year-old student as an assistant for his chemical experiments.

During his Oxford stay Hooke undertook a variety of experiments which included over 30 models for flying, some of which he had already begun at Westminster School. He improved the balance wheel for watches, time recording instruments, and methods for determining longitude at sea. In 1661 his first publication appeared at London: *An Attempt for the explication of the phaenomena observable in the XXV experiment of the Honourable Robert Boyle touching the aire.*[14]

After the establishment of the Royal Society in London, Hooke was appointed Curator of Experiments. "It was found necessary to hand over the business of experimenting to one particular person who should have various kinds of responsibility, sometimes assisting others with their experiments, sometimes making experiments proposed by others, sometimes producing an experiment of his own." It was to this Curatorship of Experiments that Hooke was appointed on 12 November 1662.[15]

His role as Curator was busy, arduous and resourceful, ever seeking new experiments for the members gathered at the Society's meetings. According to Birch, Hooke was "ordered to bring in two or three good experiments at the next meeting" and after three experiments had already been designated for the following week "Mr. Hooke was desired to think upon one or two experiments more." Anticipating the probable visit of the King during the summer of 1663 to the Society, Hooke was responsible for four experiments and five scientific instruments (ranging from the hygroscope to the artificial eye) "besides his own microscopical observations written in a handsome book to be provided by him for that purpose."[16]

The papers submitted by Hooke to the Society's greatest scientific achievement, the *Philosophical Transactions,* range from the "Rarefaction of Aire," an "Analysis of the Chinese tongue," the "Seeds of Moss," "Telegraphy," "Petrified Wood," "Vipers Teeth," the "Suspension of Falling Bodies," the "Variation of Gravity," and a variety of miscellaneous subjects.

Hooke's income was further increased by his appointment as Cutlerian lecturer. In 1664 Sir John Cutler, a former Warden of the Grocers Company, established a series of lectures which were to be delivered by Hooke at a stipend of £50 per annum. The Society, appreciating this distinction bestowed upon Hooke, elected Sir John an honorary member, "voting solemn thanks for this singular favor." Two years later Hooke was designated Professor of Geometry at Gresham College.[17]

As a result of his numerous experiments, lectures, and absorption with microscopy, Hooke in 1665 published his greatest work. The *Micrographia,* regarded by Sir Geoffrey Keynes as one of the most significant texts in the history of science, enjoyed an immediate success.

Referring to the book shortly after publication, Pepys wrote: "Hence to my booksellers and at the binders saw Hooke's book of the Microscope which is so pretty that I presently bespoke it." Once home he regarded it as "a most excellent piece, of whiche I am very proud. Before I went to bed I sat up till two o'clock in my chamber reading Mr. Hooke's microscopic observations, the most ingenious book I ever read in my life."[18]

Hooke's text continued to cause excitement at home and abroad. The Durham schoolmaster Peter Nelson declared: "I long to see the performance of what Mr. Hook has put us in hopes of his Micrographia, a Discourse to admiration pleasant & ingenious. That clear sighted Gentleman, with his glazen Eyes, hath discovered excellent things, both in ye Earth & heavens, especially in ye moon, and if there be a Way thither, I know not from whom we may best expect ye Invention, than from so Acute a Discerner."[19]

Impatiently Henri Justel, secretary to Louis XIV, inquired of Oldenburg whether a Latin edition of the *Micrographia* had been published. "If your booksellers do not wish to do it it will be done in Holland. It deserves to be done." Justel's hopes remained unfulfilled, since no Latin edition of *Micrographia* appeared.[20]

Hooke retained his Curatorship of Experiments until his death in March 1702/03. "Stricken speechless and senseless," Oldenburg had died on 5 September 1677 and Hooke succeeded him as

Secretary until 1682. Of this appointment he noted in his Diary, 13 September 1677: "To Councell at the Repository they accepted me for the Secretary pro tempore to write the Journalls without reward."[21]

As Curator of Experiments, Hooke naturally had been in close contact with Oldenburg for whom—their ethnic backgrounds opposed, their temperaments clashing—he expressed little affection. To Hooke, Oldenburg was "a strange Dutchman . . . on occasion treacherous and a villain." He was further berated by his English colleague as a "raskall" and "a Lying Dog" for not registering things brought into the Society. Shortly before Oldenburg's death Hooke rather smugly noted that the harassed Oldenburg had "fled at his sight."[22]

Despite such animosities, the correspondence of Oldenburg, like that of Hooke's fellow academicians, refers to Hooke's energy and productivity. "He is now busy about his pocket watches . . . and his new-fashioned chariot which our President [Lord Brouncker], who went in it from London to Col. Blunts house, finds not unexceptionalle," wrote Oldenburg to Boyle in January 1665/66. The Danzig astronomer Hevelius repeatedly inquired whether Oldenburg could not prevail upon Hooke to assist in "the design of a very long telescope for making celestial observations." Impatiently he sought "the knowledge and advice of Mr. Hooke, who is so very experienced in that art." From Paris the scientist Father Pardies wrote that he was aware of Hooke's "fine experiments on the refraction of different fluids," while at home his fellow academician Sir Robert Moray declared that although Hooke had absented himself from London during the height of the Plague he had not been idle. Sir Robert, however, was somewhat critical of Hooke, wishing that he would complete his many projects "rather than to learn a dozen trades, though I do much approve of time spent that way too."[23]

Among Hooke's "dozen trades" was his preoccupation with art, architecture, and printing techniques. Diary jottings allude to the purchase of paintings, prints, and drawing materials. Attracted to varied artistic endeavors, Hooke frequently visited the gilder, dyer, stainer, and quasi-book dealer Philip Barret in Moorfields. Hooke was particularly interested in this gentleman's numerous experiments in applied art, admiring his "varnish as very fine." Upon another occasion he "saw new stuff at Barrets and new printers Black." During a visit of 11 March 1673/74 he attempted "gilding flowerd shifts" which he noted "succeded." From Barret he purchased a map and admired his quadruple printing.[24]

Several Diary entries refer to his acquaintanceship with well-known London artists. A 1672 meeting with "Will Peak" doubtless refers to William Peake, member of the distinguished London art- and print-selling family whose apprentice William Faithorne the Elder later became associated with Peake in trade. William Faithorne at the sign of ye Drake without Temple Barr was one of Hooke's close friends in the London art world. Author of *The Art of Graveing and Etching,* Faithorne ranks as the most distinguished line engraver of portraits of the period, comparing favorably with Nantueil. Hooke visited ye Drake on numerous occasions. "Saw Mr. Faithorne and traced figure with Black lead on white waxen plate." With him he passed time at the various coffee-houses and at the shop purchased a copy of Felibien, *Des Principes de l'Architecture,* a set of Lombard's heads at 2sh.[25]

On 27 December 1675 Hooke visited his old master Sir Peter Lely. "Discoursed of helping the sight and of picture box. Drank rare and heady wine." Hooke mentions time passed at Bow's coffee-house with the Holstein-born sculptor Caius Gabriel Cibber. On 16 December 1674 the artist presented Hooke with a picture and together they visited the Lord Mayor.[26]

With his friend, the cartographer and engraver John Ogilby, Hooke visited the Czech artist Wenceslaus Hollar who gave the scientist an engraving of his Tangier Prospect. In 1678 Hooke purchased "Hollers 12 woemen 6d." In all likelihood the Curator of Experiments had acquired Hollar's exquisite suite "Ornatus Muliebris Anglicanae" consisting of 12 plates of attractively dressed English ladies.[27]

Upon another occasion he commented that the engraver William Dole showed him a plate of "his doing in mezzotinto. I thought it had been in Sr. Ch. Wren's way." Hooke had learned a trick in the new method of mezzotint. With Ogilby at Garaway's coffee-house he observed the cartographer's skill in "shadowing." In discussing print technique Hooke refers to the method of applying "red chalke" to the surface. Diary entries refer to his making of etching varnish.[28]

From an upholsterer in Lothbury he purchased "landskapes" and from Pepys's stationer John Cade of the Royal Exchange the scientist bought "2 quires of French paper at 5sh. pastboards for 7s.6d." Prowling through Moorfields, he picked up engravings by Le Pautre and Della Bella and at the shop of Richard Thompson he acquired 26 views executed by the Dutch artist Israel at 5sh.6d.[29]

At the premises of the printer and typefounder Joseph Moxon, Hooke discussed with the owner type and letter design, "cutting borders letters and for Roman press in copper." On 31 December 1677 he spent the afternoon with Moxon who read to him his "first monthly exercise of smithery and preface in order to license"—the first installment of his celebrated *Mechanick Exercises.* At Child's coffee-house, in the company of the bookseller Moses Pitt, Hooke explained his contrivance for printing books. To the president of the Royal Society he confided his design of tin-plates for rolling presses "and my method for printing books." Noting his home invaded by his growing collection, Hooke decided in January 1679/ 80 to remove the press from his parlor.[30]

It is not at all surprising that Hooke, a devotee of the arts, was appointed a member of the commission designated to rebuild London after the disastrous fire of September 1666. This dreadful calamity had consumed 12,000 houses, at least 80 churches, twenty-four of the Company halls, among them that of the Stationers guild. An ordinance, issued in October 1666 by the Lord Mayor, decreed that all foundations of all burnt houses "were to be cleared of ye rubbish within a fortnight, which done, Survey and Measurement of all such Foundations to be forthwith taken in hand, and yt by ye care and management of Mr. Wren and Mr. Hooke."[31]

As Surveyor of London Hooke was constantly afoot taking prospects, views, and sights. Even as late as 1690 Aubrey declared that the scientist was out nearly all the time "seldom within." His Diary entries record numerous visits to areas and edifices in need of repair or rebuilding. "To St. Martin's Church. Gave order for clearing of it; a view in Leadenhall; a sight inter Hinton and Taylor Sherbourne Lane [and] inter Grey and young fenchurch street." Hooke rebuilt the new Royal College of Physicians in Warwick Lane, Bedlam Hospital, Moorfields. A Diary reference of 22 October 1673 states: "at bridewell directed several alterations." The following Spring he viewed the sight for new Bedlam. "With Dr. Allen at Bedlam. Drew up report for him. At Bridewell. Agreed on module [model] made for Bedlam."[32]

Hooke's involvement with this work is described by Oldenburg: "Through recent months Mr. Hooke has been extremely busy in surveys for the rebuilding of this city; he is so occupied (with others) in the work of rebuilding this city that he can spare almost no time for other tasks. When that is done, he will revert to his study of color and other hidden qualities of nature."[33]

Bethlehem Hospital was located in Moorfields, a semi-rural area near Moor Gate, housing stalls, taverns, coffee-houses, and a variety of shops, some tenanted by booksellers, many of whom had suffered losses in the Fire. Hard on their luck, they had moved to this somewhat unfashionable location. Oldenburg's statement that Hooke "could spare no time for other tasks" is not quite accurate. In order to refresh himself after an arduous "sight taking" he dropped in at an ale house and frequently visited the bookshops and stalls of Moorfields. Here he found his friend the art dealer Robert Pricke, whose premises, the Golden Lion, were located at the corner of Cheapside Street next Bethlehem. From Pricke he acquired pencils as well as texts on foreign architecture. At the shop of William Birch he purchased a map delineating the seventeen provinces of the Netherlands and a copy of John Crowne's *Juliana*. Browsing in the Golden Fleece he picked up a copy of John Bulwar, *Pathomyotomia, or a dissection of the significative muscles of the minde*. At the Cross Daggers of Walter Hayes he found a few manuals essential for his current profession—surveying. It was also in Moorfields—to his great shock—that he found volumes lying exposed on the "railes" (boxes or outdoor stands) from the library of his late and revered friend Boyle.[34]

Hooke took sights in the better areas of the city—in the Strand and St. Paul's Churchyard where much damage had befallen the bookshops. A few resisted the flames; others were rebuilt. Hooke, the surveyor, found time to relax at the premises of such prominent dealers as John Martyn, Moses Pitt, Robert Scott, Robert Littlebury, and others. Here, too, he purchased many of the books which would form his notable collection. At any one of the shops Robert Hooke, well known and respected by the proprietor, could study a volume, his "glazen eyes" intent upon the text. Waller has left a scarcely flattering portrait of the physical appearance of the great scientist. "As to his Person he was despicable, being very crooked. This made him low of stature tho' by his Limbs he should have been moderately tall. He was always very pale & lean, and lately

11

nothing but skin and bones with a meagre aspect, his Eyes grey and full with a sharp sagacious Look whilst younger. He wore his own Hair of a dark brown colour very long and hanging neglected over his Face uncut and lank. He went stooping and very Fast, having but a light body to carry, and a great deal of spirits and activity especially in his youth."[35]

It is certain that Robert Hooke wore "a sharp sagacious Look" when he studied the folios and quartos of John Martyn of the Bell, his favorite bookseller. Hooke's dealings with Martyn resulted in the purchase of some of his major acquisitions. Of the specialist dealers who abetted the cause of science during the Restoration, Martyn remains in the foreground.

John Martyn, "Printer to the Royal Society"

It was at the Bell, the premises of the publisher and bookseller John Martyn, that Hooke purchased, charged, and returned books. It was here that he met his friends, and much as at a coffee-house or tavern, discussed with them matters of science or current events. Here he selected the most recent texts published and sold by Martyn, new editions of old books and foreign imports. The Bell was Hooke's favorite bookish rendezvous.

John Martyn was born ca. 1619, the son of a merchant-tailor, John Martyn of London. On 4 February 1634 he was apprenticed to one of the prominent metropolitan booksellers, Humphrey Robinson. At the conclusion of his eight-year stint in 1642 he was declared a freeman of the Stationers Company, having been sponsored by his former employer.[1]

From 1652 to 1670 the books emerging from the Bell bore the joint imprint of John Martyn and James Allestry. Although Oldenburg cared little for Allestry describing him as an "habituée of snuff," the partnership prospered.[2]

The reputation of the firm—notably that of Martyn, since Allestry died in 1670—rests upon its publication and sale of scientific books, many of which introduced new ideas to the devotees of Restoration scholarship. During this period the partners issued in addition to Hooke's *Micrographia,* John Graunt, *Natural and Political Observations on the Bills of Mortality;* the various works of the Bolognese physiologist Marcello Malpighi; the medical observations of Thomas Willis; the new progressive ideas for rehabilitation of the deaf suggested in the *Elements of Speech* of William Holder; and other works of stature. The firm published an approximate 33 scientific books carrying also in stock numerous miscellaneous treatises published at home or imported from abroad. Their great scientific achievement, however, was the publication of the *Philosophical Transactions,* the official organ of the Royal Society, whose Council at a special meeting of 26 October had appointed John Martyn and James Allestry as "Printers to the Royal Society."[3]

According to the original charter granted to the Society in August 1662, the members were permitted "to elect, nominate and appoint one or more booksellers or printers who were to publish such matters and concerns pertinent to the Society." At a meeting of 26 October 1663 Bishop John Wilkins and Dr. Jonathan Goddard were appointed to draw up a statute for the duties of the printers of the Society. On the same day the President Lord Brouncker reported:

> Because the Stationers and Printers are one and the same Company and they . . . practice both trades promiscuously the Society might choose a stationer for their printer without any violation to their charter . . . whereupon Mr. John Martyn and Mr. James Allestry being recommended to the Society, it was put to the question whether the office of the printer to the Royal Society should be conferred on the said Mr. Martyn and Mr. Allestry jointly and it was carried in the affirmative after which, those two persons were put to the ballot, and chosen.[4]

The recommendation of Martyn and Allestry may be attributed to two possible factors. By 1663 the firm had prospered and its growing interest in the publication of scientific works had doubtless attracted the attention of many members of the Royal Society. It is quite possible that the authors they had published—Willis, Graunt, and Sir John Evelyn whose *Sylva* was to bear their imprint in 1664—promoted their candidacy. Although the partners had as yet not issued the first edition of Hooke's *Micrographia,* there is every reason to believe that the bibliophile Hooke was at this time a regular visitor to the Bell. From the later entries in his Diary he appears to have regarded the shop as having been established for his own bookish eccentricities. There he browsed almost daily; purchased considerable material 'on approval,' returned an almost equal amount; made outright purchases and settled his bill several weeks later, occasionally altering it to his own advantage. Martyn appears to have indulged his customer's not uncommon or unfamiliar bibliophilic idiosyncrasies and in return the pampered customer, perhaps, promoted the appointment of his long-suffering booksellers as "Printers to the Society."[5]

By 2 November the printers' commission had been completed:

> We give and grant unto the said John Martyn and James Allestry full power and privillidge to print all such matters and business concerning the Royal Society as shall be committed unto them by the President and Council of the said Society or any seven more of them. And we do fvrther give and grant vnto the said John Martyn and James Allestry that no other person (except any duly chosen and sworn as aforesaid) shall print any of the said things, matters and businesses concerning the Royal Society.[6]

At a meeting the following week Martyn and Allestry presented themselves before the Society, where the statutes of their duties were read to them. They were afforded the opportunity of considering their honored appointment and "upon consideration having no exception to anything contained in the said commission and statutes they were sworn printers to the Society."[7]

In their official capacity Martyn and Allestry were "to print and vend such books besides catalogues and such other things as committed to them by order of the Society or Council." The partners were to abide by suggestions from the Council as to "the correctness of the edition, the number of copies printed, the form or volume, the goodness of the paper, character, figures and diagrams, the price at which books are to be sold." They were not permitted to issue any reprint, translation or digest unless approved by the Council. They were compelled to present:

> Of every book printed two copies extraordinary well bound to his Majesty and one copy to Edward Earl of Clarendon, Lord Chancellor, one copy to the President of the Royal Society, two copies to the library of the said Society, each of them fairly bound and one copy more to each of the Secretarys of the said Society.[8]

Designated as "Printers to the Royal Society," Martyn and Allestry together or alone published 16 books by members relating to exact and natural science. In addition to the aforementioned authors, these included works by Walter Charleton, Thomas Sprat, John Wilkins, Jeremiah Horrocks, John Wallis, Francis Willughby, and others. Before any manuscript could be released for publication and include the Society's imprimatur, it was examined by two Fellows who were to report "that such a book contains nothing but what is suitable to the design and work of the Society."[9]

The approved manuscript was forwarded to any one of the large London printing houses—Thomas Roycroft, John Macock, Thomas Newcomb, or William Godbid who was well supplied with plates of diagrams and mathematical configurations.[10]

An average edition consisted of 1,000 copies. In his preface to the second edition of *Sylva,* Evelyn stated that more than a thousand copies of the work had been sold in less than two years "which Book-Sellers assure us is a very extraordinary thing in volumes of this bulk." Graunt's *Natural and Political Observations* and Willughby's lavishly illustrated *Ornithologia* ran through three editions while Jerome Lobo's *A Short Relation of the Nile* and Hooke's *Micrographia* each enjoyed two editions.[11]

The popularity of these books may be attributed to their inherent value, the personal interest shown in them by fellow members, and the Bell's advertising program. Martyn took advantage of his position as "Printer to the Royal Society" and included in Number 36 of the *Philosophical Transactions* a four-page list entitled "Cataloge of some Books printed and sold by John Martyn." Although he listed books by several of the Society's members, his temerity in using the Society's official organ was scarcely appreciated by several members. The Society's "Printer" was severely castigated. John Beale criticized "ye Printer to the R.S. . . . a Rooke in chargeing us with a Lyst of such Bookes he would vend." Lambasting poor Oldenburg who had permitted the inclusion of the "Cataloge," he continued that "the loudest outcrye is against ye Printer who hath been made rich as he playes ye Mede, But we would have more Prudence, than to expose our reputation to the humour of such a sordid man."[12]

It is impossible to determine whether Martyn played the role of "ye Mede." The prices of the Royal Society texts ranged from one shilling to one pound, ten, depending upon whether the works were unbound, stitched, or bound. The most expensive volumes were Willughby, *Ornithologia,* fetching one pound, ten shillings and Malphigi, *Epitome Plantarum observationes,* bringing one pound. The high price of these two books was based upon the high cost of production, since both publications were lavishly illustrated. Malpighi's work had taken four years for the completion of both volumes.[13]

As "Printers to the Royal Society," Martyn and Allestry assumed their most responsible and exacting task, the publication of the *Philosophical Transactions,* the most important scientific journal of the time and certainly the longest-lived. Since this project was of such interest and scope it is essential that its beginnings and development be treated in its own chapter.[14]

Apparently the partners withstood the ravages of the Plague which hit London in June 1665 taking a toll of 80 stationers. They could not, however, resist the holocaust of the Fire which reached St. Paul's Churchyard. Having feared this possibility, the stationers identified their respective stocks and brought them for safe-keeping to the ancient parish church of St. Faith under St. Paul's. It was here at St. Faith, a four-aisled crypt, that the Stationers Company usually attended a service on Ash Wednesday and later retired to the Hall for "cakes, wine and ale." Evelyn declared that this ancient crypt had been filled with "magazines of books, belonging to the stationers, and carried thither for safety, they were all consumed burning for a weeke following." Within one day books valued at £150,000 had been destroyed. Pepys noted in his Diary that "all the great book-dealers are almost undone, not only these, but their warehouses at the Hall and under Christ Church and elsewhere being all burned."[15]

It was from John Martyn himself that Pepys had received an eye-witness account of the spread of the fire. Present when the flames reached St. Paul's, Martyn related that a board had been set afire, one which had been laid upon the roof instead of lead. "They took fire from the Drapers side, by some timber of the houses that were burned falling into the Church." According to Martyn, one warehouse of books had been saved despite contrary reports. It was his opinion that most of the booksellers planned to rebuild the following year, but at the present were most aggrieved at the conduct of Henry Henchman, Bishop of London, who used the stationers "most basely worse than any other landlord, saying he will be paid to this day the rent or he would not come to treat with them for the time to come and would not promise them anything how he could use them."[16]

Despite the losses sustained in the Fire, Martyn and Allestry—once reëstablished—enjoyed uninterrupted prosperity. Even as early as 1666, together, they published a second edition of Evelyn, *Kalendarium Hortense* and Euclid, *Elementa geometrica* issued by Martyn alone. Although Oldenburg declared that "Martyn had been undone with the rest of the stationers at St. Paul's and all their books burnt," this dismal statement is exaggerated. Certainly the firm lost many of its publications, but copies of works by Hooke, Evelyn, Willis, Clark, Jeremy Taylor, and issues of the *Philosophical Transactions* escaped the flames. The firm was indeed fortunate since the prospect for dealer and collector appeared most disheartening. Writing to Clarendon, Evelyn remarked: "Since the late deplorable Conflagration, in wch the stationers have been exceedingly ruined, there is like to be an extraordinary penury and scarcity of classical authors, etc. us'd in our Grammar scholes; so as of necessity they must be suddainely reprinted. This sad calamity has mortified a Company which was exceedingly haughty and difficult to manage." Pepys's *Diary* reflects the general gloomy tone. "A great want thereof there will be of books, especially Latin books and foreign books."[17]

By 1669 Martyn had sufficiently recovered to be able to supply the reader with new publications of "Latin books and foreign books." During the last decade of his career, 1670-1680, Martyn showed an increased interest in their publication and circulation. As "Printer to the Royal Society," Martyn naturally observed the predilection of its growing membership for the new science. Even before the establishment of the Royal Society, Martyn had been prepared to cater to the specialized tastes of English collectors. In 1655 he had purchased the library of the distinguished French physician Jean Riolan and promptly issued a 128-page catalogue entitled *Catalogus Librorum rei Medicae, Herbariae & Chymiae* consisting of two parts and listing approximately 3,800 books. The first section included medical, chemical and alchemical works, herbals, and a few pharmacopeia as well as "libri Magici." Part II was of a miscellaneous nature covering Hebrew, Chaldaic, Syrian, and Arabic books.[18]

With a growing demand for foreign texts, Martyn, despite the criticism of Beale, employed two numbers of the *Philosophical Transactions* for the insertion of Want Lists. The issues of 25 March and 26 July 1675 contain lists of some "Philosophical and other Curious books, desired by the Printer of these Tracts (by whom they are to be had)." The first List includes 32 titles of texts by foreign scientists: medical treatises by Franciscus Sylvius De Le Boe, Jan Swammerdam, Riolan, and the medical digests of several German *hochgelehrte*. For the wonder-working Londoner Hermes, Martyn sought the alchemical treatises of Johann Sigmund Elsholtz, Christian Adolphus Balduinus and others. His advertisement for the Danish scientific journal, *Acta medica et philosophica*, edited by Thomas Bartholinus, reflects the interest of the English academician. Can one possibly assume that Martyn obtained all of his desiderata with the exception of the *Experimentum Chymicum* of Georg Wolfgang Wedel which is the only repeat title in the July List? This second List of titles emphasizes the English demand for foreign medical and alchemical books. Specific titles are Christopher Menzel, *Lapis Bononiensis,* Friedrich Zobel, *Tartarologia Spagyricus,* Hadrianus à Mynsicht, *Thesaurus et Armamentarium Medico-Cymicum* and vade-mecums for the distillation of base metals into gold within the smoke-filled London laboratories. He also advertised for copies of the history of the German scientific society, the Collegium Curiosum sive Experimentale.[19]

As an enterprising book dealer, Martyn not only searched texts for his customers but also kept a close eye on dealers' new catalogues. He had at hand copies of William Cooper's 1673 *Catalogue of Chymical Works* and the stout comprehensive Elzevier Catalogue of 1674. It is quite possible that he had met Daniel Elzevier since he discussed the Dutch dealer with Hooke who had visited him at Aldersgate. Elzevier had traveled to England "on some small business with his correspondents of ye same profession." He had been given a letter of introduction to Sir Joseph Williamson, a customer of Martyn, who probably introduced him to the Master of the Bell.[20]

Along with Sir Joseph, other bibliophiles frequented the Martyn premises. Pepys occasionally visited stating that on 10 January 1667 he there "did meet with Fournier the Frenchman that hath wrote of the Sea and Navigation and I could not buy him and I also bespoke of an excellent work which I met here, of

China." In March he purchased a copy of Kircher's *Musurgia* and a brief Diary entry of a later date refers to the acquisition of several works of a lighter vein carried by Martyn: *"Cassandra* and some French books for my wife's closet."[21]

Other customers included Sir Christopher Wren, Sir John Hoskins, Dr. Thomas Gale, Master of St. Paul's School, Abraham Hill, patron of arts and Treasurer of the Royal Society, as well as Thomas Tompion, "Father of English watch-making." Martyn enjoyed a warm friendship with his customers, discussing the importance of a new publication, imbibing brew at Man's coffee-house, traveling with them to Greenwich and Lambeth or inviting them to his home in Bow Lane.

It was at the Bell that Robert Hooke demonstrated to Tompion his new experiment of "how to stay a falling clock-weight by a scaffold pole." The friendship of John Martyn and Robert Hooke was based on a dual relationship. Martyn was Hooke's publisher, but, above all, he was his favorite dealer who helped to develop his superb collection.

Hooke's *Micrographia,* which would win such enthusiastic praise, was published by Martyn in 1665, a second edition appearing in 1667. The scientist's *Attempt to prove the motion of the earth* was issued six years later followed by a *Description of helioscopes, Lampas, De potentia restituva, Lectiones Cutleriana* and the *Philosophical Collections,* Volume One, a continuation of the *Philosophical Transactions.*[22]

In 1674 Martyn published the scientist's extremely significant study *Animadversions on the first part of the Machina coelestis* in which he refuted certain telescopic theories of the Danzig astronomer Hevelius. The details of its publication shed some light upon author-publisher relations. On 3 December 1673 Hooke stated that he had spent the entire afternoon at home where he "Writ Lecture on Hevelius his Machina Coelestis." Within the week Martyn contracted to publish the work agreeing to pay the author twenty shillings a sheet. "Him to have the power of reprinting it at 20sh. a plate." The engraver Francis Lamb was engaged to execute the illustrations. It was not until 9 October, however, that Hooke delivered the first part of his "coppye" to Martyn. By 19 October the second signature was ready for the press. On 4 November Hooke corrected the proofs at Martyn's and a few days later gave him the fifth signature. A laconic Diary entry of 10 December

states: "Book completed about Hevelius." Two days later Hooke
visited the Bell where he took "6 Guilt 5 plaine Animadversions."
It is somewhat amazing that within two days after printing the
author received gilt calf copies![23]

Hooke's visits to the Bell were for the most part in the capacity
of an enthusiastic collector who browsed, lingered over new
publications, foreign imports and purchased "on account." An avid
collector, the Curator of Experiments was temperamental, tight-
fisted, and often delinquent in payment. He enjoyed credit with
Martyn, since he seldom paid outright for an item, eventually
settling with the proprietor but usually finding a few pence to his
advantage. After reading a book purchased from another dealer,
Hooke attempted to exchange it for a title carried by Martyn, who
occasionally remained adamant, refusing to "exchange." The
sympathy of the modern antiquarian dealer must extend to the
Master of the Bell who was the recipient of many books returned by
his over-enthusiastic customer. On 27 December 1677 Hooke
returned to Martyn "Dr. Plot's inquiries, 2 Journal des Scavans . . .
More Metaphysica 4to, Kircher, de peste, Ettmueller Respiration
4to, History of Usicocos [Usicocks] . . . Voyage de Sorbière 12mo,"
and others. Apparently John Martyn retained that state of
equanimity essential to all antiquarian dealers who realize that so
enthusiastic a customer will remain ever faithful and hopefully
solvent.[24]

It is impossible to state how many books Hooke actually
purchased at the Bell. His library contains not only Martyn
imprints but also texts imported by the proprietor from abroad.
Hooke's medical purchases from Martyn include, among others,
Regnier de Graaf, *De mulierum organis generatio;* Briggs,
Ophthalmographia "1s. not paid;" "2 books of Sir K. Digby 2s.6d.
not paid;" Gideon Harvey, *Family Physician* "1s. not paid;"
Zachary, *New Tracts about Respiration.* Acquisitions in natural
history were substantial. Hooke's Diary mentions Hagedorn,
Catechu, seu terra Japonica "1sh.," a study on the rubber plant;
Borelli, *De motu animalium;* Grew, *Natural History of Vegetables;*
Lister, *De araneis* "6d." as well as his *Historia animalium angliae;*
"Dr. Plot's books [*The Natural History of Oxfordshire*] stitchd
9s.4d.;" Willughby, *Ornithologia* as well as "Gerard Herball
3s.10d."[25]

Texts in geography, travel, and cartography provided Robert Hooke with armchair traveling and exploration he apparently preferred, for he seldom departed the squares and alleys of the city. On 8 March 1674/75 he visited the Bell where he acquired Baudrant, *Geographical Lexicon*, "30sh. not paid." An expensive purchase was Zeiller's *Topography of France* which he obtained "on account at £3.10." On another occasion he reserved copies of Edward Brown, *Travels* at 3s. and Herbert, *Travels* "12s. not paid." *The Travels* of John Ray, a set of de Bry, *Voyages* and Bernier, *Travels through Turkey and Persia* were all acquired at the Bell.[26]

On the recently "rang'd" shelves of Robert Hooke's library could be found the mathematical treatises of François du Laurens purchased from Martyn at 9sh.; a copy of *Archimedes Redivivus* at 11sh.; Schott, *Technica Curiosa*, 18sh. "not paid" which appealed to the collector's abounding technological curiosity. In the field of astronomy Martyn sold Hooke copies of Mercator, *Institutio astronomiae* and Kepler, *Epitome Astronomiae Copernicanae* for 6d. "not paid." Texts in optics, alchemy, and chemistry did not elude the collector's attention: Grimaldi, *De Lumiere* 5sh. "not paid;" Menzel, *Lapis Bononiensis* 1sh. "not paid;" Wedel, *De sale tartari volatilii* "not what I would;" Johnson, *Chemical Dictionary* 3s.6d. and Le Febure, *Book of Chemistry*. Miscellaneous purchases included Cesalpini, *De Metallicis libri tres* 3s.6d. and Evelyn's translation of Freart de Chambray, *Parallel of Antient Architectvra*.[27]

The Bell so often visited by Hooke and his associates was not only a rendezvous for the Restoration bibliophile but also a center for the exchange of letters. Oldenburg advised Lister not to continue to send his mail to Martyn but rather to him directly stating that "ye post comes as often into my quarters as anywhere else about London."[28]

Hooke obtained at the Bell not only current and antiquarian books but also numerous scientific texts imported by the owner from continental dealers.[29] In turn Martyn was active as an exporter of current writings in the sciences retaining an agent in Rouen who, in all likelihood, cleared the shipments through French customs.[30]

Martyn had established business contacts in Paris even before 1655 when he began negotiations for the acquisition of the Riolan collection. At the height of his career he enjoyed business relations with Etienne Michallat, printer-in-ordinary to Louis XIV, and the younger Jean Petit of Paris who shipped him prior to November 1672 one hundred copies of Jean-Baptiste Duhamel, *De Corporum affectionibus libri duo.* Duhamel, acting as Petit's epistolary agent, was well aware of trans-channel hazards. He continually wrote to Martyn about a long overdue shipment from London which after a five-month journey had finally arrived.

In 1673 Petit requested Martyn to send him a minimum of 6 copies of Thomas Willis, *De anima brutorum* recently published at Oxford and "the book of effluvia of Mr. Boyle when it is published." The order for Boyle's treatise was conditional—to be forwarded only if in Latin translation. Writing for Petit, Duhamel stated: "As for the English [language] I see almost no one who understands and who is competent in these sciences." Relenting somewhat, he added that Martyn should send a few copies of the English edition as well as the recent work of Nehemiah Grew. There is little doubt that Duhamel and Petit welcomed the Latin edition of Boyle's *Essay on Effluviums* published by Martyn's colleague Moses Pitt.[31]

Petit dispatched a parcel of books to Martyn through the latter's agent at Rouen in January 1673/74. In return he requested from the London dealer several works by Malpighi: 2 copies of his *De bombyce,* 24 copies of his *De viscerum structura* and 12 copies of his *Dissertatio epistolica de formatione pulli in ovo*—recently published by Martyn—as well as 4 copies of Varenius, *Geographia naturalis.* Newton had brought out an enlarged and corrected edition of Varenius which he taught to his students at Cambridge. In July 1672 he informed the mathematician John Collins that this edition would "be sold by Mr. Martin if any of your friends desire it."[32]

Martyn, well-known to several of the Parisian booksellers, was a name familiar to the Hamburg and Frankfurt stationers. Describing the content of his *Phoranomica,* the Hamburg physician Martin Vogel confided in Oldenburg in 1670 that he had consulted a German bookseller about the cost of publication. Upon seeing the bulk of the diagrams, four times as large as the text itself, the Hamburg publisher-bookseller Georg Schulz "refused to undertake to print because of the magnitude of the expense." The disconsolate author could hope for "no subvention from wealthy people [of Hamburg] to whom learning means nothing at all." Therefore he wondered whether Martyn would make a deal with Schulz "with whom he is acquainted whereby they would divide the necessary expense between them." Vogel's proposal was turned down by Martyn. He apparently envisioned little success and much expense with a book overloaded with a "bulk of diagrams."[33]

Despite his refusal to publish the *Phoranomica* Martyn retained a business relationship with Schulz. Monthly he dispatched issues of the *Philosophical Transactions* to the Hamburg dealer who in turn shipped him copies of the German scientific publication, the *Miscellanea curiosa.*[34]

The philosopher Leibniz, through the services of Oldenburg, ordered books from Martyn which were to be dispatched to Schulz and ultimately forwarded to Leibniz via Frankfurt. On 24 April 1671 Oldenburg responded to Leibniz that he had attended to his order and was shipping the books "by our bookseller Martin and Schulz to Zunner of Frankfurt as follows:

	Lib. sterl.	shil.	d.
Phil. Transact. annorum 68.69.70	1	0	0
Lexicon (Blunt)	0	4	6
Boylius de rarefactione aeris	0	0	6
Boilius Tractatus aliquot de qual. Cosmicis etc.	0	1	8
Glanville Plus ultra	0	1	6
Mercur. Librarius	0	1	6
Sum	1	10[9]	8[8]

Oldenburg suggested that Leibniz settle the account with Zunner at Frankfurt who would pay Schulz who in turn would pay Martyn.[35]

Martyn's shipment included a copy of the *Mercurius Librarius,* the forerunner of our own *Books in Print,* listing the books published in England during recent years. Among these were many of the prestigious titles issued by John Martyn at the Bell.

On 3 March 1679/80 Hooke visited Martyn. He visited him not at the Bell but at his home in Bow Lane. He came not as a customer but as a friend. Martyn had taken ill. On 5 July 1680 Hooke briefly recorded: "Mr. Martin at the Bell died." A week later Martyn's faithful friend and customer attended the obsequies. The late Master of the Bell was interred in the restored chapel of St. Faith where a monument was erected to his memory depicting him kneeling and at his side a stack of books.[36]

JOHN MARTYN, "PRINTER TO THE ROYAL SOCIETY"

There can be little doubt that John Martyn remains the outstanding publisher and bookseller of Restoration science. As "Printer to the Royal Society," he received enviable recognition. His businesslike acumen in the handling of a pampered customer Hooke and the breadth of his business dealings are admirable. His publications, a record of scientific achievement, remain a tribute to his perception of the needs of his time.

3

Moses Pitt
Publisher and Purveyor of Mathematical Books

On 2 January 1673/74 Robert Hooke "walkd to Mr. Martin" and later during the same day "bought of Pitt George Agricola de re metallica 8sh." Although later in life Hooke was to dub Moses Pitt "that raskall," he not only patronized him as a specialist dealer in the new sciences but also worked closely with him in the publication of his ambitious *English Atlas.* Pitt was a man of enterprise, engaging in publishing and bookselling, associating himself with the reëstablished Oxford University Press and investing in London real estate. He unfortunately over-extended himself and was clapped into the Fleet for debt. He was never to recover financially after this ignominy. During his more halcyon days from 1676 to 1685 Pitt ranks as a close rival of Martyn in the publication and circulation of the new scientific literature.

According to the garrulous John Dunton, Pitt was "an honest man every inch and thought of him," one who "took much delight in doing good, as if he had no other errand in the world. He had fathomed the vast body of learning, and in every several part of it was the Master. His wit and virtues were writ legibly in his face, and he had a great deal of sweetness in his natural temper." A more analytical observer, John Collins, alluded to "the good character of Mr. Pitts the stationer in Little Britain."[1]

Pitt was a Cornishman born in St. Teath, arriving in London as an adolescent. There he was apprenticed to Robert Littlebury at the Unicorn, Little Britain, a member of the Haberdashers Company. Pitt was freed after the customary seven-year period translating himself to the Stationers Company in November 1661. His activity

26

until 1667 is vague but during that year he published two books of a general nature. The following year he emerged as a specialist dealer in scientific texts. Of the approximately 160 books he published, more than a third attest to his interest in the new science. In 1669 he was located at the White Hart, Little Britain, whence he moved to the Angel over the Little North Door of St. Paul's Church.[2]

Although Pitt's publishing and bookselling programs vie to some extent with those of Martyn, the Master of the Angel was to prove himself far more optimistic in one area of the sciences. Martyn had for the most part desisted from the publication and sale of mathematical works with the exception of numerous editions of Euclid. It is difficult to understand why Pitt undertook their publication since it is well known that mathematical treatises enjoyed a limited sale. Few texts were translated into English and publishers were hesitant to market foreign originals. The mathematician John Collins bemoaned the fate of some excellent mathematical writings, informing Wallis in February 1669/70 that "Mr. Briggs *Arithmetica Logarithmica,* being too numerous an impression, has been tendered about the streets at 1s.6d. each. The like I say of Dr. Barrow's Euclid and yet at last a great number of both books together with the plates were sold by Sir Thomas Davis, Lord Mayor [of London and formerly a stationer]." Davis had received copies in payment of a debt at the rate of 1s.6d.a pair in turn selling them to the wholesale bookseller Robert Scott "who drives a foreign trade."[3]

The fact that English printed mathematical books were being hawked about the streets did not diminish Collins's interest in new continental publications and their possible availability in England. "There are many tracts of Algebra expected from beyond the sea, as that of Cheveau, an entire posthumous treatise of Tacquet which Meursius of Antwerp intends to print, two volumes in folio of Renaldinus, lastly the third volume of Des Cartes. At home Mr. Kersey hath a laborious treatise in English ready for the press, which is promised by Mr. Stephens, who will undertake it, when paper is more available."[4]

In a chatty letter to James Gregory penned about four years later, Collins dilated further upon foreign mathematical intelligence. "There is lately come out of Italy Borellus de liquidis, a physico-math. treatise, Honorati Fabri his Commentaria in Archimedes. The comment. of Borellus on Archimedes is to be printed at

Lyons, Gottignis Dioptrics; he is accounted a good geometer. . . .
None of these books are as yet come over, nor Fermats Diophantus,
which are not to be bought at Paris (there being none save are from
Toulouse)."[5]

Collins's correspondence certainly bespeaks a knowledge of
foreign mathematical texts and reflects some English interest in the
subject, referring to the fact that "none of these books are yet come
over." Mathematical treatises were imported into England by Scott
and others were published by his colleague Pitt. Collins advised
John Beale that "Mr. Scot a bookseller in Little Britain the chief
trader into France observes that England doth not vent above
twenty or thirty of any new mathematical book he brings over and
therefore to think of printing the ancient mathematicians is in my
opinion very hazardous to the stationers." Yet Scott's 1674
Catalogue of Books Imported from Abroad belies this assumption. It
is true that the section "Jus Civile" cites 224 titles and the group
"Libri Graeci" 483 works. However the same *Catalogue*
enumerates under categories "Politici" and "Res Militaris Scriptores" only 81 and 61 titles respectively. Under the heading
"Mathematici" 115 titles are listed. The mathematical works
imported by Scott from abroad include several editions of Archimedes, the *Opera mathematica* of Jean Caramuel Lobkovitz, various
commentaries on Euclid by Clavius as well as the home-bred
Dudley Digges, *Alae seu scala mathematica,* Rheticus, *Opera de
triangulis,* Schotten, *Exercitationes mathematica,* etc.[6]

The publication of mathematical treatises was costly, demanding special figures and diagrams cut for the text. The expense of
production was high and the return limited. A suggestion was made
to the impecunious mathematics-bent scholar Collins to buy his
wares in Holland for "mathematics books there in their auctions
[are] to be had very cheap." Few London printers owned type for
such specialized works. In a letter of 10 February 1676/77 to the
mathematician Thomas Brancker, Collins despaired of the lack of
specialized type. He advised Brancker that he had not given his
manuscript to Mr. [Henry] Brome of London whom he regarded as
"a person improper, he being an English bookseller little concerned
in Latin books and having no foreign trade . . . he is not
accustomed to mathematical works, and not furnished with proper
types. We have but one printer, namely Mr. Wm. Godbid in Little
Britain that is accustomed [to] and fitted for such and musick work

and besides is a very worthy, honest person." William Godbid over against the Anchor in Little Britain retained a lively establishment working five presses and employing five workmen and two apprentices.[7]

Apparently Moses Pitt had accepted Collins's earlier dictum that a bookseller of London "would print any book if he be sure to sell eighty or an hundred copies for ready money." Aware of the paucity of English printed mathematical works since the Fire, Pitt informed Wallis of his willingness to publish mathematical texts. A year after his establishment, Pitt engaged William Godbid to print for him an English edition of *An introduction to Algebra* by the Swiss mathematician Friedrich Rahn and *Exercitationes geometrica* of James Gregory in which the author had expounded the quadrature of the hyperbole, an hypothesis he had presented before the Royal Society.[8]

But it was the Savilian Professor of Geometry at the University of Oxford with whom Pitt maintained close contact. Wallis was to profit from the business expertise of the proprietor of the White Hart as publisher and bookseller. In March 1668/69 Wallis dispatched to Pitt from Oxford via "Mr. More's wagon" a bundle of books requesting their value and sale by Pitt:

5 (copies) Opera Mathematica
4 (copies) Commercium epistolicum
4 (copies) De cycloide
8 (copies) Elenchus geometriae Hobbianae
6 (copies) De correctione
3 (copies) Hobbesi puncti dispunctio

The lot can be identified as a variety of mathematical texts written for the most part by Wallis himself. The *Commercium epistolicum* is a group reply to a numerical problem posed by the French mathematician Pierre Fermat. The Hobbes treatise alludes to Wallis's dispute over the great philosopher's "mathematical imbecility." There is no indication of the price realized for the "bundle," but it is fairly safe to say that Wallis's shipment attracted few customers. According to Collins, "the stationers lost much by Dr. Wallis Work de Cycloide, De calculo centri gravitate and his Letters commercium."[9]

Wallis's *De mechanica motu* published by Pitt in 1675 remains one of his most distinguished works. Prior to its publication the author had been advised by Collins that "Mr. Pitts a stationer in Little Britain had prepared sundry tracts for the press [and] is very desirable to the undertaking of them, and to treat with you to that purpose, promising that they shall come out on a very good paper like Schooten's Miscellanies and the cuts be suitable thereto, which may be done by Mr. Marko."[10]

Despite the distinguished authorship of the work, *De mechanica motu* met a fate not too dissimilar to that of other mathematical texts. Pitt had proposed that the price be set at 15sh.6d., a suggestion rejected by the Council of the Royal Society which fixed the retail price at 14sh. Ultimately aware of the difficulty of its sale, the Council altered its decision suggesting that "those subscribers who had agreed to pay such at the rate set by the Council were also left at liberty to buy or not to buy at Pitt's rate."[11]

Wallis commiserated with the publisher's plight. He objected to the Council's proposal which had failed to realize that the work "was troublesome and chargeable to print." He further suggested that he had not "ordered more copies to my friends in the Society." On the other hand Pitt would have suffered since such a purchase for "friends in the Society" on the part of Wallis would "have prevented those from buying who are most likely to do so, which in a book of so slow a sale [as] mathematicall books usually are, is a considerable prejudice to him." Wallis repeated that the printing of the book had been "beyond what other books are of the same bulk; & ye number of the Impresssion but smal and the sale (as of other mathematick books, especially those more intricate & not for every one's understanding but slow). And considering how few are willing to undertake ye printing of books that are a little out of the common road; I would not have those discouraged that are."[12]

Undismayed by the slow sale of *De mechanica motu,* Pitt published two other works by Wallis—his *Exercitationes tres* and *De cometarum distantiis investigandis.* There is little doubt that Moses Pitt was an unshakable optimist! A letter from the mathematician Brancker to Collins written a year after the publication of Wallis's *De mechanica motu* bemoans his inability to satisfy Pitt's restless pace. "I know not whether I can oblige him so far as to move him to help me. The book I am doing for him I can finish, if he grants me a little more time. But he is in such a haste as almost discourages me to go on." Apparently Pitt was not satisfied with Brancker's *Table of numbers less than one hundred thousand* since he enlisted the service of Dr. John Pell. At Easter 1672 Pitt advertised the original Brancker text with Pell's notes and corrections. The *Tabula numerorum quadratorum . . . a table of ten thousand square numbers* was sold by Moses Pitt for "18d. stitch'd."[13]

Works of allied interest, published by Pitt, include the *Miscellanies* of the gauger Michael Dary, the astronomical writings of Jeremiah Horrocks, the *Harmonicks* of Ptolemy, *On Solids* of Nicolas Steno, *A Discourse of Local Motion* and Hooke's *Philosophical Collections,* 1680, a continuation of the *Philosophical Transactions* selling for 1sh.[14]

A year after the publication of *De mechanica motu,* Pitt published a work which aroused general scientific interest and some amusement: *Tuba Stentoro-phonica,* the Speaking Trumpet of Sir Samuel Moreland. The text, describing the amazing qualities of this loud-speaking device, was printed by Godbid for Pitt. The instrument itself was made and sold by "Mr. Samuel Beal, one of his Majesties Trumpeters in Suffolk Street." Oldenburg described the *Tuba Stentoro-phonica* as "an instrument likely to prove very useful both at Sea and Land, in conveying Humane voice, so that it may be heard distinctly, one, two, or three miles off according to the length of the instrument and the strength of ye voyce, speaking in it. The thing being in print, and to be had at Moses Pitt."[15]

Like his colleagues, Henry Herringman, John Crooke and Richard Davis, Pitt realized the economic and prestige value in publishing the writings of the most distinguished living English scientific writer, the Honourable Robert Boyle. Hence in 1672 Godbid printed for Pitt the first English and Latin editions of Boyle's *An Essay about the Origine and Virtues of Gems,* a bound copy of the English version retailing at 28d., the Latin bound at an additional two pence. Three issues of Boyle's *Essay on Effluviums* appeared the following year, the imprint indicating Pitt's new address, the Angel, followed in 1674 by the Latin version, a copy selling at two shillings. Boyle's *Tracts containing Suspicions about some hidden Qualities of the Air,* published in English and Latin, could be obtained from Pitt in 1674 and 1676. A variety of lesser treatises by the great scientist bore Pitt's imprint.[16]

Along with the publishing and sale of works on the exact and natural sciences *Plantarum Historia* ... *Oxoniensis* of Richard Morison and *The Natural History of Oxfordshire* by Robert Plot, Pitt issued several medical treatises. In 1670 he advertised Henry Stubbe, *Lex Talionis* ... *a short Way to Dr. Merret's book* ... *wherein may be discovered the Frauds and Abuses committed by Doctors professing & Practicing Pharmacy.* This admonitory treatise against illegal physicians sold for one penny. Two editions of 1672 and 1676 of the *Chirurgical and Anatomical Works* of Paul Barbette, a practitioner of Amsterdam, could be obtained from Pitt for 3s.6d. bound, while two Dutch treatises, translated into English, the one by Henry Buschofen of Utrecht, physician at Batavia in the service of the Dutch East India Company, and the other by Hendrik van Hoonhuysen, physician-in-ordinary at Amsterdam were also available. The proprieter of the Angel carried "a manual for ladies in travail. . . . Englished out of Dutch by a careful hand "selling at 3sh." Other medical compendia included *Medicina Militaris* of Raymond Minder, late principal physician of the Electoral Court of Bavaria and Imperial City of Augsburg, a *Treatise on Arthritis* of Sir Theodore Turquet de Mayerne and the *Royal Pharmacopeia* of the French physician Moise Charas. The Pitt trade-list comprised a few works in alchemy, among them two editions of the popular writings of Basil Valentine, a copy selling at 1sh., and Alexander Suchten, *Two Treatises of the Secrets of Antinomy.*[17]

Like Martyn, Pitt also published and sold works relating to geography and travel. The firm issued two editions of François Bernier, *History of the late revolution in the empire of the great Mogol,* 1671 and 1676, as well as the author's *Memoirs,* a bound copy selling at 3sh. Armchair travelers with an inclination rather than courage and purse for distant journeys could buy copies of the Sieur de Frejus, *Voyage made into Mauretania in Africk;* Joseph Georgirenes, *A Description of the present State of Samos;* Thomas Smith, *Remarks upon the Manners of the Turks;* and *Collection of several relations* by the popular French voyager Jean-Baptiste Tavernier.[18]

Pitt's stock proved a powerful magnet for Robert Hooke who was attracted to the Angel by its diversified nature. Recording visits of February 1672/73, Hooke selected a wide range of books: Dalechamp, *Chirurgie,* "Stevins Mechanicks Dutch 4d., Cardan de

Varietate fol. 2s., Des Secrets de medecin par Liebault 8vo; Quercetanus [Du Cerceau] de Spagiricis 8vo, Chouls de la Castramentatione et Bagni Antici de Greci et Romani 8vo; Paulus H[J]ovius De Romanis Piscibus, 8vo; Bellonius de aquatilibus and others. All 8 for 2s.6d. I paid him."[19]

Pitt also indulged Hooke's bibliophilic whims. At the Angel the scientist purchased 'on approval,' charged and returned a variety of texts. Having examined some of the substantial holdings of Robert Scott, he considered the purchase of Moncony, *Travels,* ultimately rejecting it. Later he visited Pitt finding a second copy which he preferred either for condition or price and acquired it at 15sh. For the *Works* of the distinguished Italian physicist Evangelista Torricelli he paid Pitt 5sh. and 3sh.10. for Grandami's treatise on the magnet. His purchases of September and October 1673 included a copy of the first edition of Boyle, *Essay on Effluviums* and "Leonardo da Vinci for 15sh." Later acquisitions comprise copies of "Boeckler's Machina . . . 35s., Diophantus 5s., 3 pieces of Snellius 6s., Hugenius [Huygens] de magnitudine circuli 1s. in all 47 sh." for which he paid not Pitt but "his man." The purchase of a significant Americanum is entered for 11 December 1675: "Northwest Fox." From the proprietor of the Angel the Curator of Experiments had bought one of the notable early voyages to North America by Luke Fox. Substantial purchases from 1677 to 1679 include among others the *Epitome* of the great astronomer Regiomontanus, the *Logarithms* of Napier at 2s. "not paid," Riccioli, *Astronomia* as well as Antonio Herrera, *Descriptio Indiae Occidentalis* at 0.6.0 "not paid."[20]

Hooke's dealings with Pitt were not solely confined to book-buying at the proprietor's premises. Pitt, like several of his London colleagues, had been lured to the recent bookselling innovation, the auction, introduced into England by the alchemical specialist William Cooper. Of the two auction sales conducted by Pitt in 1678 and 1678/79, the first and the most considerable, was held at St. Bartholomew Close, where he offered the library of the late Gilbert Voet, the Dutch theologian lately deceased. The Sale was advertised as a collection with "considerable number of other Choice Books in most Sciences, some of which have been bought out of the best Libraries abroad, and others . . . out of the most eminent seats of learning beyond the Seas." Pitt's preface is of interest for the general procedure adopted by the English auctioneer. He refers to "the several experiments of late and Sale of Books by Auction a practice which had benefitted the Buyer." After due praise of Voet's collection, he pledged himself "to observe all the Rules and Laws of Auction," changing, however, the method of payment. Pitt demanded that "all Strangers and customers of an uncertain city residence pay after the Sale." He assured prospective bidders that he would "not use any indirect way to advance or Promote the sale by commission of friends," but "would content himself with this belief; that the intelligent and ingenious will contribute by their bidding fair and reasonable prices, to make the encouragement in some measure answerable to so expensive an undertaking." One of the "ingenious" bidders at the Voet Sale, Robert Hooke, purchased 28 lots totalling £9.14.8 acquiring copies of Kircher, *China;* the *Saggi* of the Accademia del Cimento; Stevin, *Works;* the mathematical corpus of Vieta; Bassantin, *Astronomia;* a treatise on dentistry; the *Theatre d'Agriculture* of Estienne & Liebault; Scheffer, *Laponia;* a French edition of Boccone, *Richerche;* and others, all of which reflect the scientist's myriad interests.[21]

Among his auction purchases were accounts of Italy, China, and Lapland, testimonials to the scientist's intense curiosity about foreign lands. As a visitor to the London shops he displayed his interest in maps and atlases. From Pitt he took for 1sh. *A New Map of the Trading Part of America both Continent and Island* "showing also the excellent Situation of Ismus and Panama and the Island of Jamaica for trade . . . beyond all other parts of India." During the summer of 1678 Hooke borrowed from Pitt a copy of the *Description of Spitsberg* and returned his *Atlas coelestis.* The following month the collector took 'on approval' 43 maps of the French cartographer Nicholas Sanson, later purchasing an 11-volume set of Blaeu's *Atlas.* Hooke's Library included the *Atlas Major* of Jansson published at Amsterdam in 1675, the Mercator *Atlas,* 1638, 3 volumes of Merian's *Topographia,* the various atlases of his friend John Ogilby, the *Empire of the World* of Ortelius, Zeiller's *Topographia Galliae,* maps of Saxton and Speed, and the sea charts published by the marine specialist John Seller.[22]

It is not remarkable then that Hooke—surveyor, draughtsman, and collector of topography and cartography—associated himself with Pitt in one of the stationer's most ambitious schemes, the publication of an 11-volume *English Atlas* of which only four volumes were to be completed, a fifth appearing with text only. The

Auction Catalogue of the Hooke Library lists the *English Atlas* "with Mapps, publish[ed]. by Mons. Pitt. Vol. 1, 2 and 3 Oxon." In November 1680 the *Term Catalogue* carried an advertisement of "The English Atlas Volume first: Containing a Description of the Places next the North Pole, as also of Muscovy, Poland, Sweden, Denmark and their several dependencies." According to the announcement the work embodied the suggestions of Dr. Christopher Wren, Thomas Gale, and Mr. Robert Hooke, among others. The work was printed at the Theatre, Oxford and was sold by Moses Pitt at 40s. "in quires to all that are subscribers." Succeeding volumes appeared between 1681 and 1683. The production of Pitt's *Atlas* reflects the collaboration of a great scientist with a London publisher bent on a grandiose scheme.[23]

In his autobiographical *Cry of the Oppressed,* Pitt referred to his publication of the *Atlas.* "Having undertaken the printing of an Atlas, or Description of the Whole World, which will be about Twelve Volumes in Folio, Maps and Descriptions on Imperial Paper, and being much incouraged by Dr. Fell then Bishop of Oxon. I took of him the Printing-House at Oxford called the Theatre, where I have finished Four of the Volumes Containing the Description of the Northern Countries of Greenland, as also Sweden, Denmark, Muscovy, Poland and the Seventeen Provinces of the Low Countries and all the Empire of Germany, and have two volumes more almost finished viz. the East Indies and all the Turkish Empire." Pitt spared little for the production of his *Atlas.* He established a paper mill in France for the manufacture of paper in a larger size than any that was used at the time in France or Holland. The paper obviously was of such superb quality that Hooke took a sample to show to Wren.[24]

In December 1678 Pitt announced that the *Atlas* was in print at the Theatre informing his clients they could view a specimen sheet at his premises. He gave notice at the same time that "All Gentlemen who have, or are willing to subscribe to the said Atlas do forthwith pay in their subscription money; viz 40s. to the Theatre in Oxford where Receipts shall be left for them lest they lose both the Advantage and Credit of being Subscribers to so Noble a Book." These selfsame Gentlemen were later advised that "all those that have a mind to have their Coats of Arms engraven on any of the Plates shall have it done for 20s., if they please to send their Coat, as mentioned in time."[25]

Pitt's *Atlas* was to follow the Blaeu-Jansson rendition. According to an entry in his Diary, Hooke stated that he and others had "resolved about using the Dutch Mapps, but with reducing them." Pitt sought the help of Hooke and others for his ambitious publication. There is some indication that he had hoped to enlist Newton's suggestions since a letter from Hooke to Newton states that "Mr. Pitts was very joyful that you will assist him." It was, however, not Isaac Newton but Robert Hooke who actually played a major role in the preparation of Moses Pitt's *English Atlas*. He appears to have been the entrepreneur suggesting and engaging a corps of experts who were hired and paid by him on Pitt's behalf. In his multi-faceted professional capacities he was acquainted with many experts in the fields of cartography, delineation, and engraving.[26]

The earliest reference to Pitt's project in Hooke's Diary is dated 8 September 1675: "At Pits saw Catalogue of Great Atlas." "Catalogue" may be interpreted as the publisher's plan or outline of countries and maps to be included. It was not until March 1677/78 that regular consultations about the work's scope and progress are indicated. Various entries reflect Hooke's association with the venture. "To Pits, his designs for Atlas good. Mr. Pits here about his Atlas. With him to Sir Chr. Wren. At home all afternoon about Mapps." During a rendezvous at Man's coffee-house the following month, Sir Peter Wyche and a Mr. Chase submitted their subscriptions for copies of the *Atlas*. An entry of 25 May 1676 states that Hooke had introduced Pitt to one Mordant—a likely error for Robert Morden, the map-seller and globe-dealer of the Atlas. Apparently the scientist believed that Pitt might benefit from Morden's expertise who, as a specialist, could vend copies of the completed work. When Hooke on 31 July 1678 presented Pitt with his proposals for the giant scheme, the publisher agreed to give him £200 "in consideration of [his] continuance and 200 more for inspecting the work." Pitt's contract, alas, was only slightly honored.[27]

At a dinner party in August, attended by Sir Christopher Wren, Dr. Lloyd, and John Fell, the *Atlas* was the subject of discussion followed by a meeting between Hooke and Pitt the next day of which the scientist wrote: "Mr. Pitt gave me a bond to pay £200 at Michelmas next upon which I told him my contrivance for the making of Maps without graving names only pricking them on sheets by." In August Hooke began his Introduction and on the tenth of the month he received "4 sheets of North Col. hemisphere. ill and melancholy." Did this last entry reflect Hooke's e.s.p. and foreshadow the financial fiasco of that "rascall" Pitt? Later in the month Hooke visited his friend, Richards, the art dealer, a sponsor of Ogilby's *English Atlas,* purchasing from him four maps at 5sh. on behalf of Pitt who wished to use them for the project.[28]

Hooke's corps of experts for the planning, design, and engraving of the Pitt *Atlas* included the surveyor and heraldist Gregory King. For those who "had a mind to have their Coats of Arms engraven on any of the plates," he could—as a member of the College of Arms—ascertain the correct armorial bearing. Recognized cartographers were consulted and employed. The Hollander Herman Moll, who had settled in London, was engaged for the design of several maps. Hooke consulted with him upon occasion paying him on 19 October 1679 "4s.6d. for Pitts." The "Dutchman" Cramer was hired for map detail. Hooke had originally met this gentleman at Grey's Inn in 1673 when "Mr. Cramer complimented [him] much." Diary entries allude to "Mapps given to Cramer. Mr. Pitts at Childs [coffee-house] to pay Cramer Tables." At Hooke's home on 17 October 1679 together they "examined over all Mapps," Cramer returning fairly frequently to discuss the maps of Holland. "Cramer here, Maps corrected." One of the outstanding Hooke-Pitt consultants was the German Detlever Cluver who had been elected a member of the Royal Society in 1678. Mathematician, dabbler in astrology and alchemy, he won the friendship of Hooke. Cluver was consulted about the mathematical projection of the maps in October 1678 and apparently approved of the maps selected since a few weeks later Hooke stated that "Pitt told me Cluver was for the Atlas." He obviously was on the payroll since on 12 October 1678 Pitt "concluded with Cluver for 15s. per sheet."[29]

The maps were engraved principally by the artist Francis Lamb mentioned by Hooke in his Diary. "To Lamb and graver. Lent Lamb proportionall compasses." There is evidence by mid-September 1678 Lamb had spent considerable time in the engraving of the maps. "Lamb here 2 hours about Atlas. Lamb here from 8. to 3." He was assisted by Michiel Swarts, a designer, and Hooke's man Henry Hunt, known as Harry, who served as draughtsman, housekeeper for Hooke, and operator for the Royal Society.

Hooke's enthusiasm for the project apparently reached its peak in late September 1678 when he made a visit "with Pit to Prince Rupert." There is every reason to believe that this scientifically-minded aristocrat showed much enthusiasm for the *English Atlas* and Robert Hooke's new contrivance for the pricking of maps.[30]

Although Hooke continued to assist and advise Pitt faithfully he began to doubt the publisher's financial competence. An entry of 27 October 1678 reads: "Pitt engaged to make good his Bond and contract whether proceeding or not." Despite his reservations publication continued. In August 1679 Hooke received sheets F and G and was assured by Pitt the following October that he planned "to go on with my volume." Entries of February 1679/80 mention: "Mapps of Bohemia, Bavaria. With Pits at Childs. Received Preface and Proeme. At Pits Map of North Pole. Saw Pits Maps Coloured. Title-page from Pitt at Garaway mousehole."[31]

As publication day of Volume One approached Hooke realized his doubts about his publisher's financial responsibility had been justified. Although Pitt had promised payment on Lady Day, "soe soon as the first volume is finished," the scientist was to record dolefully seven months later that he had received of the promised £400 £5.5s. which with £2.5s. made £7.10s. "Gave him acquittance with soe much." No further Diary entry refers to any payment for his work on the *English Atlas*. Although Volumes One to Four of the *Atlas* were published and Volume Five, with text only, Pitt sustained great loss from his grandiose scheme—a venture which, combined with other impractical investments, was to force his retirement from trade and his incarceration in the Fleet for debt. The *English Atlas* was a bitter blow to Pitt and a sad disappointment to his principal adviser Robert Hooke.[32]

When in 1675 Pitt conceived his ideas for his *Atlas* he ranked as a successful London publisher and bookseller. In 1678 he employed "a boy" and the following year Hooke referred to "Pits his man." The latter was in all probability Pitt's apprentice Samuel Smith who in 1681 opened his own shop and eventually became bookseller to the Royal Society. Pitt owned or leased two warehouses, one in Bartholomew Close and a second at Oxford. In 1674 he issued *A Miscellaneous Catalogue of Books* listing works published in England and others imported from Holland. Two years later he published *A Catalogue of Books imported from Abroad* (in Regionibus Transmarinis) rich in texts for the English reader. Indeed, aware of Pitt's catalogue facility, Hooke, requiring a cataloguer for his own growing collection or for the library of the Royal Society, sought from him "a catalogue maker."[33]

A year prior to Pitt's first publication, John Fell was appointed Vice-Chancellor of the University of Oxford. He soon convinced the Chancellor, Archbishop Sheldon, that the Theatre at Oxford be used for the printing of books and bibles. It was at the Theatre that Pitt in 1680 issued Volume One of the *English Atlas.* Fell had long been familiar with the generosity and business career of the master of the Angel who had been a university benefactor presenting to the archives a copy of the first book printed at Oxford, St. Jerome's *Expositio in symbolum apostolorum* (1488) and copies of several Caxtons to the Bodleian.[34]

Unfortunately the publishing program of Bishop Fell had not proved successful and with the expiration of the second lease of the Theatre in 1678, he offered the London stationers his unsold stock for £3,800 as a "premium for its renewal." This offer was also made to Pitt, who with three colleagues, William Leake of Chancery Lane, Peter Parker of the Log and Star, and Thomas Guy of the Flying Horse, accepted. Pitt and his associates made a large investment. In his semi-autobiography Pitt wrote that he had "purchased from [Fell] a great quantity of Books, the value of many thousands of pounds." Pitt assumed responsibility for printing at the Theatre, his associates acting as distributors. Within four months after their agreement with Fell the stationers employed four presses at the Theatre working full time. The partners agreed "to print ... all manner of Bookes Bibles Testaments Psalters Almanacks, Lilly's grammar and all other School Bookes." Pitt stated that "in the latter end of King Charles Time [he printed] great Quantities of Bibles, Testaments, Common Prayers, etc. in all volumes, whereby I brought down the prices of Bibles etc. more than half, which did great good at that time (Popery likely to overflow us)." Although Pitt boasted an extensive publishing program the output of the partners was not considerable, issuing several editions of the *English Bible,* the *Book of Common Prayer,* an *English Psalter.* Still associated with the Oxford Press, Pitt alone published Vol. XII of the *Philosophical Transactions* in 1683.[35]

With his partners and alone Pitt published William Dugdale, *Antient Usage; Two Treatises* of the great Hebrew scholar Moses Maimonides; and the writings of others. But the competition was strong. England was flooded with Bibles and Testaments, many imported from Holland where they were cheaply printed. During the course of his Oxford association, Pitt invested heavily in property in the Westminster area. In 1683 he visited Ireland for a considerable time, apparently hoping to sell there some of the University imprints. Upon his return, the partners demanded from him some hundreds of pounds. Pitt was held responsible for the failure of the publishing venture. "They locked up my Oxford warehouse, mortgaged my estate to my Lady Jones for 3800 [pounds]." In addition, a relative, the stationer Adiel Mill, who Dunton believed should have been "a stranger to Pitt," demanded £62.6sh. for paper which Pitt declared he had paid. Taking advantage of his plight, Mill advanced him money on exorbitant terms for building projects, demanding in return his "stock of books, atlases, atlas paper, Copper Plates, Pictures, Printing Presses, letters, etc. which all came to several thousand pounds."[36]

Having abandoned the Oxford Press project, Pitt continued to publish alone or in partnership with several London booksellers. Through 1685 he still maintained his premises at the Angel where he sold not only books but also pictures and maps. In 1684 he announced publication of a *Collection of Travels through Turkey into Persia and the East Indies . . . being the Travels* "of Monsieurs Tavernier, Bernier and other great men." About the same time he advertised *The Picture of Her Royal Highness the Princess Anne of Denmark* and *A Large Map of the great Level of the Fennes* by Sir Jonas Moore Knight, "Pasted, coloured 30s.," Sir William Petty, *Maps of Ireland* "being an actual survey of that whole kingdom. Price in sheets 50s." Pitt's interest in science had not lapsed. In May 1685 he advertised "Leipsick Transactions for the years 1662, 1663, 1664 and for January, February, March, April 1685." The master of the Angel had imported issues of the *Acta eruditorum,* the organ of the German scientific society, the Collegium Naturae Curiosa.[37]

On 30 November 1685 the popular London auctioneer, Edward Millington, conducted a sale of "ancient and modern English books" at Petty Canons Hall. The owner of the property was Moses Pitt, bookseller. A few weeks later at Ave Maria Lane, Millington disposed of the remainder of Pitt's holdings: "several sorts of Bibles," stock available from his former association with the Oxford Press which he had apparently saved despite his creditors' claims. In 1686 Pitt moved to Duke Street where he probably remained until 1688 when he published the *Reports* of Edward Bulstrode.[38]

Shortly thereafter the former affluent publisher and bookseller was arrested for debt and confined to Fleet Street where he composed his semi-autobiography, *The Cry of the Oppressed Being a true . . . account . . . of the sufferings of debtors* issued in 1691. Apparently the ebullient spirit of Moses Pitt had not been completely stifled by imprisonment, since in 1696 he wrote *An Account of one Anne Jeffries who was fed, for six months by a small sort of airy People, called Fairies.*[39]

Poor Pitt may have derived some comfort from a world of fantasy. His last years had been spent in the atmosphere of reality where he had confronted the betrayal of his partners, the loss of his once prosperous business and long days within the dank walls of the Fleet. He had grown old and disillusioned in the profession to which he had richly contributed. Although his aggrieved customer Hooke had dubbed him "that rascall," Pitt, nonetheless, had supplied him and his circle with many significant scientific texts written at home and abroad.

4

William Cooper, Alchemical Specialist

On 3 September 1674 during a visit to Pitt, Hooke "talkd with him and wife about Mr. Cooper." The gentleman in question, William Cooper, was a stationer located at the Pelican, Little Britain. Little is known about Cooper's background. He is one of the few London booksellers of the period not mentioned by the effervescent John Dunton in his *Life and Errors*. Even Hooke refers infrequently to Cooper—a fact which is extremely odd, since the proprietor of the Pelican was a specialist in the publication and sale of alchemical books, a subject of some interest to the Curator of Experiments. Cooper's reputation rests on his comprehensive *Catalogue of Chymicall Books* and his role as the first London book auctioneer.[1]

Cooper's introduction to his *Philosophical Epitaph* (1672) offers some glimpse of his years before he entered the book trade. Apparently he had suffered a violent personal religious upheaval which transferred his faith to astrology. Either he had been ill or in some difficulties with the authorities since he refers to the year 1652 as "a living grave." It was the antiquary Elias Ashmole who appears to have rescued him in 1662 from his troubles. Ashmole, "the greatest virtuoso and curioso that ever was known and read in England before his time" was deeply interested in astrology, alchemy and chemistry, having composed his *Theatrum Chymicum*, a collection of poems on alchemy. He obviously exercised much influence upon Cooper, a kindred spirit, who emerged in 1669 as a specialist dealer in alchemy and chemistry. During that year Cooper published two works bearing identical titles— *Secrets Reveal'd* by the alchemist George Starkey and the other by a fellow adept Eirenaeus Philalethes. Exclusive of his numerous auction catalogues, Cooper was to publish until his death in 1689 a total of 44 books.[2]

Cooper was familiar with the masters of alchemy at home and abroad. In the introduction to his *Catalogue of Chymicall Books* he boasts that he had viewed and perused all of the 200-odd titles therein listed with the exception of nine. If true, Master Cooper's knowledge of his subject was extensive. After the publication of a less comprehensive *Catalogue,* he claimed that he was in a position "to give a larger and more satisfactory account of the Titles, and several Editions of these [books]." He further displayed his familiarity with pertinent subject matter of the *Philosophical Transactions,* since he included in his 1675 *Catalogue* 111 titles of articles published therein during the past ten years, "those having any dependency upon chymistry, the Study of Nature by Art to the Animal, Vegetal or Mineral Kingdoms."[3]

His Introduction reflects his familiarity with the *Bibliotheca Chymica* of the Frenchman Pierre Borel of which Hooke owned two copies. Cooper's expertise is further evinced by his translating and editing several alchemical texts. A 1670 English version of Johann Friedrich Helvetius, *A Briefe of the Golden Calfe, or the World's Idol* is attributed to Cooper. His edition of Eirenaeus Philalethes, *Ripley Reviv'd,* includes a Latin text by Cooper, *Porta prima de calcinatione* and a list of Philalethes's writings. In addition he edited the *Aurifontina Chymica* of John Frederick Houpreght (1680), the *Collectanea Chymica* (1684) and the *Works* of the Arabic scientist Geber.[4]

It has been said that the seventeenth-century alchemist spent more time in scribbling than in experimenting. In his *Bibliotheca Chymica,* Borel cites 4,000 alchemical and chemical authors past and present, an exaggerated claim. Yet it was a century still questing the universal remedy of the alkahest, this fabled solvent— the shortcut to gold! Sir Kenelm Digby searched Germany and Scandinavia, while Evelyn wrote during his continental tour that he had visited "Frier Nicholas at the Convent of Challiot, who being an excellent chymist shew'd me his Laboratorie, a rare Collection of Spagyrical remedies ... he shew'd me a raritie some ... of Antinomie." At a later date the mathematician Oughtred visited Evelyn stating that he thought "water to be the philosopher's first matter, and that he was well perswaded of the possibility of their Elixir." Viewing the royal library at Windsor in September 1680,

Evelyn was most impressed by the "processe of the philosopher's great Elixir represented in divers pieces of incomparable Miniatures ... the Discourses in High Dutch." Oldenburg informed Boyle in 1658 that he was sending him "the Arabic inscription and the proportion to open gold for the price of £100 sterling."[5]

There is some indication that Hooke and John Aubrey hoped to establish an alchemical society in London. A Diary entry of 14 July 1676 states that he had been "with Aubrey to whom I spoke of the Rosicrucian Club. He named Tonge." Aubrey, in all likelihood, had proposed Israel Tongue, the future associate of the infamous Titus Oates. A week later, when Hooke visited Tongue with Aubrey, he found him a "surly fellow" and the club came to nothing.[6]

Although no formal alchemical club existed in London, there was an avid interest on the part of Hooke and his fellow academicians in metallurgy, a science which embraced the transmutation of metals—the search for gold and infinite riches! The fact that William Cooper published and sold alchemical books and issued specialized catalogues on the subject indicates a prevailing predilection for the subject.

In 1672, the year of his publication of his *Philosophical Epitaph,* Cooper's reputation as a connoisseur in the fields of alchemy and general science appears to have been well established. Writing from Utrecht, one F. Oswell informed Oldenburg of some new texts by the physicians Barbette and Bartholinus and a pharmacopeia of Schroder. He requested that Oldenburg "present his service to Mr. Cooper." Cooper's major contribution to alchemy and chemistry was not to appear until 1675 when he issued his *Catalogue of Chymicall Books* to be followed later by writings of major alchemists. His trade-list was highlighted by the compositions of the high priest of alchemy, George Starkey. This adept is of considerable interest, having been born in the Bermudas and graduated from Harvard College as a physician. He declared that while pursuing his practice in America he met the mysterious Eirenaeus Philalethes who initiated him into some of the secret methods of transmuting precious metals. He emigrated to England where during the 1650s he engaged in the sale of quack medicine, styling himself "a philosopher made by the fire and a Professor of that Medicine that is real not Histrionical." In addition to his *Secrets Reveal'd* 1669 and 1678, Cooper published Starkey's

Exposition upon Sir George Ripley's Preface, Exposition upon Sir George Ripley's Epistle, Ennaratio Methodica, Opus Tripartitum, Exposition upon Sir George Ripley's Vision, A breviary of Alchemy and *The Secret of the immortal liquor called Alkahest.*[7]

Other Cooper imprints in the field include a collection of 15 alchemical treatises, the aforementioned *Aurifontina Chymica* of John Frederick Houpreght, edited by Cooper, the *Chymical Secrets* of Sir Kenelm Digby "published [edited] since his death by George Hartmann Chymist and Steward to the aforesaid Sir Kenelm," the *Collectanea Chymica* and the *Works* of Jabir Ibn Haiyan known as Geber. In 1658 the Master of the Pelican published *One Hundred Fifty Three Aphorisms* by the celebrated Franciscus Mercurius van Helmont translated into English by Christopher Packe who styled himself a "Philo-Chymico-Medicus." The work, selling at 20sh., was offered on fairly attractive terms. The customer was expected to pay 10sh. following delivery and subscribers for six copies were given one gratis. The following year Cooper issued the *Works* of the renowned Johann Rudolph Glauber. Metallurgy, an adjunct of alchemy, is represented on the Cooper trade list: Thomas Houghton, *Rara Avis in terris;* Hugh Platt, *History of Subterraneal Treasure; The ancient Laws, Customs and orders of the Miners in Mendipp Forest* and *Two Ephemerides for the year 1687* by the great astronomer Halley.[8]

Although Cooper rarely ventured outside his special field, he published in 1674 *A French Grammar . . . how to Read and Write it perfectly . . . both in French and English.* "Published by the Academy for the Reformation of the French Tongue," the work sold for 1sh. In 1685 Cooper again evinced an interest in philology issuing *Minerva, The High Dutch Grammar* "teaching the Englishman perfectly easily and exactly the Dialect of the High German Tongue."[9]

Cooper's *Catalogue of Chymical Books* (1675) remains his most important contribution to publishing history. It reflects not only his predilection for alchemy and allied subjects but also his awareness of public demand since in his preface he "take[s] the boldness to inform the Reader that most of the Books contained in these Catalogues (with many others of this Subject in Latine . . .) are to be sold by Will. Cooper at the Sign of the Pelican in Little Britain, London."

Cooper's *Catalogue* is of extreme significance as the first bibliography in English relating to alchemical and chemical texts. Arranged in three parts, the work lists in the first two approximately 200 books published in England during the sixteenth and seventeenth centuries, many of which had been translated from the original into English. The third part consists of titles of articles from the past ten-year run of the *Philosophical Transactions.* Hence the *Catalogue* remains a substantial guide to the *materia alchymica & chymica* which appeared in England prior to 1675.[10]

The writings of well- and lesser-known specialists are cited: the *Secrets* of Alexander of Piedmont; the *Three Books of Occult Philosophy* of Henry Cornelius Agrippa; the popular *Theatrum Chymicum Britannicum* of Cooper's inspirational master Elias Ashmole. Well-known to the English adept was the *Mirror of Alchemy* of Roger Bacon published in 1597. *Of Natural and Supernatural Things* by the popular Basil Valentine bore the imprint of Moses Pitt. The first English edition of the *Tyrocinium-chymicum* of Jean Beguin of Lorraine appeared in London in 1669 having been translated into English by Richard Russell. A work of some rarity is the *Aurora chymica* (1665) of the English physician Edward Bolnest, part of the impression having been destroyed in the Fire of London. Hence copies were scarce at the time of publication of Cooper's *Catalogue.* Other items include Samuel Boulton, *Magical but Natural Physick with a Description of the very Excellent Cordial of Gold* and the *Basilica Chymica & Praxis* of Oswald Croll, a follower of Paracelsus. Hooke may have purchased his copies of Agrippa, Beguin, and Croll from Cooper.[11]

Other works by Englishmen enjoyed a ready market: *The Treatise of Aurum Potabile* of Nicholas Culpepper; Digby's *Choice and Experimental Receipts* and his *Discourse touching the Cure of Wounds by the Powder of Sympathy;* as well as the *Mosaicall Philosophy* of the physician, astrologer, and alchemist Robert Fludd—another work in the Hooke collection. Rosicrucianism appealed to many of Cooper's customers. Its followers believed themselves possessed with the deepest knowledge of the transmutation of metals. Although John Heydon, the astrologer, denied any close affiliation with the English Rosicrucians, he nonetheless averred that his writings interpreted their philosophy. Many Heydon works are listed by Cooper: *Wise-man's Crown or the Glory of the Rosie Cross, Hammegulah Hampaaneah or Rosi Crucian*

Crown, Theomagia or the temple of wisdome, Harmony of the world and *El havarevna or the English Physitians tutor in the Astrobolisms of Metals.* Cooper listed *the Unlearned Alchymist, his Antidote* by Richard Mathews who also sold his composition "at his house by the Lyons Den at the Tower, next Gate to the By-Ward." Along with the text the customer could obtain a potion made by the author who supplied directions for its use.[12]

Paracelsians noted mention of the master's *Key of Philosophy* and his *Chymical Transmutations* as well as his *Archidoxes.* The *Catalogue* cites numerous writings of the alchemist Thomas Vaughan who adopted the pseudonym Eugenius Philalethes (not to be confused with Eirenaeus Philalethes): his *Anthroposophia Theomagia, Magia Adamica, Euphrates or Waters of the East, Lumen de Lumine, Man-Mouse taken in a trap, Aulae lucis* and others. Significant studies were Joachim Poleman, *Novum lumen medium,* the *New Light of alchymie* of Michael Sendivogius and naturally the miscellaneous contributions of George Starkey and George Ripley. Works of other authorities were the *Store-House of Physical and Philosophical Secrets, Secrets of an open Entrance to the shut pallace of the king containing the greatest treasures in Chymistry, Philosophia Maturata, or the pratick and operative part of the Philosophers Stone, Four Patents granted by King Henry the Sixth . . . for finding Gold & Silver;* the writings of both Helmonts, father and son; the *Hieroglyphical Figures of the Philosophers Stone* of Nicholas Flammel, one of the most renowned of all adepts whose pursuit of the profession had been inspired by an alchemical book written on leaves made of the bark of a tree.[13]

Cooper's *Catalogue* achieved additional stature by its inclusion of the writings of the greatest and most popular English scientist Robert Boyle. The catalogue cited many in first editions: *New Experiments Physico-Mechanicall Touching the Spring of Air* (1660); one of the greatest of contemporary and future chemical treatises, *The Sceptical Chymist* (1661); *Certain Physiological Essays* (1661); *Hydrostatical Parodoxes* (1661); *Experiments and Considerations touching Colours* (1664); *Experimental History of Cold* (1665); *An Essay about the Origine & Virtue of Gems* (1672); *The Origine & Forme of Qualities* (1666); *Essay of Effluviums* (1673), and others.[14]

For his specialist client on the prowl for gold and the great alkahest, Cooper cited several metallurgical treatises: *The Booke of the Art of Metals,* the first complete edition of Alvaro Alonso Barba translated into English by the Earl of Sandwich—of importance for its reference to America; Sir John Pettus, *Foedinae Regales;* Robert Love, *Compleat Historie of Animals and Minerals;* Paracelsus, *Chymical Transmutation;* and several others. Medical texts, pharmacopeiae, treatises on balneology and pertinent articles from the *Philosophical Transactions* complete the *Catalogue of Chymicall Books* compiled and published by William Cooper.[15]

An innovative specialist, Cooper realized the value of advertising new as well as old publications. A list of 35 titles is appended to John Frederick Houpreght, *Aurifontina chymica. A Caveat for the Protestant Clergy, if Popery be restored* scarcely reflects Cooper's alchemical predilection. It does indicate English fear of the return of the Roman church to the realm. The Houpreght appendix includes Spenser's *View of Ireland* in folio. Written by the poet Edmund Spenser, the *View* was first published inaccurately by the Irish historian James Ware as an appendix to his *Historie of Ireland.* No other edition had been published at the time of Cooper's advertisement. Apparently the *View* had been detached from the *History* and sold separately, a practice, alas, not uncommon in today's antiquarian market.[16]

There is no way to determine Cooper's income from the sale of books in alchemy and chemistry. Hooke mentions few outright purchases from the proprietor of the Pelican. On 8 August 1679 he acquired from Cooper "Scheiner's Opticks 4s. and Snellius Observationes Hassicae 1½s. paid." The Auction Catalogue of Hooke's Library refers to a few Cooper items: the treatises of Scheiner, Houghton, *the Compleat Miner* and Fromond, *Meteorologicae libri 6.*[17]

Cooper's role as a specialist bookseller in alchemical and chemical texts is rivaled by his career as the first English auctioneer. He introduced this method of bookselling into England encouraging a host of imitators and successors. Thus he played a double role in the history of English bibliophily.[*]

---

[*] For Cooper's role as auctioneer, see Chapter 6 of this work.

5

Book Stalls of Duck Lane and Moorfields

Hooke apparently spent little time at the shop of William Cooper. On the contrary he passed many hours searching for a good buy—a sleeper—in the jumbled quarters of Cheapside, notably the warrens of Duck Lane and Moorfields. Like all eager bibliophiles, he sought a bargain and here he hunted new and antiquarian books. As London surveyor, he was afforded ample opportunity since he took sights in Aldersgate and Moorfields.

In his analysis of the seventeenth-century English book trade, Dunton remarks: "It would be tedious and unconscionable to go through all Cheapside, Paul's Churchyard, Little Britain and Duck Lane to describe every Man, Woman and Sucking-Child, Bookseller, Auctioneer, Stitcher, Hawker, &c." A visitor to Duck Lane, Pepys refers to his "passing through the booksellers." Neither the diarist nor Hooke specifies by name a single dealer in this concentrated warren of books and book people. Their journals afford tantalizing clues "To Duck Lane at first shop . . . at second shop . . . at third shop." The impression is given of small shops or stalls adjacent to each other, their wares haphazardly assembled—some displayed in the open in crates or on rickety shelves. It is only through the imprints of these denizens of Duck Lane and Moorfields that their persons are reanimated—their anonymity shed—their proprietorship of the Crown, the Black Raven, the Bible, the Anchor, the Golden Ball reëstablished.[1]

From a study of an approximate 19 book dealers active in Duck Lane during the Restoration it becomes apparent that the majority had met some adversity and had sought this less stylish area to pursue their profession. Some few, once again prosperous, deserted the neighborhood for a more distinguished address.

Although Dunton avers the honesty and character of the Duck Lane dealers he repeats their misfortunes in business and their general hard luck. Thomas Axe of the Blue Ball known as "Honest Tom" had met withe grave losses. "No man is more contented with his little, and so patient under any disappointment: but, notwithstanding his losses in trade, I believe Mr. Axe will get money enough." A little-known bookseller Frank Hubbald had "been unfortunate." Nonetheless "his courage and wisdom carried him with unwearied course through both Hemispheres of Prosperity and Adversity." Comparing the dealer Thomas Yates with himself, Dunton remarked that he had also suffered losses but "was still as honest as ever." William Whitwood was dubbed by Dunton "a rolling printer." He may have earned this sobriquet either because he dealt in engravings or because of his many moves from the Swan to the Golden Lion, the Golden Ball to the Golden Dragon next door to the Crown Tavern.[2]

Having lost stock and household goods in the Fire, many were compelled to seek new quarters. Joshua Coniers, originally of Long Walk near Christ Church, had set up at the Black Raven, Duck Lane, while his colleague Samuell Thompson of Bishops Head, friend and bookseller to many of the Royal Society academicians, confessed that he had suffered much in the wake of the Fire. William Thackeray of the Old Bailey had relocated at the Sugar Loaf, Duck Lane.[3]

Once financially recovered, the auctioneer Millington abandoned Duck Lane, moving to nearby Little Britain and later to Cambridge. Thomas Sawbridge, publisher and bookseller, left his old area for the Flower de Luce, Little Britain.[4]

The majority of the Duck Lane coterie were booksellers who lacked capital essential to publishing. A few were tangential to the trade. Anderson, a weaver, together with the almanac maker Thomas Streete, sold some of the mathematical works of Oughtred. Thomas Axe was binder, bookseller, globe-dealer, and auctioneer.[5]

Much of the Duck Lane stock—according to Hooke's Diary entries—comprised foreign and early English scientific texts. It is quite likely that many of these books were at the time in little demand and had been bought up quite reasonably in lots from some established dealers in St. Paul's Churchyard, indifferent to their content, or at auction. The small, little-known specialist in antiquarian science could scarcely vie with the dealer in the ever-popular modern firsts who offered his clientele the latest in Dryden, Cowley, Congreve, Waller, and other "in" authors.

To supplement his stock the Duck Lane bookseller searched beyond London. Nicholas Boddington of the Golden Ball traveled "much in the country." Apparently his greatest asset, according to Dunton, was "his satisfaction to belong to a beautiful wife." The Stourbridge Fair lured several denizens of the area. Here Millington conducted his first country sale in 1684 selling a collection of English and foreign books. The *Bibliotheca Sturbichiana,* copies of which were distributed gratis at all the Cambridge coffee-houses, included 2,200 lots. The Sale proved eminently successful and was repeated the following year. Among its visitors was William Shrowsbury of the Bible, Duck Lane, who, Dunton declared, was "a constant frequenter of the Stourbridge Fair."[6]

Pepys, an habitué of Duck Lane, appears to have been attracted to its crowded precincts not merely for bibliophilic but more so for amorous reasons. It is true that in February 1667/68 he acquired at one of the shops a copy of Athanasius Kircher, *Musurgia* for 35sh., "a book I am right glad of, expecting to find great satisfaction in it." Another visit resulted in the purchase of a copy of Montaigne, *Essays* in English. On the prowl for a copy of Mersenne, *L'Harmonie Universelle* he searched the area. "It is not to be had, but I have given order for its being sent for." As compensation he purchased a copy of Descartes, "his little treatise on musique," in all likelihood the English translation (London, 1653). Pepys's entry is of interest since it indicates that the Duck Lane dealer either enjoyed good relations with the larger London music firms or maintained contacts with the French trade which could provide him with a copy of his desideratum.[7]

Although Samuel Pepys, Secretary of the Admiralty and bibliophile, purchased a copy of the *Lives of the Saints* of Jacobus de Voragine, his behavior on the day of acquisition, 10 April 1666, was scarcely saintly since either before or after the sale he tarried to embrace the bookseller's wife. This damsel—and not the folios and octavos of Duck Lane—continued to beckon Pepys thither ... "passing through Duck Lane ... only to get a sight of the pretty little woman I did salute the other night, and did in passing." Returning to the area he bought one work in Spanish and "there did I endeavour to see my pretty woman that I did baiser in las tenebras a little while depuis. And did find her sola in the bookshop but had not la confidence par a aller a elle, but still another time." The "pretty woman" in question was the wife of William Shrowsbury, proprietor of the Bible. Upon several later visits Pepys "espied his belle femme," but had "no opportunity para hazer con her." His passion, alas, was cooled when, upon a feigned business call to the Bible, 23 October 1668, he discovered his "belle femme . . . so big-bellied that elle is not worth seeing." There is no evidence that his future viewing in Duck Lane was confined to literature![8]

Unlike Pepys, Hooke certainly did not seek "les belles femmes, big-bellied" or otherwise within the shops and stalls of Duck Lane. His Diary entries refer to the purchase of books offering but one clue only to the identity of a bookseller—none to a "pretty woman." To specify exactly the names of the shops frequented by Hooke it is necessary to eliminate those Duck Lane dealers who sold virtually no science. Hence the bibliophilic sleuth must stalk the area and investigate the activity and publications of Samuell Thompson, William Shrowsbury, Thomas Sawbridge, Joshua Coniers, and William Isles.

It is certain that Hooke was personally well acquainted with Samuell Thompson of the Bishops Head, Duck Lane who in 1661 published the scientist's *An Attempt for the explication of phaenomena*. Thompson, originally from Burfield, Shropshire, arrived in London in 1634 when he was apprenticed to Joyce Norton and Richard Whitaker who freed him in January 1641. Nothing appears to be known of his activity during the following seven years. In 1648 he set up at the White Horse, St. Paul's Churchyard, suffering reverses in 1666 from the Fire, thence apparently moving to the Bishops Head, Duck Lane. According to the records of Richard Smyth, Secondary of the Poultry Compter, "On Oct. 16 1668 (at midnight) Sam. Thompson bookseller in Duck Lane obit. a good husband and industrious man in his profession."[9]

During his approximate twenty years in business Thompson published at least forty books half of which are scientific in content. These include texts in physics, medicine, alchemy, and mathematics. With the establishment of the Royal Society, Thompson published, in addition to Hooke's treatise *Of phaenomena*, John Wallis, *Hobbius heautontimorumenos*, Gilbert Clark, *Tractatus de restitutione corporum*, James Gregory, *Optica promota*, Gideon

Harvey, *Archelogia philosophica nova,* and medical treatises of Everard Maynwaring. In 1668 Thompson crowned his literary production as one of the publishers of the first edition of *Paradise Lost,* the title-page in fourth state.[10]

Before the Fire, Thompson had entertained high hopes of publishing the Latin version of the *Observations on the fixed stars* by the Persian astronomer Ulugh Beg who had established an observatory at Samarkand in 1420. The findings of Ulugh Beg were considered to be the most accurate before those of Tycho Brahe. The manuscript of his *Observations* had been deposited at Oxford and aroused keen interest among the Royal Society astronomers. Thompson had apparently suggested a plan for publication which Wallis had considered not sufficiently comprehensive. In a letter of 30 April 1664 addressed by Wallis to Oldenburg, he remarked that "there may possibly be a mistake in Mr Thompson's comprehension, as thinking onely of a Latine translation, & not of ye Persian to be printed with it." It is quite obvious that John Wallis had little idea of the cost of exotic type or of the difficulty in procuring it. Actually Ulugh Beg's *Tables* were published in Persian the following year by the well-established Oxford dealer Richard Davis—two copies of which were eventually acquired by Hooke.[11]

It was at Thompson's shop that the mathematician John Collins informed his colleague James Gregory that he had read through a copy of his *De quadratura circuli ex hyperbole.* "He [Thompson] hath sent the other to Dr. Wallis." During a visit to Padua, Collins kept in touch with Thompson.[12]

As a bookseller Thompson not only imported foreign scientific texts but also kept abreast with current English scientific publications. Like several of his colleagues, he appears to have issued catalogues or lists of available material. During a visit to his premises Oldenburg noted that the proprietor expected "within 4. or 5. dayes ye delivery of Kircher's Mundus Subterraneus. I perceive ye price will amount to 50sh. at least, and yet but one volume. I find also, by his Catalogue, yt yesame Kircher has publisht a Scrutinium Physico-medicum Pestis." Had not Pepys during a bibliophilic foray in Duck Lane found a copy of Kircher's *Musurgia* which had cost him 35 shillings? The texts of the Jesuit Athanasius Kircher had been printed in Amsterdam and Rome and were probably exported as a lot to a general London clearing house. In October 1665 Oldenburg informed Boyle that it was Thompson's wont "to acquaint [him] with the new Books, yt come abroad." The Secretary of the Royal Society expressed some annoyance that Thompson had "neither then or afore told [him] anything of Galilaeo's second Tome, but I shall ask him about it, God willing, ye next time, I passe yt way." Oldenburg was no doubt alluding to Thomas Salusbury's version of Galileo, *Mathematical Collections,* published by William Leybourn in 1665.[13]

During the Plague when Martyn and Allestry suspended the publication of the *Philosophical Transactions,* taken over for a brief period by Richard Davis of Oxford, Boyle suggested that Davis send copies to Thompson for circulation in London.[14]

It was at the sign of the Bible, Duck Lane, that Samuel Pepys "did baiser" the proprietor's wife in "las tenebras." During this romantic interlude it is quite possible that the lady's spouse William Shrowsbury was scouting books in London, attending the Stourbridge Fair or even discussing the desiderata of his somewhat exacting customer Robert Hooke. Although Hooke does not specify a visit to the Bible, his purchases suggest that a goodly number may have been bought from Shrowsbury, the principal publisher of the jurist, scientist, and philosopher, Sir Matthew Hale. The constant exchange of merchandise among members of the London book trade is attested by Hooke's Diary entry of 23 December 1676: "Sent to Mr. Martin for Sir Ma. Hales book." Martyn had ordered copies of Sir Matthew's texts from Shrowsbury. In addition to Justice Hale's works, Shrowsbury stocked various antiquarian scientific texts.[15]

Of the proprietor of the Bible, Dunton somewhat rhapsodically writes: "The morning of his life was clear and calm, and ever since his whole life has been a continued series of honesty; then no wonder he printed for Judge Hales. He merits the name of universal bookseller, and is familiarly acquainted with all the books that are extant in any language. He keeps his stock in excellent order, and will find any Book as ready as I can find a word in the Dictionary. He is a great Ornament to the Stationers Company, and may justly be called Venerable for his heavenly aspect wherein gravity and Sweetness are all compounded."[16]

From 1672 to 1688 William Shrowsbury was active at the Bible, Duck Lane, where he published an approximate 18 books, the majority of which represent the writings of Hale. Shrowsbury's first publication, *Stereometrie, or the Art of Practical Gauging* by J.

Smith "Philo-Accomptant" selling for "3s.6d. bound" appeared in 1672. Hale's scientific texts include his *Essay touching the Gravitation of non-gravitation of fluid bodies,* "bound 1sh.;" *Observations touching the Principles of Natural Motion* and his most significant work, *The Primitive Origination of Mankind.* A balneological treatise *Spadacreno-Dunelmensis, or a short Treatise of an antient Medicinal Fountain, or Virtioline Spaw, near the city of Durham* "bound 1sh." bore the 1675 imprint of Shrowsbury who seven months later issued *A Tryal of Witches Held at the Assizes of Bury St. Edmunds.*[17]

Hooke's Diary records at least six visits to Duck Lane and there can be little doubt that he found much of interest at Shrowsbury's premises. On a buying venture of 17 December 1672 he refers to the purchase of "Descartes epistles 6sh., Leotauds Cyclomathia etc. 3sh., Dutch book 1sh., Fioravantys trades 8d." He had obviously acquired the London 1653 edition of Descartes' *Epistolae.* Pepys had earlier referred to his acquisition of "Descartes his little Treatise of Musique." The Hooke Library included the Latin and English editions of Descartes' *Compendium of Musick.* Vincent Leotaud's *Cyclomathia ... Libri III* had been published at Lyons in 1633 and two English editions of different works of Leonardo Fioravanti had appeared in London in 1652 and 1659.[18]

Hooke offers the bibliophilic detective one clue in his search for the identity of yet another Duck Lane dealer. On 16 April 1674, he writes: "Bought [books] next Blew Anchor in Duck Lane." Thomas Sawbridge was the proprietor of the shop next the coffeehouse, the Blew Anchor in Duck Lane. He published several scientific writings including a few of the draughtsman and mathematician William Leybourne, a close friend of Hooke.[19]

Thomas Sawbridge, a member of the successful stationer family, began as publisher and bookseller at the Anchor, Duck Lane in 1655 continuing for 37 years during which he issued and sold a variety of scientific texts. He published two editions of Joseph Darling, *The Carpenters Rule made easy* "bound 2sh.," Henry Coley, *Clavis astrologiae elementa,* three editions of Palladio, *First Book of Architecture;* and two editions of Hodder, *Arithmetick* at 1s.4d. each; and other miscellaneous texts. Obviously Sawbridge's varied stock appealed to the multi-faceted interests of Robert Hooke. In his specific reference to "the [shop] next Blew

Anchor," Hooke cites the purchase of "Clusius variorum planta-rum Historia 6d ejusdem exoticarum libri 10s. cum observationibus Bellonii 4s. Cardanus de proportionibus & Algebra 2s. Paid him by Harry." The scientist had acquired the highly prized botanical treatises of Charles L'Ecluse, his *Variorum plantarum historia* published by Plantin at Antwerp in 1601 and his *Exoticarum libri* of 1605, the mathematical treatises of the ever-influential Jerome Cardan. Apparently Hooke had sent his assistant Harry Hunt, also operator of experiments at the meetings of the Royal Society, to settle the account.[20]

Hooke's Duck Lane purchase of 23 July 1675 is described as "Albert Durers works for 4sh." Although he may have acquired the recently London-published *Albert Durer revived: or, a book of drawing, limning, washing or colouring of maps and prints,* a work most useful to Hooke, the "map pricker" and artist, the Hooke Auction Catalogue cites only a copy of Duerer's "De symetria." *De simmetria partium in rectis fermis humanorum corporum libri* was published at Nuremberg in 1528, a work of singular significance to the world of art.[21]

A sizable purchase of 13 books is mentioned by Hooke on 24 August 1675—"all in 8° 2s.6d." The collector, indeed, knew a bargain! These titles could have been obtained either from Saw-bridge or Shrowsbury. The lot includes among others the *Historia Vitae et Mortis* and the *Historia de Ventis* of Sir Francis Bacon, published in London in 1623 and 1671 respectively. Other titles mentioned are "Digges Calendar, Burning London, Hood of the Sector, Wright of the Sphere, Finaeus de Horologii, Gellibrand of the Variation of the Needle, Shakerley against Urania practica, De la Main, Circles of Proportion, Sir Christ. Heydon Astrology, Street & Childreys Almanacs for 1653." The majority of these titles are of English origin. Leonard Digges, *Prognostication ... contayn-ing rules to judge the weather* appeared in several editions from 1578 to 1605; *London's Flames* was a recent publication (1667) detailing the ravages of the great Fire. Thomas Hood's *The Making and use of the sector* was published by Windet in 1595 and *The Description and Use of the Sphaere* appeared in 1598 and 1631. Oronce Finé's *De solaribus horologiis quadrantibus libri quatuor,* an important continental text by the celebrated French scientist, issued in 1560, is listed exactly in the Hooke Auction Catalogue. Gellibrand's *Discourse mathematical of the variation of the magneti-*

call needle and Shakerley's *Anatomy of Urania Practica* were printed in London in 1635 and 1649. *Grammelogie or the mathematical ring* was the work of the English mathematician Richard Dalamain, while Christopher Heydon's *Defence of Judiciall Astrology* appeared at Cambridge in 1606.[22]

In late December 1675, Hooke refers to a book-hunting jaunt in Duck Lane "at the first shop west." The character of his purchases suggests that he had again visited Shrowsbury's premises, since among other items he acquired "Harriots Algebra 1s.6d., Snellius triangulis 6d., Schooten Sines Secantes Tangentes, R.S. Arithmetick 6d., Shakerley's Tables 2sh., Against Galilaeo 2 tracts 6d." Of these works three had been published in England prior to the Restoration and may have been picked up by Shrowsbury at the Stourbridge Fair.[23]

A bookbuying trip of 11 December 1675 reanimates the bookish aspects of Duck Lane. Here Hooke browsed in three book stores: "the first shop, the second shop, the third shop." The scholar-detective is frustrated by the anonymity of ownership; the collector is titillated by the image of a vast sea of books! The "first shop" may have been that of William Isles, publisher of a single work which is listed in the Hooke Auction Catalogue: Lucas Jacobsen Debes, *Faeroae et Feroae reserata,* London 1676. *A description and history of the Faroes,* islands off the Danish coast, had been translated into English by the Scotsman John Sterpin who was to render a most faulty Latin version of a part of the *Philosophical Transactions.* Published by Isles in 1676, the work sold for 2s.6d. Hooke states that he had purchased at the same shop a first edition of Oughtred. A letter of Collins to Francis Vernon refers to one Isles, a bookseller in Duck Lane who had "bought some of Oughtred's books." In addition, Hooke selected "a written map," a copy of the *Optics* of the Arabic scientist Alhazen, and the *Logarithms* of Napier.[24]

His bibliophilic passion still running high and his purse still fat, Hooke proceeded to the "second shop" which might have been the Black Raven owned by Joshua Coniers, a post-Fire resident. The few books published by Coniers are of a miscellaneous scientific nature: *Meteorologia* by William Cock "Philomath;" *A Guide to the young Gager* by Simon Jones; almanacs of Thomas Street and Robert Anderson; as well as several texts by the astrologer Henry Coley. Hooke appears to have been quite discriminating during his visit selecting only one work: Thomas Digges, *Alae seu scalae mathematicae* (London 1573). The browser completed his day's rounds at the "third shop," possibly that of William Whitwood of the Golden Ball who had been hailed by Dunton as a "rolling printer." Whitwood had begun publishing at another Duck Lane premise, the Golden Lion, when in 1669 he issued *Two Discourses: the first concerning the different Wits of Men, The Second the Mysteries of Vintners* . . . "Delivered to the Royal Society. Price "bound 2sh." Other Whitwood imprints include books on travel, medicine, archeology, and miscellaneous subjects. It was at this "third shop" that Hooke selected a variety of texts: Pellisson, *Relation contenant l'histoire de l'Academie Françoise;* Jacques Billy, *Nova Geometria;* Bartholomaeus Pitiscus, *Trigonometria;* and one of the many works of the Italian scientist Ulysses Aldrovandus.[25]

If Hooke's bibliophilic thirst had not been sufficiently slaked by Duck Lane attractions he could have easily slipped through Aldersgate to Moorfields near Moor Gate and London Wall. This somewhat rural area, drained in 1527, had during the early reign of James I been converted into a partial recreation center with attractive walks. Here the militia paraded "with pykes and bowes in bluw clokes garded with red." Studded with windmills, small shops and stalls, ale- and coffee-houses, it appealed to Hooke, Pepys, their fellow academicians and the general public for relaxation on a pleasant day. Here Pepys enjoyed the wrestling matches between north and west countrymen; witnessed several times a merry performance of Ponchinello; bought a set of compasses at the shop of one of the instrument-makers; sought out a pretty damsel or discussed the snow and drabness of Russia with his friend Mr. Pargiter. During the Plague and the Fire refugees sought haven here from the spreading infection and the onslaught of the flames. "I went forth and walked toward Moorfields to see . . . whether I could see any dead corps going to the grave," wrote Pepys in August 1665 and a little over a year later during the height of the Fire he discovered the area "full of . . . poor wretches carrying their goods there, and everybody keeping their goods together by themselves."[26]

It was at Moorfields that Robert Hooke, city surveyor and architect, rebuilt Bethlehem Hospital in 1676 which in Evelyn's opinion "was magnificently built and most sweetly placed in Morefeilds since the dreadful fire of Lond." The area was fast becoming a patchwork of new buildings which included shops and stalls. During his numerous visits there Hooke "viewed Lands at Cripplegate and Bunhill Place;" ate bacon at the Windmill and imbibed ale at the Sun, Moor Gate. Moorfields lured the scientist professionally and bibliophilicly. Like Duck Lane, this less affluent area attracted booksellers who had met with adversity. Their stocks, similar to those of the Duck Lane professional, comprised largely antiquarian books appealing little to the collector interested in new English and French novels, smart plays, and sumptuous bindings.[27]

The bookshops and stalls of Moorfields, probably less numerous than those of Duck Lane, appear to have had a greater attraction for Hooke. His later Diaries from 1688 to 1693 indicate frequent visits and often an unsuccessful book bag which is indicated "MF[0]." Like the publishers and booksellers of Duck Lane, their Moorfields colleagues remain for the most part anonymous. With the exception of Hooke's specific reference to the art specialist Robert Pricke and the premises of the Golden Fleece, the remaining stationers of Moorfields are reanimated only through the meagre publications and the titles acquired by Hooke. In the latter case association of specific books with specific dealers is conjectural.

The somewhat careless attitude of the Moorfields dealer toward his jumble of books is suggested by two terse entries of 21 and 23 March 1692/93 in Hooke's later Diary: "In MF saw neer 100 of Mr Boyles High Dutch Chymicall books ly exposed in Moorfeilds on the railes. Till 11½ in MF saw many of Mr Boyles German chemicall books." One can only deduce that the books which had once belonged to one of the greatest English chemists lay exposed on shelves or crates in front of a stall or shop subject to the moods of weather, proprietor, and customer. Boyle died in December 1691. A year later a nonconformist divine Zachary Merrill wrote that he had seen the late chemist's library "containing 330 fol. 801 qtos 2440 Oct. and 12. most of y^{m} well bound. They may be had for 3 or 400£s (tho' worth 1000) because they must not be sold by Auction." The Library was to have been sold from the house of Boyle's late sister Lady Ranelaugh. Evidently no sale transpired and once the house was closed, some of the books were sold to Moorfields dealers. The remainder were dispatched to Tom's coffee-house where, together with the library of the arms-painter Silvanus Morgan, they were put up for public auction—notwithstanding the statement of the Rev. Mr. Zachary Merrill. Hooke records on 28 March 1693 that he had "read a Catal. of Morgans and Boyles books at Toms." It certainly may be concluded that Hooke attended the auction sale of the books of his late revered friend![28]

Long before Hooke had espied Boyle's books "on the railes" in Moorfields he had prowled about the area searching for books satisfying his many interests. In June 1672 he acquired a copy of Hugh Plat, *Jewel House of Art and Nature* followed by the purchase of "Bulwars Muscles." The latter was bought at the Golden Fleece whose proprietor Richard Southby was a fairly inactive stationer. Credit is given to him by Dunton for "having a Wife of a good Fortune." Despite his wife's presumed estate Southby had established himself in Moorfields. According to Dunton, he had also run a coffee-house, since "it was not his luck to get estate by Authors; and I wish he may get it by Coffee." Perhaps Hooke sipped a strong brew while flipping through the pages of Bulwar, *Pathomyotomia, or a Dissection of the Significative Muscles of the Minde.*[29]

Art, architecture, and print specialist, Robert Pricke was located at the Golden Lion, corner of New Cheapside next Bethlehem in Moorfields. Obviously Hooke could readily visit Pricke before or after work on the construction of Bethlehem Hospital. Here Hooke acquired books on perspective, the arts and pencils for drafting. Fluent in French, Pricke had translated several notable architectural treatises: *A New Treatise of Architecture according to Vitruvius from the French of Julien Mauclerc* and Jean Barbet, *A Book of Architecture* "adorn'd with 150 copper plates." Other Pricke publications certainly attracted Hooke the surveyor interested in texts for the rebuilding of London: *Ornaments of Architecture* described as a manual for "Painters, Carvers, Stone-Cutters and Plaisterers" "sold at 5sh;" Henry Coggeshall, *Timber Measure* and *The Store House of Architecture.*[30]

Pricke's architectural list included a work of considerable influence. In 1669 he translated from the French and published *A Nevv Book of Architecture wherein is Represented Fourty Figures of Gates and Arches Triumphant* originally compiled by Alessandro Francini, the Florentine engineer of Louis XIV. A copy is listed in the Hooke Auction Catalogue and it may be assumed that Hooke had obtained in addition from Pricke his copies of the works of Vitruvius, Alberti, Boeckler and others.[31]

Among the Pricke imprints is his 1670 translation of Pierre Le Muet, *The Art of Fair Building*. It is interesting to note that Hooke acquired the first French edition (Paris 1623) as well as Pricke's English version. According to his Diary he purchased this translation and a copy of Philip Vingboon, *Gronden der vornaemste Gebowen*, (Amsterdam 1675) not from Pricke but rather from "Thomsons, Bedford Street." Richard Thompson was a specialist in *objets d'art* and mezzotints. According to Hooke, "a curious inlay'd table" had attracted him to his shop.[32]

During a visit to Pricke on 7 October 1675, Hooke remarked that there he had seen "Palladio Englisht." It may be assumed that Hooke had later obtained the English version from its translator, his friend, the book and map dealer, Godfrey Richards who published the work in 1683. Richards declared he had been inspired to undertake this translation and publication of Palladio because "of the scarcity of books of Architecture in English and the zeal which he discovered our Ingenious Artists have to entertain anything of that subject." The Hooke Library also included two Italian editions of Palladio.[33]

The Hooke Diary entries shed light not only upon his personal taste but also upon the interchange of books among dealers. Although he was a faithful customer of Pricke, he purchased Le Muet's *Art of Fair Building* from Thompson and the "Palladio English't" from Richards.

In Moorfields Hooke also searched for technical texts. In all likelihood, Hooke obtained from the publisher-bookseller William Birch a copy of Michael Dary, *Miscellanies;* Leybourne, *Panorganon or a universal instrument;* and miscellaneous works attesting to his manifold interests: *A true and faithful account of the four chiefest plantations* by Samuel Clark of Grendon-Underwood, Bucks.; *A description of the seventeen provinces* and for diversion John Crowne's *Juliana*.[34]

There can be little doubt that Hooke found books and technical accessories at the shop of Walter Hayes of the Cross Daggers. Available to him were copies of Leybourne, *Use of the semi-circle,* Walgrave, *Decimal arithmetick,* Twysden, *Use of the general planisphere,* and Seth Partridge, *The description and use of an instrument called the double scale*.[35]

Hooke's quest for technological texts resulted in the acquisition of two extremely important works: William Ames, *Philosophemata Technometria* (1646) at 5d. and the handsomely illustrated Spanish edition of Jacques Besson, *Teatros de los Instrumentos.*[36]

A prestigious mathematician, Hooke prowled Moorfields for books in the field finding Charles de Bouvelles, *Geometrie pratique* (1547) at 3½d., Michael Constantius Psellus, *Calculus* (1558) at ½d., and the contemporary text of Johann Friedrich Rahn, *Introduction to Algebra.* Conversant with marine science, he bought a copy of A. Van Berlicom, *Treatise on Longitude* and the English edition of Libert Froidmont, *Meteorologica* at 2d. As an excellent astronomer and dabbler in astrology, he naturally purchased Welper, *Epitome Astronomiae* and some "astrology books." Throughout his life he evinced curiosity about the occult and it is not surprising that during a Moorfields jaunt he willingly paid 14d. for a copy of Cardan, *De subtilitate* and 1sh. for *De justificatione Daemonum* of Pico della Mirandola.[37]

A Diary entry of 22 March 1692/93 states that he paid 6d. for "2 Dutch chymick books"—in all likelihood works from the library of his late esteemed friend Robert Boyle—books that lay exposed "on the railes" of Moorfields.[38]

It is not at all surprising that the hypochondriac searched Moorfields for wondrous cures and remedies. Here he paid 2d. for Cardan's *Ars curandi parva* and Juan Fragoso, *Discursos de las cosas aromaticas de la India Oriental.* If the Eastern aromatic spirits of Señor Fragoso failed to allay Robert Hooke's chronic catarrh, the botanical texts of William Hughes surely afforded some pleasant fragrance. In April 1663 he picked up copies of Hughes, *Compleat Vineyard* and *Flower Garden.*[39]

Hooke's bibliophilic migrations seldom took him beyond his familiar haunts. Yet his great intellectual curiosity bore him beyond deepest sea and highest peak. His mind inquired into the remote, hazardous, the unknown. He had searched Americana at the premises of Martyn and Pitt and tracking through Moorfields he bought copies of Sir Ferdinand Gorges, *America Painted to Life* and *The Reformed Virginian Silkworm* by his fellow academician Samuel Hartlib.[40]

The shop of Robert Littlebury, dealer at the Unicorn, Little Britain, was in close proximity to Moorfields. Dunton declared he had traded with Littlebury of Newport Street, "a man of composed and serious countenance."[41]

Littlebury was active as a London bookseller and publisher for almost forty years, 1650-1688. Apparently quite well versed in biblical literature, he was asked by Robert Scott in 1685 to evaluate the collection of the late Edmund Castell, the noted Semitic scholar. With Scott he appraised "the Bibles and other Oriental parts of Holy Scripture 30 folio volumes amongst which the Polyglot Bible, the Interlineary Bible of Arias Montanus, those of Buxtorf, Castalio, Luther's Dutch Bible, Tyndale's English translation, etc. at £20 which also included 140 octavoes, a Turkish and Ethiopic New Testament estimated at £11.6sh.8d valued and appraised what books were given to my Lord of London including 100 Lexicons compleat at £242.10s."[42]

Littlebury emerges as a London bookseller in 1650 when he sold for the Commonwealth publisher William Dugard copies of the library manual, *The reformed librarie-keeper* by John Durie—one of which was to be acquired by the Curator of Experiments. The ties between Littlebury and Dugard appear to have been fairly close since upon the latter's death he bequeathed to Littlebury five pounds for the purchase of a mourning ring.[43]

Although Littlebury issued a succession of sermons and religious texts he also published the *Complete Works* of Malpighi (1686-1687) and the *Orbis descriptio* of Dionysius Perigetes (1688). He also carried a stock of scientific texts, many imported from the continent. Hooke somewhat sceptically noted in his Diary of 5 July 1675 that Littlebury "profesd to send to Paris to his son for any books." His son may have been studying in Paris or remained in the French capital as his father's agent. By the end of 1675 Littlebury's holdings necessitated the publication of a stock catalogue.[44]

In all likelihood Hooke's earliest contact with Littlebury was professional. On 18 July 1673 he visited the dealer to "view his house." The following November he returned to Little Britain for a different sort of "viewing," the study of Littlebury's copy of Tycho Brahe's *Machina Coelestis.* Hooke apparently mulled over its purchase since he did not buy it until December for 10sh.[45]

In 1674 while browsing at Littlebury's premises he purchased copies of "Mersenne, Harmonicks, french 35sh., Scheiners Rosa urina 3sh., Laet, De genie [*De Gemmis Lapidibus*] 2sh., Horker 2sh., Gunther [*De balneis*] 1sh., french arch[itecture]. 1sh. in all

£3.15sh." A few days later he added to his collection a copy of Robert Anderson's *Angular Sections.*[46]

During 1675 Hooke was a fairly regular visitor at the Unicorn investing in the *Belopeecea* of the Alexandrian mathematician Ctesibus, Hero's writings, and an astronomical treatise of the French scientist Charamont, the *Steganographia* of Bortas, and other works.[47]

There is evidence that Hooke was somewhat ambivalent in his purchase of a prize volume owned by Littlebury who in turn sold it to another customer. A Diary entry of 13 December 1675 angrily states: "Missd Polyplice for 3sh. Littleberry a dogg." Indeed Hooke had missed the opportunity of adding to his collection a copy of the great 1499 Aldine *Hypnerotomachia Poliphili,* one of the most beautiful books of the Renaissance. Had Hooke haggled over the price or arrived at the Unicorn too late for purchase? Apparently he was fortunate enough to find another copy which is listed in the *Bibliotheca Hookiana.*[48]

Evidently the scientist's avidity for books counterbalanced any personal resentment since he was back at the Unicorn in January 1675/76 buying significant texts by Kepler, *Selenographie* 2sh., his *De Novis Stellis,* 3sh., a copy of Snell, *Erastothenes Batavus* 2½sh.[49]

Hooke's later Diaries, 1688 to 1693, make brief mention of Littlebury. The Master of the Unicorn was now an elderly man. His activity had waned and his son had probably long departed Paris. Hooke found few foreign imports or English treatises in his fields of interest. He turned his attention to those smaller dealers with more desirable stocks.

Hooke's Diaries shed new light on ephemeral members of the book and instrument trade who eked out an existence by an incidental sale, living precariously on the professional fringe. "Bought of Moran Street's Sphere 2sh., at Lyes paid 1s. for Speidell's Logarithmotechnica." From the bookseller and instrument-maker Henry Win (or Wynne), Hooke purchased several antiquarian texts: an edition of Euclid edited by John Dee; Andreas Schoner, *Gnomica* and Henry Briggs, *Logarithmicall Arithmeticke* at 5sh. Win was established at Chancery Lane where, according to the author Henry Bond, he had experimented with the magnetic inclinatory needle. Hooke stated that he had seen "Dipping Needle at Wins" and informed him to send Lord Ranelaugh weather-glasses.[50]

Taking views at Fish Street Hill, he took time to inspect the stock of the widow of Dixy Page, specialist in books on surveying and marine science. Page had begun business as publisher and bookseller at the Anchor and Marriner in East Smithfield. There is evidence that among Hooke's early purchases from him was a copy of Reginald Scot, *Discovery of Witchcraft.* Dixy Page died before 1675 and his widow moved to Fish Street Hill. Although her firm was small, she provided Hooke with essential texts in her husband's specialties. Here he obtained works by the gauger John Newton; Edward Perkins, *The Seaman's Tutor;* and in September 1675 a *Sea Grammar* and Henry Maynwaring, *Sea Dictionary.*[51]

Hooke's bibliophilic ardor led him to a variety of firms in the search of scientific texts. Yet there can be little doubt that he savored most keenly those jaunts to Duck Lane and Moorfields with their jumble of books, their dealers recounting past glories, Micawbers anticipating a brighter morrow. Relishing the passion of the chase, Hooke wandered into the Golden Ball, the Blue Ball, the Crown Tavern, the Bishops Head, the Golden Fleece, the Bible, and scouring Moorfields found "on the railes . . . Mr Boyles high Dutch Chymicall Books" of which he purchased two. There he took his sights, surveyed areas in Cripplegate and Bunhill, built Bethlehem Hospital, visited his friend Robert Pricke at the Golden Lion. At the Windmill he downed a beaker of ale with a rasher of bacon, later strolling along a neatly laid-out walk with his friend, the astronomer Edmund Halley, discussing the stars and planets and perhaps the new edition of Dr. John Wilkins, *A Discovery of a New World in the Moon.* The congeries of minor publishers and booksellers clustered in Duck Lane and Moorfields played as interesting a role in the development of Robert Hooke's Library as the more prestigious stationers in St. Paul's Churchyard, Westminster, and the Strand.

6

Book Auctions and Auctioneers

ALTHOUGH Hooke delighted in his rambles to Duck Lane and Moorfields he took equal relish in the auction and tempo of the "rooms" of the recently established London auction houses. The method of selling books by auction had been introduced to London by William Cooper, the alchemical specialist. This innovative system—practiced on the continent—may have appealed to the Master of the Pelican for several reasons. The auction pace was far more spirited than the occasional visit of an hermetically-minded customer to the shop in Little Britain. A public auction sale also provided Master Cooper with additional income.

On 31 October 1676 Cooper conducted his first auction at Coxes Court, Paternoster Row, the home of the deceased collector Lazarus Seaman. For the occasion he issued the first known English book auction catalogue, *Catalogus Variorum et Insignium Librorum instructissime Bibliothecae Clarissimi Doctissimique Viri Lazari Seaman.* The Catalogue announces the place and date of the sale held jointly with the London bookseller Edward Brewster of the Crane.[1]

Although Hooke entered this event in his Diary 30 October 1676, in all likelihood having received a copy of the catalogue, there is no indication that he attended the sale. He did, however, record the results. "The auction began at Dr. Seamans in Coxes court. The books yeld £800 for which the booksellers proferd £400." In short time the Curator of Experiments was to become an inveterate auction buff. In his crabbed hand he left a memorandum of 56 book sales held between August 1686 and August 1689, many of which he attended.[2]

There is evidence that Cooper compiled the Seaman and subsequent catalogues since a note in a later catalogue states that "the present was taken by Phil. Briggs and not by W. Cooper, but afterwards in part methodized by him, wherefore he craves your excuse for the mistakes that have hapned, and desires that the Saddle may be laid upon the right Horse." Briggs, a minor bookseller of Mermaid Court, Amen Corner, retired in 1672. Apparently in financial need, he had assisted in cataloguing books for an upcoming sale. He could, alas, gather few crumbs of comfort from Cooper's remarks.[3]

The Conditions of Sale, completely modern in concept, became the model for future auction catalogues. By way of introduction Cooper declared that "it hath not been usual here in England to make Sale of books by way of Auction . . . but it having been practised in other Countreys to the Advantage both of Buyers and Sellers; it was therefore conceivd (for the encouragement of learning)." Cooper believed it to be of advantage to have specific editions listed in the catalogue thereby permitting the prospective bidder to become acquainted in advance with the material. The customer might "depute any one to buy such books . . . as they shall desire" and "if any manifest difference should arise that then the same Book or Books shall be forthwith exposed again for sale and the highest bidder to have the same." Cooper averred that all books were perfect and were sold as such, "but if any of them appear to be otherwise before they be taken away, the Buyer shall have his Choice of taking or leaving the same." Payment was to be made upon delivery or "within one month's time after the auction is ended." The Sale was to begin at 9A.M. and again at 2P.M. "and this was to continue daily until all the books be sold."[4]

The contents of the Seaman Catalogue of approximately 5,000 books bear little resemblance to the *Catalogue of Chymicall Books* compiled by the auctioneer William Cooper. The owner of the collection had been a Puritan divine, master of Peterhouse, "a learned nonconformist" who had erected a chapel in Meetinghouse Yard, Silver Street, Holborn. His Library included major works of the Church Fathers, Bibles and psalters, some classics and a few items of American interest. *The Holy Bible* "translated into the Indian Language . . . Turn[ed] by the servant of Christ who is called John Eliot," published in 1661 at Cambridge by Samuel Green & Marmaduke Johnson fetched 18sh. Johann Huttich,

Novus Orbis Regionum Insulatum Veteribus Incogniti Scriptores (Basle: 1555) brought 5sh.—a copy of which enhanced the Hooke Collection. The first edition of the *Works* of Homer, published at Florence in 1488, was sold for 9sh. Buyers could acquire these and other items over a period of eight days excluding the intervening Sunday. The Seaman Sale concluded on 8 November 1676. Hence about 700 lots were sold daily—a feat exhausting to auctioneer and bidder![5]

The Seaman Sale was apparently extremely successful since Cooper was to write that: "the first attempt of this kind by the sale of Dr. Seaman's Library [gave] great Content and Satisfaction to the Gentlemen who were Buyers and no great discouragement to the Sellers." He had been encouraged to conduct a second auction, that of the library of the late Rev. Mr. Thomas Kidner of Hitchins, Herts.[6]

The Kidner Sale began on 16 February 1676/77 at the King's Head, Little Britain. Despite Cooper's optimistic endorsement of the auction medium there had been some growing opposition to this method of bookselling. In his Introduction to the Kidner Catalogue he states that "in the hopes of receiving such encouragement from the learned, as may prevent the Stifling of this manner of Sale, the benefit (if rightly considered . . . [is] equally balanced between Buyer and Seller.)" Hence it was of mutual advantage despite the grumbling of the opposition—probably those booksellers who saw in the auction inroads into their own business—a persistent grievance! The Conditions of Sale for the Kidner auction are identical with those of the Seaman Sale with the exception of one innovation—books might be viewed before the commencement of the auction. Cooper also introduced an attractive sales pitch favored by contemporary auctioneers. A special item was set in small capitals, e.g., ROBERT ABBOT, DEFENCE OF WILL. PERKINS AGAINST THE CALUMNIATIONS OF DR. BISHOP, London 1606—a work of great rarity. The Kidner Sale consisted of nearly 1,400 lots comprising texts similar to those sold at the Seaman auction.[7]

Cooper was to conduct at least 20 auctions alone or with the stellar auctioneer Edward Millington, who was to outshine his preceptor as a man of wit and eloquence. For the average sale Cooper issued a catalogue either at his own expense or that of the consignee which was for the most part distributed among the trade. At the time of his fourth sale—the Library of the Admiralty

THE SCIENTIFIC BOOK TRADE OF RESTORATION ENGLAND

lawyer, Dr. John Godolphin and others, held 11 November 1678—
Cooper reviewed the general acceptance of the auction as a *modus
operandi*. The preface to the sale catalogue of the holdings of
Phillip de Cardonell, a sycophant of Charles II, held 6 June 1681,
indicates that Cooper had begun to use his own premises at the
Pelican for auction purposes. He was to become quite arbitrary
about hours and the necessity of punctuality. Bidding was to begin
at 8 A.M., "if there be but twenty Gentlemen present." He advised
prospective buyers to arrive in time "since many have confessed
they have lost the opportunity of buying for themselves by coming
or sending too late, and afterwards would have given double what
they sold for if they could have had them."[8]

The Cooper Sale of the Library of Dr. Nathan Paget, held 4
July 1681 at the auctioneer's premises, reflects Cooper's interests:
books on alchemy and chemistry, the writings of Cardan, Paracelsus, Agrippa, Fludd, Van Helmont, Lull, Basil Valentine, and
others. In all likelihood the late Dr. Paget had frequented the
Pelican and purchased from the stock or the *Catalogue of
Chymicall Books*. The *Catalogue* of the Walter Rea Sale held at the
Pelican, 19 June 1682, is of singular interest for its list of previous
auctions held in London by Cooper and other dealers. Cooper
states in his Introduction that he had wished "to gratifie the
curious whose genius may lead to make perfect their Collection."
Therefore he had caused "to be printed the names of those persons
whose Libraries have been sold by Auction, and the series of the
time when." For the late seventeenth-century English bibliophile
and for an appreciative posterity, Cooper lists 30 sales including the
present. Will Cooper was surely aware of the acquisitive instinct
and collecting passion of the bibliophile. He repeated the list of
auction sales in a catalogue of 14 February 1686/87, informing the
bidder that he wished "to gratifie those Gentlemen, whose Curiosities may lead them to make perfect their Collections ... I have
caused to be printed those Persons whose Libraries have been sold
by Auction and the Series of the time when." The List records 74
sales beginning with the first of Lazarus Seaman and concluding
with the present. It is quite possible that Robert Hooke was one of
"those Gentlemen whose Curiosit[y]" led him "to make perfect"
his "Collection" acquiring those catalogues not in his Library
which he "rangd" and rearranged.[9]

The auctions of the libraries of the Rev. Mr. Chace and the physicians Dr. Christopher Bathurst and George Tonstall afforded Cooper the opportunity to vaunt in his catalogue their special contents which were largely alchemical and medical. Protesting that it was not his custom "to make long harangues to set off the goodness of our Books (I have no reason to question the Judgments of the Buyers) but yet I thought it not impertinent at this time to acquaint the Reader, that there is a very good Collection of Chymicall as well Medicinall, and likewise of Philologicall as well as Theologicall Books."[10]

The largest auction sale of books conducted by Cooper and Millington was that of the huge stock of the Oxford publisher and bookseller Richard Davis. Davis had been one of the most active stationers of the time and interim publisher of the *Philosophical Transactions.* He issued many of Boyle's works and other notable texts. By 1688 the competition of younger more active dealers had apparently caused Davis's business to decline. In need of money, he put up his stock at auction. During the three sales, comprising most of Davis's holdings, approximately 80,000 books were sold. The Davis Sale was the first held in Oxford and was announced in a catalogue: *Catalogus variorum in quavis Lingva et facultate insignium tam antiquorum quam recentium Librorum Richardi Davis Bibliopolae,* which was apparently published at Davis's expense. Copies of the auction catalogue were available gratis in London not only at the Pelican but also at the premises of colleagues and coffee-shops: the Queens Arms in Pall Mall, the Acorn, St. Paul's Churchyard, the Blackboy in Fleet Street, the Three Pigeons over against the Royal Exchange, the Posthouse in Russell Street, Covent Garden, and at Mr. Davis's own house in Oxford as well as at Cambridge coffee-houses.[11]

It was not Cooper but Davis who wrote the preface to the first Sale Catalogue in which he somewhat speciously declared that the auction was being held for "the benefit of the University of Oxford." He acknowledged the favors that had been bestowed upon him by "the worthy heads of that famous and celebrated Body of Learning" who he hoped "will further, and promote the sale . . . by . . . Auction." Following an analysis of the various kinds of books to be sold, Davis "leaves all persons to judge for themselves" and concludes with the promise that "it [the auction] shall be managed with all fairness . . . and though I am extremely sensible, that let my friends be as kind as they please, I must be a considerable loser in the disposal, yet the single consideration that my books will be dispersed amongst you, and are sold for your advantage, perfectly expiates the sense of it, and makes me cheerfully subscribe myself as I really am, your humble servant Richard Davis."[12]

The Sale began at 8A.M. lasting until 11A.M. resuming at 1P.M. until 5P.M. on 22 April 1686 at "Mr. Newman's house over against St. Michael's Church." Conditions of Sale were as usual but "all Gentlemen buyers [were] requested to give in their names and the Colleges or Halls they belong to, to the end that every Person respectively may have Justice done him in the buying and the delivery of the Books." The *Catalogue* of the first Davis Sale contained 10,168 lots or apparently 30,000 books representing a variety of subjects from "Libri Theologici" to "Libri Mathematici," romances, novels, and the common law of England. The Sale lasted approximately two weeks, Sunday excluded.[13]

The second Davis Sale, 4 October 1686, was again conducted by Cooper and Millington at Mr. Newman's house in Oxford. In his Introduction Davis flattered the University body, hoping once again that his books would be dispersed among its members. Ingratiatingly he stated that he would not "willingly expose any of them elsewhere, so long as I find your favorable acceptance." He trusted that "this way of sale by auction" would give them "the greatest Content and Satisfaction." There is every reason to believe that the faculty and student body found great "satisfaction" from a selection of 8,534 lots or an approximate 25,000 books.[14]

After a lapse of over a year and a a half, Cooper and Millington conducted the third Sale of the Davis stock. Probably during this lengthy interval, Davis had hoped to recoup his fortune which, alas, had continued to dwindle since in his Introduction to the *Catalogue* he refers to recent misfortunes. The material now offered was similar to that of the preceding sales and Davis hoped that customers would find items not "much inferior." The collection consisted of 7,071 lots or an approximate 25,000 books. It is quite possible that the Oxford bookseller had not consigned all of his stock to auction but had reserved some of his rarer material for offer to special customers. The Davis Sale Catalogues, nonetheless, are an index to the size of the holdings of a former prosperous university bookseller who had either over-extended himself or was unable to meet competition.[15]

The auction catalogues of the Cooper Sales were distributed among members of the profession, one of whom was Martyn of the Bell. During a visit there, Hooke studied "Cooper's Catalogiae." It is quite surprising that Hooke in his Diary alludes to only one Cooper Sale. Visiting the Pelican on 30 July 1679, he discussed "3 books of auction." These lots were apparently acquired at the Cooper Sale of 2 June 1679 which comprised several properties including much of the stock of the bookseller Richard Chiswell. There the scientist purchased Kircher, *Mundus subterraneus* at 27½sh., Fromond, *Opera* at 2sh., and Caneparius, *De Atramentis cujuscunque generis opus* at 2sh.8d.[16]

William Cooper had conducted his last sale, the third part of the Davis books, on 25 June 1686. He was shortly thereafter to disappear from the auction rooms and the larger world of books including the "libri alchymici" he so loved. He died before 6 November 1688, since an auction held that day at Popes Head Alley states that copies of the catalogue could be obtained from various dealers among them the Widow Cooper, Little Britain.[17]

Cooper's role was readily filled by the "fine, facetious" Edward Millington who in time was to overshadow him as the leading expert in the field. Little is known of Millington's early years. There is no evidence that he had received any formal education, and despite his practical knowledge of the auction trade he displayed little scholarly book learning. He was ignorant of the time sequence of printing history since he classed Aldus Manutius among the "original printers." He casually attributed the date of origin of an edition of Roderic Zamorensis to 1450—pre-Gutenberg claim! Nonetheless he was to exhibit much professional ability and personal charm.[18]

Departing the Pelican, he set up at the Bible, Little Britain. Like most Restoration stationers, he was a dealer in "old books" and a modest publisher, issuing William Seaman, *Grammatica linguae Turcicae* (1670) and George Thompson, *Experimenta.*[19]

To some his role as an auctioneer is far over-shadowed by his presumed association with John Milton. According to Jonathan Richardson, editor of *Explanatory Remarks on Milton's Paradise Lost* (1724), Milton had lodged with Millington. "One that had often seen Milton told me that he used to come to a house where he lived, and he also met him on the street led by Millington, who was so famous an auctioneer about the time of the Revolution and since.

The man was a seller of old books in Little Britain, and Milton lodged at his house three or four years before he died. About 1670 I have been told by one who knew him that he [Milton] lodged some time at the house of Millington the famous auctioneer some years ago, who then sold books in Little Britain and who used to lead him by the hand when he went abroad." It is known that Milton lived in at least eleven houses—some temporary lodgings. Accounts of the time describe the poet as being led about the street near the Bunhill house "a slender man slightly under middle height, dressed in a grey cloak and wearing sometimes a small silver-hilted sword, looking in feeble health, but with his fair complexion and lightish hair, younger than he [Millington] was." Milton's association with Millington has not been refuted. Milton apparently lodged with him during 1670 returning to his home in Artillery Walk, Bushnell Fields, a small house with a garden. There he remained with his wife, the former Elizabeth Mishnull, until his death.[20]

To the poet's alleged benefactor, Millington, Dunton had attributed "a quick wit and wonderful fluency of speech . . . a man of remarkable elocution . . . sense and modesty." Apparently he was also a man of compassion and literary appreciation since he assisted the great poet in his missions to town.[21]

During his career of 18 years Millington conducted at least 42 recorded public sales of books and prints. In the "List of Catalogues of Book Sales Held between August 1686 and August 1689" compiled by Hooke, many anonymous sales are cited. There is every reason to believe that Millington conducted several of them since Hooke himself refers to a few Millington auctions not mentioned in the standard work by Lawler.[22]

Much of contemporary auction practice can be gleaned from Millington's prefaces to his catalogues. Dunton declares that in addition to his fluency in speech he displayed "much comedy in his business approach. 'Once, Twice, Thrice,' as can be met with in a modern play. Turning upon his audience he mockingly queried 'Where is your generous flame for learning? Who but a Sot or Blockhead would have money in his pocket and starve his Brains?'"[23]

An Elegy on the Death of Mr. Edward Millington The Famous Auctioneer by Thomas Brown, 1718, affords additional information on the style and rhetoric of this estimable gentleman. He apparently conducted sales standing behind a desk, mallet in hand. His many talents are related in Brown's amateurish verse. Through his "fine, facetious pleasing way,/The Author's genius and his wit display;/ Then in his hand another piece he takes,/ And in its praise a long harangue he makes;/And tells 'em that 'tis writ in lofty Verse,/One that is out of print and very Scarce."[24]

Like all members of his clan, Millington strove for a high opening bid: "Five Pound, Four Pound, Three Pound, he cries aloud/And holds it up, expose it to the Crowd." Master Millington surely indulged in financial flights of fancy since few books of the period brought even a pound. Hooke acquired at the Pitt Sale of 1678 a lot of 28 items for £9.14.9. Accepting reality, Millington did not refuse a penny or even a half-penny bid raise.[25]

The Millington sales usually took place in London at "the Auction House" in Warwick Lane, directly opposite Warwick Court or Dr. Coxes Rents; at "the Auction House" over against the Black Swan in Ave Maria Lane, Ludgate; at Petty Canons Hall on the North Side of St. Paul's Churchyard entering Paternoster Row; at Brydges Coffee-House in Popes-Head Alley or at the house of Mr. Thomas Ward at the Boar's Head in Cornhill.

Customarily sales began at 9A.M. lasting until noon, recommencing at 2P.M. until 5. Occasionally the hours were altered to satisfy professional groups. In order to comply with the visiting hours of physicians, Millington offered a different schedule for the sale of the libraries of Drs. Christopher Terne and Thomas Allen held 12 April 1686. To avoid any conflict with their routine, the hours were altered to 10A.M. to 12P.M. and 3P.M. to 6. The auctioneer admitted that earlier specialized sales had been unsuccessful "either through the forgetfulness of the Gentlemen of the Profession as to the time or by Reason that the hours of Sale have interfered with their business. This Experiment is made intentionally accomodated of the supposed leisurable time of the practicers of that Noble Science."[26]

Like Cooper, Millington compiled catalogues for the preparation of which assistants, probably journeymen or impecunious booksellers, had been engaged. Apparently they were not overzealous in their work and upon occasion Millington apologized for the inaccuracies in catalogues which had been "taken in hast, and by several hands, which hath often many, and some material mistakes." Careless compilation elicited criticism and in a preface to the Massauve Collection, 1 February 1687/88, Millington deplored the negligence of his staff, urging the collector to collate books purchased. His comments are somewhat ambiguous since he suggests that if customers "desire a fit person . . . they shall be assisted with one for their purpose on the most reasonable considerations." One conjectures why this "fit person" had not originally been engaged by Millington for preparation of his catalogues.[27]

Millington's prefaces to his catalogues reflect some nefarious practices on the part of the buyer, some still bemoaned by members of the profession. At the George Lawson Sale, 30 May 1687, Millington warned the idle visitor who successfully bid upon items later refusing to pay or remove the material. The irate Millington intended to suffer "no further loss from such practices." He threatened to prosecute such individuals according to law "if forthwith they do not send for their books, or give reasonable satisfaction." Apparently this threat delivered early in his career proved of little avail. At a sale held six years later he again alluded to the losses incurred because of bidders who refused to pay for their books. Determined to end this malfeasance, he decided upon an additional condition of sale: "All Gentlemen Buyers [were] to give in not only their Surnames, but Christian, as also to their Place of Abode with the Signs they live or lodge at." The proposal was made to protect his own losses and those of serious customers unable to obtain books through fraudulent practice. As a further measure to discourage such behavior, Millington decided to charge 6d. per catalogue "which method we have now taken . . . for the better accomodation and more prudent distribution than formerly of copies." The payment "shall be allowed (if demanded) to any persons . . . that shall buy or cause to be bought for them to the value of ten shillings."[28]

Although the majority of Millington Sales included the literary properties of deceased divines and gentlemen of letters, some were of specialized material like the holdings of the physicians Terne and Allen; the law library of the barrister John Collins, late of Gray's Inn sold by Millington on 2 July 1683 at the first house on the left hand in Flying-Horse Court in Fleet Street. The books were advertised as "the compleatest Collection of the Common and Statute Law Books, ancient and modern, that hath hither to been published or perhaps will ever by exposed to sale by way of auction . . . there being no less than three editions of that famed Book of the

Customs of Normandy, two of Stebunhithe and Hackney, and of the Charter of Romney Marsh, of the Tinners of Cornwall ... which is invitation sufficient to all gentlemen of the gown to buy upon this Occasion what they cannot so easily meet with or not at all find."[29]

Readers of Millington's prefaces may find some spirited jingoism in addition to his bookish enthusiasm. In a sale of *Choice English Books in Divinity, History, Law, etc.* held at Brydges Coffee-House, 16 June 1684, Millington offered for the first time books entirely in English. In his preface the auctioneer stated: "This Catalogue consists perfectly of English Authours, which I rather for once essayed to expose to sale by way of Auction, thereby to convince the World, that all learning and useful knowledge is not contained in Foreign Languages."[30]

Millington was the first to introduce book sales to the provinces. He declared that his country auctions were held for the "diversion and entertainment of the gentlemen of the town." Such towns included Tunbridge Wells, Norwich, Cambridge, St. Albans, Chelmsford, Abingdon Hatfield, Wells, and smaller communities.

His first out-of-London sale was conducted in 1684 at Tunbridge Wells where "the books could be viewed at the Tea-House upon the Walks." He was quite convinced since "Auctioning having elsewhere met with a good acceptation it is not doubted that the Gentlemen of Tunbridge will also encourage the first Essay of it amongst them."[31]

The *Bibliotheca Castelliana,* the library of the well-known Oriental scholar Dr. Edward Castell, certainly attracted Cantabrigians. It was the first book sale held in Cambridge, June 1686, at the house of Robert Skyrings at the Sign of the Eagle and Child over against St. Benedict Church. The library of the late professor of Arabic included rare works in Semitica, Orientalia, and Judaica.[32]

Millington, a clever business man, gauged popular taste, the shifting moods of the collector. Aware of the increasing sophistication of the English bibliophile, who traveled abroad to view and to buy choice books finely bound in red morocco or delicately tooled calf, Millington announced in a sale catalogue of February 1687/88 that "some of the valuable books are of the Great Paper and most of them as to their binding sufficiently inviting answering the present mode, and commendable fashion of most bookish gentel-men's libraries being generally curious and richly bound."[33]

Observing Millington's success, new auctioneers entered the field. The man of "fluency and wit" confronted increasing competition. With contempt he referred to his rivals' "swelling and fulsome prefaces, to empty and trifling catalogues [which] have nauseated the learned and intelligent readers." At the same time he announced he would no longer include lengthy introductions to his catalogues since "prefaces to Auction Catalogues have of late been censured more customary than instructive, and that the buyers set up for better judges of the Editions, Use, Scarcity of the books exposed to Sale than the men of the profession. I am resolved to humour the Age, to say as they say, to let them believe, as they please, to think as they list." He further resolved to trouble the collector no longer "with any characters or descriptions unless I am satisfied the books do truly deserve them."[34]

Obviously experiencing some difficulty in locating literary properties, Millington held on 4 May 1689 a graphics sale referred to by Hooke as *A Collection of Drawings & Prints.* In his *Elegy on Millington,* Brown alludes to his print sales: "Come, put it in, a fine Original,/Done by a curious hand, what stroakes are here,/Drawn to life: how fine it does appear!/O lovely piece! Ten pound, Five pound, for shame,/You do not bid the value of the frame;/How many pretty stories could he tell,/To inhance the price, and make the Picture sell." Millington alludes to an auction of *Paintings and Limnings* at Tunbridge Wells which had been "readily received and freely entertained by persons of all quality." Although at the St. Edmondsbury Fair of 23 September 1689 Millington sold some books, he also featured in his Sale Catalogue "Artificial Rarities, the latter including Roses, etc. extremely natural, all sorts of Perfumes for Rooms brought out of Italy, Hungary waters, Chocolate, Best Spanish Snush [snuff]. Essences and all Sorts of Powders for the Hair greater and lesser quantities." One may wonder to what extent Edward Millington exercised his "wit and eloquence" in his disposal of "snush" and hair powder.[35]

In his preface announcing this country fair Millington had hoped to attract the local gentry. In his London "rooms" he had gathered literati and scientists—among them the enthusiastic Curator of Experiments to the Royal Society. From entries in his Diary, Hooke attended a minimum of 10 Millington auctions between 1688 and 1693, and, in all likelihood, additional sales which are cited anonymously. An enthusiastic auction buff, he mentions visits to four sales on 5 April 1689—certainly one must have been to the "Auction House" of Edward Millington. Several Diary allusions mention the perusal of Millington catalogues and later the viewing of books. At a Millington Sale of 9 April 1689 he purchased two works of the medical author Glisson for 6 shillings, paying an additional 18 for Marsham's *Diatriba chronologica*. At a November 1689 auction he successfully bid on copies of the "High Dutch Vitruvius 2 shillings" and the "Low Dutch Linschoten 26 pence." Present at an early December 1689 Millington Sale, Hooke acquired the *Description de l'Amerique Septentrionale* of Nicolas Denis, copies of Scaliger, *Cyclomathia,* and the *Dictionarium Hebraicum* of Sebastian Muenster. Several entries of 1693 mention his reading of Millington catalogues and visits to his "rooms," where he stated that on 16 June "books sold extravagantly dear."[36]

A Hooke Diary entry of 25 March 1688/89 mentions the catalogue of the *Bibliotheca Gulstoniana,* the library of Dr. William Gulston, Bishop of Bristol, a sale which had taken place the previous June. Since Hooke collected auction catalogues he probably picked up a copy of the Gulston holdings at Millington's. The entry continues "at Hussy's with Waller."[37]

Robert Hooke was a fairly frequent visitor to the auction rooms of Christopher Hussey who conducted bookselling and publishing at the Fleur de Luce from 1685 to 1705. Although Dunton describes Hussey as "a downright honest man," declaring that he had a large stock of books that are "very scarce," Hussey remains an ephemeral figure in the Restoration book world, emerging as an auctioneer rather than a bookseller, a role ignored by the estimable Mr. Dunton. As a publisher, he issued a few books, all of which were certainly of interest to the city surveyor and draughtsman Robert Hooke: John Holwell, *A sure guide to the practical surveyor* (1678); John Kendal, *The measure of time* (1684); Thomas Everard, *Stereometry made easie* (1684). Two other titles enhanced Hooke's large holdings in exploration and travel: Baudier, *The history of the court of the King of China* (1682) and Samuel Newton, *An idea of geography* (1695).[38]

It was not at his shop but rather at Sam's Coffee-house in Exchange Alley that Hussey conducted his public sales. Hooke in his "List of Catalogues of Book Sales" cites seven Hussey auctions:

Choice English Books, August 1688; *Scarce Books Most English,* January 1688/89; *English & Lat[in] Books,* Jan. 1688/89; *Engl:Lat[in] French Books,* March 1688/89; *The Library of Dr. Chr.Thomas,* April 1689; *Ye Lib: of Mr. Jo. Oakes,* May 1689; and *Ye Lib. of Mr. Tho: Chambers,* May 1689.[39]

Hooke's Diaries refer repeatedly to Hussey catalogues, the viewing of books and purchases. At the auction of 22 January 1688/89 he successfully bid on copies of Dee, *Monas,* 7d. and the *Aphorisms* of Hippocrates at 2sh.6d. Two days later he acquired a copy of Richard Simon, *Critical Enquiries into Editions of the Bible* for 4d., the *Hebrew Dictionary* of Santes Paganini; copies of works by Vives and Theocritus at 3 and 5d. respectively. At a March 1688/89 sale he obtained a variety of texts including a Spanish dictionary, a copy of the Holland edition of Euclid for 3d. and a German travel book entitled *Welsche Reiss-beschreibung.* During the same month Hooke discussed "Hussy new catalog" and an unsuccessful auction visit which is noted "0" (zero). Hooke somewhat dolefully comments that he had arrived too late for a Hussey Sale, but during visits from May to September 1689 he successfully bid on copies of Euclid edited by Barrow at 21d.; a copy of *Areopagitica;* the *Travels* of Pietro delle Valle at 9sh. and the *Lexicon Arabicum* of Golius for 10sh.[40]

Few London auction sales eluded Hooke's attention. A Diary entry of 2 November 1689 states: "pd Mr. Hook auction 3sh.1d." The scientist Hooke had acquired a lot of miscellaneous texts from the bookseller and quasi-auctioneer Nathaniel Hook of the King's Arms, Little Britain. As an auctioneer, Hook attracts attention for his sale of French books held 13 May 1693. Although it was attended by the Curator of Experiments he acquired nothing, purchasing, however, at a sale held the following month 8 books whose authors and titles are not indicated.[41]

Nathaniel Hook did not specialize solely in French books. The entries in Robert Hooke's Diary attest to the purchase of miscellaneous works, among them "Martinius, *China* at 20sh.; Gesner 13½sh.; Zwinger 2sh.2d.; Pitiscus tables 1s.; Rheticus 2s.6d.; Bullialdus 7d. in all 40s.3d."[42]

The Library of Richard Maitland, the Fourth Earl of Lauderdale, the greatest sale of the late 1680s, was dispersed at the sign of the Bear by Benjamin Walford, bookseller and auctioneer. In Dunton's opinion, Walford was "a very ingenious man and knew books extraordinary well." The Maitland books, prints, and drawings were sold by Walford in two sales, 30 October 1688 and Collectio Secunda, 28 October 1689. Entitled *Catalogus instructissimae Bibliotheca nobilis cujusdam Scoto-Britanni, in quaevis Lingua et facultate insignium,* the collection is described by Walford as the property of "a Person of Quality, who in his Travels beyond Seas made himself very well acquainted with the most eminent Authors of all Sciences, and was curious in collecting both the best editions and the fairest copies, which considered with their bindings do far excel any books that have hitherto been exposed to public Sale."[43]

To this auction of "the fairest copies and the best editions" came the London collectors and among them Robert Hooke. There is evidence from the scientist's Diary that the Maitland Sales lasted for months since he attended eleven sessions from 26 April to 6 June 1689. On 6 April he states: "To Maitland sale. viewd books." His purchases included two important treatises relating to American botany: Hernandes, *Novus plantarum Mexicanarum historia* at 4 shillings, 6d. and Cornutus, *Canadensium plantarum historia* (Paris 1635). Other acquisitions reflect the scientist's interest in medicine and optics for he obtained copies of Johann Wecker's *Practicae medicinae generatio* (Basle 1585) for 4 shillings, 6d.; Giovanni Baptista Porta, *De refractione optices* (Naples 1598) at 1 shilling and the *Optics* of Euclid at half the price. It was at the session of 6 May that Hooke paid £8.15 for a copy of one of the works of the Italian naturalist Ulysses Aldrovandus. This appears to have been one of the highest prices ever paid by Hooke for a single item. But then he may have succumbed to auction fever—a very costly malady. Despite this sizable investment he was back at the sale of 8 May where he successfully bid on a copy of Zahn's ophthalmological treatise for 11½ shillings, which he later found to be imperfect and returned the volume to Walford. Although he commented that "prints sold dear" at the 3rd June session, he returned three days later to purchase a copy of *The Tempest* for 2½ shillings. Hooke apparently accumulated his purchases, having them sent directly to his residence at a carriage cost of 3d.[44]

The scientist attended a few sessions of the second Maitland Sale during the late autumn of 1689, stating: "To the Bear Auction, viewd folios." On 15 November he purchased a copy of Simplicius in Greek at 18d. and a Greek and Latin Plotinus for 18½ shillings.[45]

Other smaller London book sales attracted the Curator of Experiments, those of John Bulord, Nathaniel Rolles, Benjamin Sherley, and Joseph Shelton of the Peacock in the Poultry. The book auction had become an ancillary of the English book world—a system which, according to Millington, was "so well approved of ... for the general benefit and gratification of the learned."[46]

Hooke states that he had attended four auctions within a day. Public sales were rapidly becoming a threat to the bookseller and a boon to the collector. The bibliophile was now presented with a free competitive system of book buying. The Conditions of Sale introduced by the auction's progenitor William Cooper, and observed by Millington and later auctioneers, differ little from those maintained by present day houses. Cooper averred that all books were perfect and were sold as such, "but if any of them appear to be otherwise before they be taken away, the Buyer shall have his Choice of taking or leaving the same." Payment was to be made upon delivery or within one month's time after the auction ended. Millington introduced the charge of 6d. per catalogue—a practice which still prevails—but the current price tag would surely boggle the commercially-minded Edward Millington. The irritating habit of the bidder to abandon purchases still persists, rankling auction houses and under-bidders. The Conditions laid down by Cooper and Millington for the conduct of public sales are for the most part still observed.

Above all the passion, the excitement, the competition which suffused the "Auction Houses" of Warwick Lane, Petty Canons Hall, and Ave Maria Lane still invest the "rooms" of today. Auction fever is one contagious malady which has remained incurable by the high priests of bibliophily throughout the past three centuries!

7

Domestic Circulation
Exportation and Importation of Foreign Books

Hooke's purchases at the shops of Martyn and Pitt, the stalls and quarters of Duck Lane and Moorfields, the "rooms" of Cooper, Millington, and Hussey indicate the availability of a substantial corpus of domestic and foreign scientific texts in London. The conveyance of such material locally and overseas depended upon a variety of transportation media. The publication of English and foreign scientific works resulted in a lively exchange of books between the homeland and the continent.

A network of agents—ranging from a local porter to a Danzig shipper, from a Berwick carrier to an Amsterdam broker, from the Royal Mail Service to a Calais agent, from a member of a diplomatic suite to the Governor of New York—assisted in the circulation of books throughout the Island, across the Channel, and to the New World. The various methods of transportation—slow, cumbersome, circuitous, threatened by the caprice of the elements, the moods of shippers, the violence of pirates—proved nonetheless effective.

Porter service was the most direct method of local delivery. Eager to acquire copies of Boyle's recently published *Physiological Essays,* Oldenburg engaged a porter to bring the books from Warwick Lane to his home in Pall Mall. Although the fee is not specified, he informed the Danzig astronomer Hevelius in August 1669 that he had paid porters 4sh.6d. for bringing books from the customs house to his quarters. Hooke frequently indulged in porter service for transporting books from auction houses to his home, the charges varying from four to eight pence, obviously depending upon the distance, the size, and weight of the package.[1]

Portage was limited to the city confines. For more distant deliveries the customer relied on carrier service or the Royal Mail delivery. Two active carrier firms maintained service between London and Oxford: Bartlet at ye Oxford Arms in Warwick Lane, whose wagon or coach was popularly dubbed "Bartlet's Flying Coach" and Moor of the Saracen's Head at Newgate. Of the two, Wallis considered Moor "as much ye more careful." Both companies retained warehouses in the capital where merchandise could be stored for a period of time. The run between London and Oxford usually took overnight and there appears to have been at least one weekly delivery. Having missed the carrier, John Collins was compelled to wait until the following week for a parcel to be sent to Oxford.[2]

Mills, the Burford carrier, "who lyes at the Cross-Keyes in Whitecross Street," was recommended as one who "would safely forward any package of bulk [and] convey shipments as safely as the Post though not so speedily." John Loft, "inning at ye White Horse without Cripplegate," is mentioned as a carrier between London, York and Tadcaster. This gentleman apparently shared quarters with the Hereford carrier "well known to every porter in town." The London carriers, Burnhill and Will Pell, also hauled freight to York, competing with Loft. Customers could deposit merchandise at Pell's address, the Red Lion, Aldersgate Street. In November 1689 Hooke referred to a carrier with premises at the Swan, Holborn Bridge.[3]

The drivers of "Bartlet's Flying Coach" and the teamsters heading for Hereford, York, Burford, and Tadcaster were confronted with difficulty and danger. The roads were muddy and rutted, slippery and often icy or flooded; the highways unsafe, infested with bandits. Frequently dissatisfied with their pay, the drivers demanded supplementary fees. Oldenburg wrathfully exploded to Boyle that in addition to the carrier's charges he had been compelled to pay the porter's charge. He accused both services of collusion. He declared that he had most painstakingly examined a shipment discovering that "a piece of ye cover [had been] torne out just where ye words 'carrier paid' are most wont to be written; which made me suspect a Cheat. I refused to pay yt Part of ye demand, shewing ground of my suspicion to ye she-porter yt brought yt to me, who would putt it upon ye being rubbed of in ye sack among ye things. But it was too artificially done, to be laid upon such an accident, wch made me persist in my denyall."[4]

The carriers appear to have been a very independent lot refusing to work during inclement weather and reserving holidays for themselves. Referring to their unconscionable behavior, Boyle declared: "Ye county carryers at this Tyme of ye year [December] as little stay for any Body as ye Winds or Tydes."[5]

If dissatisfied with "Bartlet's Flying Coach," or the unreliability of the average carrier, the customer could always select the water route from London to Oxford which, of course, proved a far slower method of travel. Sir Robert Moray complained that a copy of Hevelius's *Prodromus cometicus,* which had long since been dispatched from London to Oxford, had as yet not arrived. "Mr. Boile I think will send to Abinton [Abingdon] to enquire after it, for the boate comes thither from London."[6]

The impatient could, of course, always resort to His Majesty's Royal Postal Service whose celerity had been highly vaunted by Hooke's fellow academician Henry Powle. It was during the reign of Charles II that the modern postal system was developed. Henry Bishop, Master of Posts, devised a plan by which "a stamp is putt on every letter shewing the day of the month that every letter comes to the office, so that no letter carrier may dare to detayne a letter from post to post which before was usual." By 1680 William Dockwra, a London merchant, and Robert Murray, an upholsterer, established a special local postal service in the capital as their own private commercial enterprise. They set up 450 receiving offices for mail with sorting areas and direct delivery to the recipient. Letters and parcels were conveyed by the Dockwra service from one part of London to another for a penny, thus setting the precedent for the "penny post."[7]

Regular mail could be dispatched throughout the kingdom as well as overseas. Henri Justel, future Secretary of Louis XIV, requested Oldenburg in May 1666 to forward by post to Paris copies of the recently published *Opera* of William of Blois. The package was to be addressed to the postman of Calais who in turn was to direct it to the attention of M. Guibert of Paris. Justel was to find the charges exorbitant.[8]

Not only were postal fees considerable but mail delivery between England and France was considered "uncertain and tedious." Furthermore the Restoration postman—despite Master Bishop's injunctions—was indifferent to his responsibilities. Justifiably annoyed, Oldenburg informed Boyle that the letter carrier "instead of delivering yr and other inland-letters yester-night, delivered ym not till this day in the after-noon." Writing to René François Sluse, Oldenburg remarked that he would have sent him the *Works* of Hobbes and Wallis "if the Postman would burden himself with so large a Package."[9]

Since individuals found the international mail service not only expensive but also unreliable, they sought other agencies. Commerce in books depended upon several media: brokers, travelers, members of the diplomatic suite and the stationers themselves.

Henry Daems (or Dames) of Amsterdam proved to be a reliable book broker receiving and forwarding texts. Eager to obtain the *Mesolabe* of Sluse, Oldenburg advised the author in June 1668 that as soon as the work came off the press, he was to urge the printer or bookseller to send fifty copies of it to Henry Daems . . . who "will pay the price on the nail." Daems was to arrange for the careful packing of the shipment and to send it to London in care of the merchant George Coward. "We only ask you to admonish your bookseller to set a fair price on these copies." The following October, Sluse complied with Oldenburg's instructions, requesting his bookseller to forward fifty copies of the *Mesolabe* to Daems.[10]

This Amsterdam broker was known to several of the coterie of English scientists. Collins dispatched a shipment of Wallis's *Mechanica sive de motu,* the *Lectiones opticae* of Barrow, and the *Exercitationes geometricae* of Gregory to Daems eventually to be forwarded to Sluse.[11]

Daems enjoyed a good relationship with the great Dutch publishing firm of Elzevier. This giant house, with its many branches and agents, apparently took care of some of the shipping for Daems who naturally paid the firm for its services.[12]

Established at Calais, a merchant Varges acted for a time as agent for the handling of an extremely important collection of books sent from London to Paris. The librarian of Louis XIV, Pierre de Carcavy, assisted by Justel, had decided to increase the holdings of the French Royal Library. Oldenburg had been requested to submit a list of recent English scientific publications from which both gentlemen selected a sizable number. The overburdened Secretary of the Royal Society was further petitioned "to send every important book published in [England] during the last twelve years." Replying to this munificent order, Oldenburg commented that the Fire in all likelihood had destroyed a considerable number of books and moreover those available were "only sold at exceptional prices." In February 1667/68 Justel informed Oldenburg that he was sending him "a bill of exchange for the purchase of the books. Be so kind as to buy them and have them packaged and addressed to Mr. de Varges, merchant at Calais, to be forwarded to M. Justel, the King's Secretary for M. Carcavy, Royal Librarian and at the bottom put 'For the King.'" The name of this most august addressee would certainly prove a sufficient deterrent to any interception of the shipment![13]

A month later Justel thanked Oldenburg for the trouble he had taken, informing him that M. de Varges would not fail to forward the package safely. "Do not trouble to obtain receipts from the booksellers. It is enough you are so kind to buy us the books we ask for." Justel's confidence in M. de Varges's integrity was short-lived. A letter to Oldenburg states that the Calais agent had proved to be somewhat dishonest. "I beg you not to send anything further for me. He seems not to be very scrupulous."[14]

Travelers and merchants en route to the continent or stationed abroad occasionally acted as factors for the delivery of books. A Delft business man Willem Bleyswyck, who had visited England, offered to act as the agent for the shipment of a work by William Neile intended for Huygens. Oldenburg advised Huygens that he had taken advantage of the offer of "this meritorious gentleman" and was forwarding the text. The English physician Robert Swale, visiting Paris, delivered to Carcavy a copy of Sprat's *History of the Royal Society,* while Samuel Free, an English merchant at Hamburg, sent to London a mixed bag of continental scientific texts. Apprehensive that a selection of recent Italian books had not reached London, Malpighi asked Oldenburg to inquire of Francesco Teriesi, a Florentine business man in London, whether he had not received the package which included among recent treatises a copy of Mengoli's work on music. The renowned physiologist was even more disturbed by the delay of a shipment from London of copies of his *De Bombyce* printed by Martyn for the Royal Society. His fears were allayed by a note from Oldenburg which stated that, according to a recent advice, the package had reached Leghorn aboard a vessel bearing the insignia 'Fama,' its master, one John Noble. The bundle had been addressed to two English merchants of the city, Thomas Death and James Skinner.[15]

Members of the diplomatic corps were occasionally pressed into service to convey books to the cities of their assignment, subsequently to be forwarded by local agents. Oldenburg expressed relief that a long overdue package had been delivered by "a certain noble friend now doing the State's business in Holland." As early as October 1660 the French engineer Pierre Petit had displayed great interest in recently published English scientific books. In a lengthy letter to Oldenburg he inquired about a Latin edition of Browne's *Pseudodoxia Epidemica* and the posthumous works of Bacon, the philosophy of Hobbes and "everything he has done except the Politics and De homine which I have." He also requested copies of Oughtred's *Circles of Proportion* and Foster's *Astroscopium* and *On Planetary Instruments,* "which I am told may be had at Thomsons." He assumed that one pistole for the lot would prove sufficient and requested the package be sent through the kindness of Mr. Fouquet, "the brother of the Surintendant," namely the Marquis de Belle-Isle.[16]

Justel advised Oldenburg in March 1667 that he had the opportunity of sending him a recent book by Father Fabri through the help of the servant of the Earl of Aylesbury, later dispatching a text by Saumaise through the office of Henry Jermyn, English ambassador to Paris. Sir John Dodington, the English ambassador to the Republic of Venice, was in frequent contact with Oldenburg about books, suggesting that if he planned to send books to Venice they were to be "directed for Mr. Humph. Sydney at Livorno, for me, by any shipp yt comes into the Straytes or leave it wth Mr. Geo. Ravenscroft a Merchant wellknown in Great St. Hellens, and he will convey it to me."[17]

Eager for the weekly numbers of the *Gazette de Londres,* Pardies requested Oldenburg to send him issues and supplements. Addressing the harassed Secretary of the Royal Society in June 1672, he stated: "Please wrap these Gazettes and adress them to M. le Duc de Bethune, Gouvernour de Calais."[18]

Hevelius received a copy of Wallis, *Mechanica* and issues of the *Philosophical Transactions* through the services of Thomas Henshaw, secretary of the English Embassy at Copenhagen. It was to this same gentleman that one Mr. Flexny, a servant of the Duke of Richmond, brought copies of Boyle's *Booke of Gemmes* which Henshaw regarded as "ye most pleasing divertissements . . . in this tedious, dull place."[19]

With the constant press of inquiries from his many foreign correspondents about recent English scientific publications, Oldenburg himself often served as a most expeditious shipper. Justel had ordered a copy of Shelton, *Tachygraphy,* Pell, *Algebra,* and a book by Wilkins. "Please send the price of the books . . . so that I may see that you get the money. If Mr. Morland's machine does not do division it cannot be of importance, and no one would have any regard for it. Our French dont work as hard and are not as precise as the English."[20]

Like Justel, Pardies, involved in the development of the Royal Library, requested Oldenburg in October 1671 to send "all the books printed in England in the past six or seven years dealing with mathematics or physics either in English or Latin." He specifically ordered the writings of "Mr. Hooke, Mr. Barrow, Mr. Boyle, Mercator, Gregory, etc., of Mr. More and above all the whole of your Philosophical Transactions collected from the beginning. And you will oblige us in sending them afterwards as they are printed. There is no need to send bound volumes; they will be bound here after our fashion."[21]

Matthias Paisen of Hamburg had received in 1669 from Oldenburg an attractive package of new English scientific works: "the Continuation of Boyle's Experiments On Air. Lower's De corde, 2 shillings, Sydenham, Methodus curandi febres with the appendix, 2 shillings, Wallis, Gra[mmar] and Malpighi, On the Silkworm, 7 shillings."[22]

A few shipments from Oldenburg crossed a far greater expanse of little-known space—the stormy waters of the North Atlantic. On 12 November 1668 the Governor of Connecticut John Winthrop thanked Oldenburg for his gift of Sprat's *History of the Royal Society* and "many sheetes of those phylosophicall transactions" remarking that the package had passed from "London to Amsteldam [sic] and hence to New Yorke in the hands of Heere Peter Stuivesant." It was only through the care of a "trusty friend" that the books eventually reached Winthrop. Several years later Oldenburg sent the governor a package of recent scientific publications which included "1. Mr. Boyles new Tracts about ye wonderful rarefraction and condensation of the Air. 2. Monsr. Charas's New Experiments upon Vipers. 3. The Transactions of 1670." At the same time the Secretary of the Royal Society remarked somewhat tactlessly that he had received the "cranberries sent from New England which unfortunately tasted of ye Caske, or else they would have been very good."[23]

Overworked and often unable to attend to shipping personally, Oldenburg in all likelihood assigned the shipping of several requests to Martyn and Allestry. Martyn's continental dealings seem to have been concentrated upon France and Germany. He did considerable business with the Parisian stationers Jean Petit and Etienne Michallat as well as with Gottfried Schulz of Hamburg and lesser dealings with Friedrich Zunner of Frankfurt. Oldenburg informed the Breslau scholar Philip Sachs à Lewenhaimb that he "would have gladly sent a copy of each issue of the *Philosophical Transactions,* did not Martin, our bookseller at whose expense they are printed here, send them every month to Gottfried Schulz of Hamburg where they can easily be procured." In exchange Schulz sent Martyn issues of *Miscellanea curiosa,* organ of the German scientific society, the Collegium Naturae Curiosorum. Writing to Oldenburg in August 1672, Martin Vogel of Hamburg had expected to receive from London, along with the "life of Galileo, a copy of Robert Morison [*Plantarum umbelliferum distributio nova*] which would conveniently have been added to the books John Martin sent our Schulz."[24]

Martyn apparently took little nonsense from his foreign colleagues. Immediate payment was demanded. A note from Oldenburg to Leibniz suggests that accounts were to be settled promptly, "if not Mr. Martin will make difficulties the next time."[25]

Allestry appears to have been a fairly active importer. Searching for a copy of Kircher's *Mundus subterraneus,*—copies of which Oldenburg had located at the premises of Samuell Thompson—Sir Robert Moray stated that "Allestree hath none of them [Kircher] as yet for ought hee knows, but he hath four bales come in at the Customshouse lately, hee knew not from whence when I spoke with him."[26]

Ever concerned about the fate of his London published writings, Malpighi was much relieved when informed by Oldenburg that six copies of his *History of the Silkworm* had been sent by

Allestry to a Florentine bookseller, Francesco Passarini. The package had been shipped via Leghorn aboard "the vessel 'The Royal Defence' its captain [named] Bonneel." Searching London for mathematical texts, Collins declared that Allestry was expecting books out of Italy.[27]

Oldenburg objected to Allestry's "snuff-pinching." Apparently he was faulted for more serious reasons since Malpighi advised Oldenburg that he not only had not received a shipment due from Allestry but he also wished to warn him that "Mr. Allestry is not well with the Italian booksellers."[28]

Robert Scott of the Princes Arms was regarded by his contemporaries as one of the largest buyers from the continent, "obtaining his stock at great expense from most parts of the world." As an importer of foreign books, he made frequent trips abroad. He counted among his customers His Royal Highness Charles II, Samuel Pepys, and Robert Hooke. The scientist alludes to several foreign works acquired from Scott: "Pardies, Mechanicks 3s., Schooten's Miscellany 6sh., a French Anatomy, 2sh.6d., De Chaulnes, Cursus mathematicus." In 1674 Scott issued his important miscellaneous catalogue consisting of an approximate 6,500 titles, most of which had been acquired abroad. The *Catalogue* covered sections on medicine, natural history, chemistry and physics, with larger divisions devoted to theology, the classics, history, and literature. Although he cannot be classified as a specialist in science, Scott was an importer and exporter, a visitor to the French and Dutch markets, the Frankfurt Fairs and particularly Paris where he retained an agent and warehouse.[29]

Hooke purchased not only from Scott but also from a small coterie of French booksellers, in all likelihood Huguenot exiles in London who, maintaining relations with colleagues in their former homeland, sold to the English trade and private collectors. Of the group, Jean Cailloue was the most active as a London publisher and bookseller from 1688 to 1700 with premises in the Strand. In stock he carried travel literature, novels, miscellanea, and stationery. It was at this shop that Hooke saw "strang marbled paper," stating that he knew "how to make it."[30]

Obviously Cailloue had a sufficiently sizable English and foreign clientele since he issued a catalogue of French books. Hooke apparently enjoyed a fairly close contact with him indulging in several of his bookish antics at his shop where he studied his stock of novels, borrowed, and returned a copy of "M. Moll a book on Russia." During a January 1693 visit the scientist spent part of his time transcribing the contents of "4 academy French books." From France, Cailloue imported current literary and scientific journals. From him Hooke purchased vol. 13 of Jean LeClerc, *Bibliothèque Vniverselle et historique* for 2 shillings, later paying 6d. for an issue of the *Journal des Sçavans.*[31]

Anthony Boudet, a member of the French exile bookselling group, published a single known work by William Darrell. Occasionally Hooke visited his shop where he acquired Tachard, *Voyage to Siam* and a set of Adrian Baillet. *Jugemens des Savants* which Boudet had imported from France in 9 volumes was purchased at 22½ shillings. Hooke noted on 21 January 1688/89 "Boudet packing."[32]

Certainly known to Cailloue and Boudet was another exiled French stationer, a certain Behgal also known as Biagen or Behagen who maintained a shop in St. Paul's Churchyard. Hooke visited him in 1693 buying a bound run of the 1691 *Journal des Sçavans*. There he also picked up a treatise on the navigation of rivers and Davity's *Voyages.* Behagel died in May 1693 and, according to Hooke, his "goods [were] gon" by mid-July. Of the group Cailloue alone remained in London donating to the Royal Society a gift of six books.[33]

Actually this small coterie of French London refugee dealers were importers—seldom exporting English scientific books abroad. They do not belong to the group which accepted this responsible and challenging task of export: e.g., Oldenburg, a "trusty friend," member of a diplomatic suite, a traveler, a broker. In a concerted effort to bring to the continent the recent publications in English science they all confronted almost insurmountable difficulties: disease and fire, caprice of the elements, mood of the seaman, the derring-do of pirate, shipwreck, the violence of war—impedimenta beyond human control.

The London Plague of 1665 naturally affected the entire London book trade. Boyle was to write six months after its initial onslaught that "for ought I can learne ye Sicknes has so interrupted & impaird ye Trade & correspondency yt was wont to be driven by ye way of London betwixt all ye parts of England yt Diurnalls are ye only printed things yt have any thing near as quick & generall Vent as formerly; & yt too, as well upon ye Account of their being now printed in halfe sheets of Paper." Oldenburg referred to the "deadnes of Trade and Correspondency." Alluding to the toll of the Plague among members of the Stationers Company, he declared that "Many Printers being carried away among ye rest, by this sad Contagion wch God be blessed, is now faln to 152."[34]

During the height of the epidemic Oldenburg agreed with Boyle that the publication of a catalogue of "anti-pestillentiall Medicines" would prove a public boon. He suggested that it be printed at Oxford since "the London stationers and printers" had retreated to the country as well as others. The lack of craftsmen, of course, delayed the publication of books. Boyle's *History of Cold* could only be issued as soon as compositors could be found "wch of ye Trade have dyed in very great numbers."[35]

The Plague which had so ravished London later decimated parts of Flanders and northern France. Justel suggested that any shipment from England be sent by way of Calais because of the contagion at Rouen, while Sluse remarked that the pestilence had befallen Liège for the past four months "making our neighbors suspicious of our trade."[36]

The Fire of London was further to exacerbate the English book trade. Shops, warehouses, and stocks in the area of St. Paul's were for the most part consumed by the flames, destroying the livelihood of many small stationers and crippling the activity of larger firms. Martyn declared that his colleagues planned to rebuild admitting that they were being treated most basely by their landlord, the Bishop of London.[37]

Once commerce between the English and foreign book markets reopened, the Italian physicist Lorenzo Magalotti remarked that shipments depended not solely on the prompt departure of a vessel but rather "on the kindness of sea and wind." Martin Vogel had entrusted a parcel of books to the seaman Henry Herring bound for London. His patience was to be sorely tried. "I heard yesterday that [Herring] had not departed hence because of the freezing of the Elbe." Not only ice floes barred the way of outbound vessels but also the intense cold gripping northern Germany impeded sea traffic. The few ships that departed northern ports were for the most part compelled to return.[38]

Probably even more dreaded than possible icebergs and frostbite was the eventuality of shipwreck. Concerned about the delay of a long overdue shipment from London, Paisen informed

Oldenburg that he had not received the package entrusted to the sailor John Herne "and I dont know whether it will ever come to my hands since he suffered a shipwreck near Spiekeroog." Hevelius referred not to shipwreck but to piracy at sea when marauding Scotsmen stole two ships "with all our goods." Alluding to the boarding of the free vessel, the "Bocuder van Stockholm," by pirates, he stated that among the items taken were "40 reams of the most excellent paper for which he had paid 150 Imperials." What literary pirates!!![39]

"Si bellum dixeris, omnia male dixeris" [if you speak of war, you speak of every evil] declared Governor Winthrop in November 1688. During the recent Anglo-Dutch War, an English vessel departing New England for home had been seized by the enemy. To protect their merchandise, the English had thrown overboard all letters and writings that "they might be sure, none of them should find what goods were in the ship." Obviously they had thrown the manifest overboard—but what else—what unknown American incunabula had found a watery grave?[40]

Eager to obtain certain works by Boyle, Spinoza was informed that "this unlucky war" prevented their transmission. A later letter to the Dutch philosopher alluded not only to the misery of the Plague but also to the calamities of "this most dreadful war, bringing with it a very Iliad of ills and all but extirpating human kindness from this world." A Dutch scholar bemoaned "the furies of Mars (who now happens to hold sway) paying no heed to our commerce with the Muses." With some resignation Duhamel in 1672 remarked: "If peace is made books will be worth more, for the largest trade is in the North, but this will be in God's good time."[41]

Despite such hazards—just as English books continued to be exported abroad—so continental texts were imported into England. There is little doubt that the Italianate Englishman bought his books not only in Italy but also in his homeland. Five catalogues of Italian books were published in England between 1628 and 1647. In 1657 Octavian Pulleyn issued a catalogue of general foreign texts while the great 1674 miscellaneous catalogue of Robert Scott offered the reader not only belles-lettres but also a variety of old and current scientific works.[42]

Although continental shipments to England encountered the same snags as English exports to Europe, a general knowledge of foreign scientific publications prevailed in England. New books reached the homeland, while the curious stay-at-home could scan the Book Sections of the *Philosophical Transactions* for particular desiderata.

Through his correspondents scattered throughout the principal cities of Europe and a few in the New World Oldenburg was apprised of the most recent works. He requested Auzout to inquire "about books in philosophy upon which the best minds of Italy are now at work. I am told that Mr. Viviani composes the Life of Galileo; that Mr. Borelli writes a treatise De incessu animalium, Mr. Oliva de fluido ... Mr. Malpighi De visceribus, the Abbe Falconieri On Tactics, Mr. Capponi on all Philosophy, and Mr. Travagino the same."[43]

The holdings of Martyn, Pitt, Cooper, Thompson, Littlebury, and Scott attest to the prevalence of scientific texts in England. As early as 1655 Martyn had imported from Paris the Riolan Collection issuing a catalogue of its contents. His Want Lists reflect English curiosity about numerous obscure foreign texts, while Hooke's sizable purchases indicate the feasibility of obtaining foreign books in London.

At the premises of Samuell Thompson, Oldenburg had read his recent catalogue announcing forthcoming texts from abroad: Kircher, *Scrutinium Physico-Medicum Pestis* and Steno, *De Musculis et Glandis.* He informed Boyle that he had noticed little else of interest with the possible exception of an astronomical work by Johann Hocker.[44]

Collins, ever on the search for new mathematical texts, informed Oldenburg of the availability of scientific books "at a bookseller in Hamburgh"—in all likelihood the shop of Martyn's colleague Gottfried Schulz. Collins had seen the dealer's catalogue which included the writings of Leibniz, Strauch, Bartholinus, and others. "There are other Books in ye Booksellers Catalogue which I doe not much desire unlesse cheape." An English traveler may have brought the catalogue to Collins's attention or it is quite possible that dealers were exchanging catalogues.[45]

The importation of books into England follows much the same pattern as the exportation process involving use of similar media, broker, members of the diplomatic corps, friends, authors, and continental booksellers.

Henry Daems does not appear to have played a considerable role in forwarding books to England although he had shipped 50 copies of Sluse's *Mesolabe* to England in October 1669. Oldenburg also advised Sluse to send to Daems "any really good books in physics and mathematics that recently have seen the light in your neighborhood and nearby Germany, then you will be so good to have them sent to Henry Daems at a convenient opportunity." The material—some of which was acquired by Collins—was to be stored in Daems's warehouse until the English mathematician was sufficiently solvent. Oldenburg requested Sluse to procure for him at least 12 scientific texts to which he was to add a copy of Joseph Hebraeus, *Bibliotheca Mathematica et directio ad scientam mathematicas* and Alessandro Marchetti, *Exercitationes mathematicae* recently issued in Italy. Were Sluse to encounter any difficulty, Oldenburg suggested that there might be a "supply of these and similar books at the Frankfurt Fair. I earnestly beg you to add to (the aforesaid titles) a list of those authors of good repute who have written about mathematics in German or Flemish."[46]

At a later date Oldenburg importuned Sluse to arrange that "a single copy [be sent] to London of each of the notable books in mathematics and physics." They were to be sent to Liège or the vicinity. "We will endeavour to recompense you cheerfully whether with books or money, as you shall choose."[47]

Sending a package to London, Malpighi used as agent a certain Verbecke who shipped 17 books by several notable Italian scientists: Marchetti, Rossetti, Montanari, and Riccioli.[48]

Members of the diplomatic corps were pressed into service as agents for the forwarding of literary properties. Regardless of the renewal of hostilities against England on the part of Louis XIV, the English scientific world continued its interest in foreign publications. Oldenburg realized that there would be some interruption of "our philosophicall commerce—the Marchant trade" being seriously affected. He urged an English gentleman, "yt intends to come . . . with our ambassadour . . . to bring over such Curious Books as are to be found in Paris, Redi, De Vipera, Mariana, dela Chine, Descartes, de Homine in French, Petit des Cometes." The following year Arthur Capel, Lord of Essex, English Ambassador to France, brought to England copies of Pascal's *Traité du Triangle Arithmetique* and a *Relation du Voyage de l'Evesque de Beryte par la Turquie, Perse, Les Indes.*[49]

Collins in March 1672 importuned the assistance of the English secretary at the Paris Embassy, Francis Vernon, to purchase books for him. Vernon complied reporting to Collins that he had sent him "Much of those books you writ for as I could at that time procure. They cost

	L.	R.
The third volume of Descartes his Letters	6.	0
The two Mecaniques at 45ʳ	4.	10
Pascals Triangle arithmetique	1.	5
Le Père Labbé s Bibliotheca Bibliothecarum	1.	10
In all	13.	5

At the time Vernon mentioned some annoying French bookselling practices. He had experienced difficulty in obtaining the third volumes of Descartes apart from the rest and the *Mecaniques*. "They bind up here the Specimina and Dioptrics, and it is hard persuading them to sell it without." It still is!!![50]

The interest of the English academic in Italian research spurred Oldenburg to engage the assistance of Sir John Finch, English Resident at the Medici Court in Florence. He dispatched to Sir John a list of desiderata demanded by English scientists—books by Italian scholars among them: "Archimide redivivo a Giovanni Battista Hodierna in 4to. at Palermo 1644: with some Optick Treatises and his Ephemerides of ye Motions of Jupiters Satellites; L'Antanalise Di Salvador Grisio, or Grisius agst Maghettii Romae 1655; A new Treatise agst Vincent Viviani de Maximis et Minimis, Mengoli Arithmetica; Mutio Oddi delle Horovoli [Horologi], and others." Oldenburg hoped at the time for direct business contacts between Italian and English booksellers. "If the Italian stationers would be prevaild wth to take care of sending some Copies of these Books into England, it would very much gratifie the Curious here."[51]

Friends and academic associates brought with them to London requested texts. Returning from Paris, Wren carried in his luggage copies of Redi, *Treatise on Vipers* and Petit, *On Comets*. In an optimistic mood Oldenburg advised Boyle in February 1665/66 that he "daily expected more than one friend from Paris to bring along several Treatises I have looked out for these 12 month." In a later letter he was more specific about the books which had just arrived from the continent: Borelli, *De vi percussionis* and Steno, *De Myologia*. "Mons. de Launary hath transmitted to me his printed

96

Essay De Lieu du Temps et du Vuide which the Royal Society Secretary found both 'acute and learned.'"[52]

As a young man the Dutchman Nicolas Witsen had visited and enjoyed England. He returned to Leyden to study law, later travelling to Russia. Hence it is not surprising that he forwarded to Oldenburg a package which included a copy of the Russian alphabet, a sketch of Novgorod made some years earlier and a Dutch narrative about Ceylon written by Philip Baldaeus. Occasionally authors sent copies of their books and even their portraits. The French physician François Sylvius De Le Boe sent to England copies of his *Praxeos medica idea nova* as well as "a couple of copies of his portrait" engraved by Christopher van Dalen which he declared had been requested by some Englishmen. Apparently this portrait caused some slight stir in London circles since a crayon copy was to be found among the papers of Sir Christopher Wren.[53]

Although Oldenburg seldom ceased his litany about the paucity of foreign *materia scientifica* reaching England, it appears certain that he was quite incapable of realizing the loss of two American "incunabula" which never arrived in the motherland. To the complaining Oldenburg, Governor Winthrop had dispatched copies of the *Indian Dialogues* of John Eliot and "the sheet called the Indian A.B.C." Neither ever arrived in England. Apparently the governor had deposited the texts at the Boston wharf for shipment. Upon ascertaining their non-arrival in England, he declared "Had there been the opportunity of any ship ready I should have seene them delivered on board my selfe, but it is to my great disadvantage in reference to conveiance into England that I am so farre from ye port whence the ships returne."[54]

Surmounting almost impossible impedimenta books safely traveled the rough seas of the Atlantic and the stormy passage of the Channel waters. Traffic between the New World, the continent, and England existed. The successful circulation of scientific books in England and on the continent may be attributed to a variety of factors—basically to man's innate desire to learn, to become acquainted with the new, the unknown. His curiosity was abetted by a host of media—from the local porter and carrier to the cross-Channel and cross-Atlantic vessel bearing the newest scientific publication and artifact. Although brokers, travelers, members of the diplomatic corps eased the burden of transportation, they could in no way lessen the hazards of the age: plague, fire, the threat of the elements, shipwreck, piracy, and intermittent warfare. Despite multitudinous delays and threats to this international commerce, communication among scientists succeeded—their inquiries and experiments enriching the minds of all men committed to the study of an ever expanding intellectual horizon.

In May 1693 a shipment from Germany reached London. It had been sent not from Hamburg or Frankfurt to Henry Oldenburg but from Leipzig by Otto Mencke to Isaac Newton. The package contained copies of the *Acta Eruditorum,* the scientific organ of the Collegium Leipsicum. Newton sent a letter of thanks to its editor and publisher, Mencke, acknowledging receipt of the issues "right up to the month of June 1691. and afterwards the rest of the months of August of the year 1692 inclusive with supplements."[55]

The *Acta Eruditorum* contained learned articles and announcements of recent scientific books. It served as a forum for the exchange of ideas within Germany acquainting German intellectuals with scientific accomplishments. To some extent it followed the design of the *Philosophical Transactions.* It lacked, however, the depth and continuity of the English journal which remained not only the standard work for all subsequent learned periodicals but the greatest general scientific achievement of the Restoration.

8

The Philosophical Transactions

At a meeting of the Royal Society in March 1664 it was ordered that "A Journal be entitled The Philosophical Transactions . . . to be composed by Mr. Oldenburg to be printed the first Munday of every month, if he have sufficient matter for it." The 'copy' was to be reviewed by delegated members, printed in four sheets in folio and published by John Martyn and James Allestry."[1]

On 6 March 1664/65 the first number of the monthly *Philosophical Transactions* appeared. Although the Journal received the Society's imprimatur, it was really Oldenburg's private venture by which he vainly hoped to derive an annual income of £150. Such financial ambition was to be dashed and his association with the *Transactions* was often frustrating and vexatious.

The "peculiar" temper of the first secretary clashed with the personality of the London publisher associated with the production of the *Transactions.* Oldenburg declared Martyn to be "morose and fickle" and his behavior "mightily tedious." He highly disapproved of Allestry's "snuff-pinching" and distrusted the efforts of the Oxford publisher Richard Davis during his association with the periodical.[2]

Prior to the outbreak of the Plague, the *Transactions* appeared on the first Monday of the month in quarto format averaging about 16 pages—not the projected sheets in folio. An issue included approximately five articles, news items from foreign correspondents and a section "Of some philosophical and Curious Books that are shortly to come abroad" which alerted the public to the forthcoming texts in a variety of scientific fields: new titles by Boyle, Lister,

Hooke, and the foreigners—Regnier de Graaf, Redi, Malpighi, and a host of others.

The *Transactions* continued regularly through the publication of no. 5, July 1665, when the Plague had already hit London and printers and readers fled the infected city. An announcement in this issue reports suspension of the periodical: "The Reader is hereby advertised, that by reason of the present Contagion in London, which may unhappily cause our interruption aswel as Corresondencies as of Publick Meetings, the printing of these Philosophical Transactions may possibly for a while be intermitted though endeavours shall be used to continue them, if they may be."[3]

Not only the disheartened Oldenburg but several members of the Royal Society hoped for resumption of the *Transactions* publication. They were to be ultimately successful in obtaining the services of the Oxford publisher Richard Davis who was established close to Oriel College. A letter addressed to Oldenburg, 11 October 1665, by Sir Robert Moray, surely raised the spirits of the dejected editor. Discussing a recent dinner party at Oxford hosted by the Savilian Professor of Mathematics, John Wallis, and attended by Boyle, himself, and others, Moray declared that "amongst other Discourses at Table I mentioned the printing of your Philosophical Transactions here, they all were instantly for it: and without lossing time having pitchd upon Mr. Davyes they sent for him." With the arrival of this gentleman in the afternoon "in 2 words it was agreed that he would print them." Realizing that it would not be possible for him to sell as many copies as the London publishers, Davis demanded a "Proportionable abatement." He was informed by Moray that Martyn and Allestry had paid Oldenburg "3 lib. for every printed sheet" and had issued 1200 copies. Davis agreed to print an edition of 1000 copies. Oldenburg was encouraged to resume 'copy' in "as many sheets printed as you think fit, though I think it will do well to go on with the same number as you was at."[4]

By the end of October 1665, Davis was prepared to distribute copies of the Journal. The quality of the paper used was not as good as formerly. Moray informed Oldenburg that it was the best to be had. Of the 1250 copies printed, he wrote "fifty [half] are for you, the other half for presents &c. 200 the publisher Davis to keep by him. And the rest are to be sold." At the same time Boyle advised the London editor that he had informed "Mr Davis yt wee expected on yor behalfe two Dozen of Copys of ye Transactions, wch will be here wellcome to many of ye Curious."[5]

The first issue of the *Philosophical Transactions* printed at Oxford by Davis—Number 6—appeared 6 November 1665. It included Davis's brief announcement: "An opportunity being presented to revive the Publishing of these Papers, which for some Moneths hath been discontinued by reason of the great Mortality in London . . . it hath been thought fit to embrace the same." Davis certainly did not undertake the publication with alacrity. He had been cajoled into the venture by the pillars of the Royal Society whose favor he naturally wished to retain as a publisher of scientific texts.[6]

At a time when London was still suffering from infection, the average reader was disinclined to intellectual pursuits, especially the reading of scientific and technical discourses. Davis found the *Transactions* a slow seller. Of the first number he had not been able to dispose of more than 300 copies, sales not meeting his overhead. Oldenburg received nothing. Nonetheless, he agreed to continue the venture. A letter dated 19 October 1665 from Oldenburg to Boyle reflects Davis's business acumen. He suggested that the Journal have a wider distribution: "He [Davis] thinks, London being like to be open now for Commerce, if he do send 3. or 4. active Stationers in severall quarters of ye Towne; and besides to Cambridge, Exeter, Bristoll, etc. item into Ireland, Scotland; a far greater number should then goe off." Oldenburg added that when Davis shipped copies to Samuell Thompson he was also to send copies to "Booksellers about ye Exchange, (for there I find, they are inquired after) and to another about Dunstans in Fleetstreet. and to another about Westminster, and so disperse ym to ye chief parts of ye Citty, especially now Carriers begin to return hither."[7]

Unfortunately the combined suggestions of Davis and Olden-burg did not accelerate the Journal's sale. The Secretary of the Royal Society blamed the slowdown upon Davis, who, he believed, had not applied himself "seasonably enough to despatch a competent number of Copys to ye Country Carriers." In a gloomy note Boyle admitted that Davis was loath to publish additional issues since he had a considerable backlog. Publication could only continue "upon such Termes as may be very Preiudiciall to ye Transactions for ye future."[8]

Davis's negative attitude prompted Oldenburg to vent his venom on the fraternity of stationers and to air his own pessimism. "I wish only, there be no collusion among ye Stationers, and yt ye deadnes of Trade and Correspondency into wch the reassuming of ye printing of these papers is fallen, may not prove too great a prejudice to ye dispersing of ym for the future." A letter addressed to Boyle, 24 March 1665/66, reflects Oldenburg's deep concern about the fate of his *Transactions:* "I wonder somewhat at Mr Davis, yt he should make such a noise, among our Stationers, even by letters, concerning ye Transactions and ye scarcity of their vent: Me thinks he does what he can to decry ym, and he has already effected so much, yt, if they goe on to be printed, I shall be ye worse for it by 40.sh. a month; wch is a great losse to one, yt has no other way of subsistence for serving the Society." Oldenburg assured Boyle that he had never pressured the Oxford publisher and was certain that the issues published by Davis amounted to £20.10. He was at a loss to comprehend Davis's attitude since readers were again seeking copies of the *Transactions.* He himself could locate no copy of Number One. "ye Stationer alledging he can find none of ym in his ware-house." He proposed that Davis send to London available issues since "they may in a little time be dispersed if ye Towne remains in health, and then sure his clamorous complaints may be satisfied. What was hoped, might have brought me in about 150. lb. per annum, English and Latin together, will now scarce amount to 50. as the matter is like to be ordered, especially since the Stationers, by reason of Warr, refuse to print the Latin." Oldenburg's criticism of Davis may be ill-founded. The Oxford publisher had suggested a broader base for the circulation of the *Transactions.* Oldenburg suffered a lingering distrust of the stationers' corps. There can be little doubt that the sale of the Journal was affected by loss of readers during the Plague.[9]

Despite his enmity toward members of the publishing craft, Oldenburg must have experienced some relief when Martyn and Allestry resumed publication of the *Philosophical Transactions* with Number 9, February 1665/66. With difficulty the periodical had survived the effects of the Plague and Davis's apparent indifference. Now in September 1666, the publishers were to be confronted with a business calamity of disastrous proportions. The Fire of London of September 1666 swept the booksellers' quarters, leaving in its wake blackened stumps of their former Hall, water-soaked and charred remains of books and issues of the *Philosophical Transactions.*

Oldenburg regarded the Fire as a personal calamity and while the flames consumed the area he wrote to Boyle: "I shall find it very difficult to continue ye printing of ye Transactions; Martyn and Allestry being undone with the rest of ye Stationers at Pauls Churchyard and all their Books burnt . . . besides, yt ye Citty lying disconsolate now, it will be very hard to vend them at ye present." This gloomy conjecture must be discounted. It has already been indicated that books and issues of the *Transactions* escaped the disaster, since Martyn in his 1670 Catalogue advertised *A Compleat Collection of the Philosophical Transactions of the Years 1665, 1666* and it is not too difficult to secure early runs of the *Transactions* in the current antiquarian market.[10]

Oldenburg's tribulations seem endless. A letter to Boyle of 18 October 1666 alludes to the loss of his wife and subsequent funeral expenses. In addition he was constantly harassed by the conduct of the stationers of St. Paul's who, suffering from the loss of stock, insisted that he give them "the Transactions of the month freely, yf yt will doe them any kindnes, or, at least be any encouragement to ym to continue. which they say it will." The complaints of Oldenburg continued unabated. At the end of October 1666 he informed Boyle that "to this very houre I have got none yet to print them." He had unsuccessfully attempted to enlist the services of John Crooke of the Ship to undertake the assignment promising him the publication of "some good vendible books." Despite his many disappointments, he was happy to hear from Paris that "our Transactions goe on, notwithstanding the spoyle by ye late fire."[11]

It is somewhat puzzling that Oldenburg was still concerned about the future of the *Transactions* once Martyn and Allestry had resumed publication. Apparently Davis still retained an Oxford agency "exspect[ing] downe some copies of the October [issues], there were sent 2. or 3. pacquets containing some douzens of ym to Oxford," as Oldenburg informed Boyle.[12]

The friction between Oldenburg and Martyn continued. Although the proprietor of the Bell was regarded by Oldenburg as "scrupulous afresh, to continue ye printing of the Transactions," he apparently had informed the editor that he was sustaining a loss from their publication. Annoyed and frustrated, Oldenburg once again fulminated against the stationers' corps. "The morosity and fickleness of these men is mightily tedious to me. I wish I had another way of subsistence." Referring to Martyn's so-called high-handed tactics, he expostulated: "Mr. Martyn deals very mercinarily with me; for knowing, that others will hardly undertake the printing of those papers . . . hath constrained me to abate the rate yet lower, so that, after ye proportion, he allows me, I shall hardly bring it to 30 lb. a year." Oldenburg constantly referred to his reduced financial condition. "I have some ground to believe," he wrote to Boyle in December 1667, "that there are persons who think, the Transactions bring me in sufficient revenue. But I will make it out to any man that I never receaved above 40lb. a year upon their account (and that is little more, than my house-rent). And now by a new agreement, I have been obliged to make, I shall not bring it to above 36lb. a year at most."[13]

There is no doubt that the editor had grounds for complaint. The publishers and booksellers obviously disliked this stiff-necked German "of peculiar temper." Bred in a rigid social caste, a man of education and vast erudition, he regarded with contempt men of lesser social rank and education. Yet one must have sympathy for Oldenburg who was not only victimized by the calamity of Plague and Fire but also financially exsanguinated by the publishers and some seeming indifference to the Journal itself. In June 1666 the naturalist John Beale wrote that he had observed a prevailing apathy toward it on the part of the trade. "In Blanford, & other cheife Townes of Dorsetshire; & in Bristoll, Wells &c. I found ye Stationers under a Prejuduce, or averse agst them: And yu well know, yt we have often discoursed & found yt some others, perhaps not a few of ye R S are somwt unfriendly or unassisting in ye spreading of them."[14]

Despite an indifference to the circulation of the *Transactions* "in Blanford, & other cheife Townes of Dorsetshire," the Journal enjoyed an enviable position in some "cheife" cities of the continent—Paris, Hamburg, Danzig, Rome, Florence, Amsterdam—its reputation enhanced by the correspondents Oldenburg had established in these key intellectual centers.

To present to the public a comprehensive periodical replete with news of current scientific experiments and investigations, new publications and activity, Oldenburg realized that he must have reports of the most recent scientific progress from agents abroad. Even prior to the publication of the *Transactions,* Oldenburg, in his role as Secretary to the Society, had established relations with a Parisian correspondent, the astronomer Adrien Auzout. "I have lately offred me a new correspondence at Paris for all ye news and Curiosities of France and Italy. He expects nothing for a returne, but ye communicating to him what considerable books are continually printing in England, whether in English, Latin, Greek etc. and some generall account of ye Progress and performances of ye R. Society. He hath already promised to send me ye observations, wch one of ye very best Philosophers of Paris hath made upon ye new book of Optick Glasses, yt are so much cried up."[15]

Once the *Philosophical Transactions* were firmly established, Oldenburg hoped for a widespread chain of corresponding agents. In a letter to the great benefactor of the Royal Society, Henry Howard, he expressed his hope that "we might obtaine some Philosophicall Correspondents in ye chief Cittys of Italy and particularly at Florence, Pisa, Bologna, Milan, Venice, Naples, Rome." The editor hoped for reports from such eminent scientists as the mathematicians Michelangelo Riccio, friend of Galileo; Giovanni-Domenico Cassini of Bologna; Gilles-François Gottignies, the Jesuit astronomer; the medical writer Honoré Fabri who taught at Rome; the well-known physician Francesco Redi; the physicist Giovanni-Antonio Borelli; the engineer Manfred Settala; the famous optical instrument-maker of Rome, Giuseppe Campani. He regarded these gentlemen "to be no inconsiderable persons for such a commerce; and they may be assured, yt I shall make it a part of my study to make some return."[16]

Information from abroad shortly cluttered the editor's desk. Boyle was advised in December 1667 that Oldenburg had received "very many letters and papers stored with philosophicall matters from Antwerp, Dantzick, Sueden, Poland, ye Bermudas, and Holland." In particular, he stressed the reliability of [Richard] Norwood of the Bermudas, "a solid, knowing and sober man. Tis he, from whom I have communications come from yt place." By mid-December 1667 he somewhat complacently informed Boyle that "I have no less at present than 30. correspondents partly domestick, partly forrain." A week later he excitedly announced that he was "like to enter into a Correspondnce with the excellent Carcavy, a great Mathematician, and one that knows most of ye Intelligent and Curious Men in the world, his French Maj'ties

Bibliothecarius, and the Chief Director of ye new Experimental Academy at Paris."[17]

The London editor suggested that once Ercole Zani, the Italian astronomer, had returned to Italy from a London visit, he "should be so good as to keep up a regular correspondence with me communicating in it . . . news of what novel and unusual things come forth in Italy with respect of philosophy, mathematics, optics, mechanics, chemistry and botany." He was also to send new books dealing with such subjects by vessels sailing out of Leghorn for England, addressing the packages to some Italian merchant dwelling in London. Boyle expressed satisfaction with Oldenburg's contacts especially pleased that he planned to establish correspondence with Rome "that being the chief center of intelligence; nor is it unwelcome news to me that you are likely to receive, from time to time an account of what will be done in the academy at Caen." Not all correspondents, however, were satisfied with their role. Dodington at Venice complained that "in ye two yeares & halfe yt I have been yr correspondent I have expended some Eight pounds or more on Bookes & Postage on yr Accompt." He demanded recompense in the form of a book, namely a set of Goltzius's *Works*.[18]

Many foreign scientists, despite their meagre English, eagerly awaited the *Transactions,* anticipating the variety of articles, scientific news, and book reviews. The range of subjects was varied and its scope was indicated by the contents of the first issue: "An Account of the Improvement of Optick Glasses at Rome;" "Of the Observations made in England of a Spot in one of the Belts of the Planet Jupiter;" "Relation of a very Monstrous Catt;" "Of a particular Lead Ore in Germany;" "Of the new American Whale-fishing about the Bermudas;" "A Narrative concerning the Success of Pendulum Watches at Sea for Longitude;" "A Catalogue of the Philosophical Books Published by Monsieur de Fermat Counsellor at Toulouse lately dead." Numbers contained articles by Boyle, Ray, Willughby, and foreign scientists. Many of the subjects presented by Hooke for discussion at the Society's meetings later appeared in the *Transactions.* His contributions include among others: "An Answer to Monsieur Auzout's Considerations," his research on artificial respiration, his observations of the planet Jupiter. Two years after Oldenburg's death in 1677, Hooke became editor of the Journal from 1679 to 1689, changing its title to the

Philosophical Collections. His work on the marine barometer was published during the last year of his life, February 1700/01.

It was the hope of foreign readers that for a better understanding the *Transactions* be translated into Latin. Boyle was confident that a Latin edition would be profitable and feasible. He informed Oldenburg in March 1665/66 that if the Journal were translated into Latin, he wished to be advised beforehand so that he might render assistance. Encouraged by Boyle, for whom he had the highest regard, Oldenburg toyed with the idea, discussing the possiblity with Martyn, suggesting a small letter for a Latin pocket edition.[19]

Actually a Latin version of the *Philosophical Transactions* was to be undertaken a few years later for a brief period, not by Martyn at London, but at Copenhagen by the publisher Daniel Paulli. Oldenburg had been advised by Martin Vogel that the translation had been begun by a "Scotsman who, it seems to me, [is] ill-suited. As I hear he has already resigned the employement, perhaps because he does not understand everything equally well. I send the first sheet. The printing has not yet proceeded beyond four sheets. They intend to make a start with the year 1669, because they have heard that you intend to take up the same task."[20]

John Sterpin was the Latin translator of the *Philosophical Transactions.* Although he called himself a Scotsman, he had been born in France, lived in England, and later migrated to Denmark. He declared that he owed much of his education to England and hence should interest himself "much in the glory of it, and specially of the Royal Society, as its chiefest ornament." Oldenburg was informed that Sterpin had been prompted to undertake the translation "to satisfye the desires of the knowing world . . . who often complained that your Philosophicall Transactions were not intelligible to them." The errors in the translation were ascribed not to his own lack of comprehension but rather to the inability of the corrector "for haveing suffered some faults though not very many to enter in the impression."[21]

Oldenburg announced the Latin version and its numerous errors in No. 75, September 1671 of the *Philosophical Transactions.* Enforced by the criticism of Vogel who had not envisioned "such enormous errors," Oldenburg advised Sterpin in April 1671 to discontinue his translation of the periodical.[22]

Foreign scientists and readers, however, continued to clamor for a competent Latin version of the *Transactions*. English was not a universal language and some potential subscribers were deterred by their lack of the tongue. The Polish astronomer Hevelius aptly expressed the hopes of many continental scholars: "All foreigners wish that your Philosophical Transactions might be printed in Latin as soon as possible, seeing that it is of importance to the whole world of learning." The French physician Jean Denis aspired not only to a Latin text but also to a French translation which would "be sold throughout France for the benefit of the many curious readers who understand no English, and who are grateful to read good things in French rather than in Latin." Denis was later to reverse his opinion and regret that the Journal had not appeared in Latin since it would have sold "largely in France, Germany, Italy and other distant countries."[23]

Continental demand for a recognized Latin version of the *Transactions* was to be met. The booksellers Boom of Amsterdam commissioned before January 1672/73 one Christopher Sand to render a Latin text. Sand, a German by birth, had worked as a press corrector in Holland, later settling in Hamburg where he styled himself Secretary of the Resident of the English King, Sir William Swan. Here he began his translation. His correspondence with Oldenburg regarding problems in translation relates largely to the interpretation of English words and expressions. By 28 February 1672/73 he informed the English editor that "almost everything is printed, for I have not done the beginning of the translation from the year sixty-six. It has been published in a continued series from the year sixty-seven past the halfway mark, and soon the whole will be published." Brashly he remarked: "I do not make bookselling my business. I sell my services to anyone for money. I am paid a ducat for one sheet of Latin."[24]

The Sand version appeared as *Acta Philosophica Societatis Regiae in Anglia anni MDCLXVI* (Amsterdam: Boom, 1672), a title offensive to Oldenburg who considered the periodical his own private venture, not the publication of the Royal Society. The Sand version found a ready market among the scholarly set unfamiliar with English. The Dutch physician Nicholas ab Hoboken expressed the sentiment: "Our people (being clumsy in the English language) certainly very much desire and long for a continued translation of each and every part."[25]

Dodington believed that the *Transactions* should also appear in Italian. He informed Oldenburg in April 1672 of "a worthy, inquisitive studious friend who is resolved to translate and print them at Padoa incouraged to do it by many hundreds who will contribute to ye Charge. I hold it a duty to man, & my Country, to promote ye knowledge of ye one, & Honor of ye other." Despite the diplomat's worthy sentiments no Italian text appeared.[26]

Those scholars "not clumsy in the English language" continued to enjoy the *Transactions*. From remote Hartford in New England, Governor John Winthrop referred to the long-awaited arrival of "many sheetes of those phylosophicall Transactions (the excellent fruit of your indefatigable industry, the world's benefit, the publication of them)." Eagerly the young German scientist Matthias Paisen of Hamburg begged for all issues published. "I will take it upon myself either to return you the money you expend in London (with thanks) or to recompense you with books purchased here on your behalfe."[27]

Hevelius, a member of the Royal Society, was a faithful subscriber receiving copies from Oldenburg who advised him in August 1669 that he was sending him numbers 16 to 49 with the exception of number 27 stating that "the bookseller has no more copies of it; he is to have that number and others reprinted in the near future." Number 27 was surely a sellout for it included the French physician Jean Denis's famous "Letter concerning a new way of curing sundry diseases by transfusion." The Dutch scientist Christian Huygens impatiently awaited the issues which his father was to bring to Holland from London and requested Oldenburg to send future issues "so from now on the collection of them I am making will be complete."[28]

English and foreign subscribers could not complain about the price of the *Transactions*. A single issue averaged six pence. Although it would be expected that Hooke—as Curator of Experiments, future editor of the *Transactions,* and mainspring of the Royal Society—should have received his copies gratis, this was not the case. According to his library holdings he paid varying prices for individual issues and runs of the Journal. Occasionally he received a complimentary number. In March 1672/73 he acquired 8 issues for 18sh. This amount appears to be extraordinarily high since a run for 1675 cost him only 18 pence. The mathematician John Collins was advised that 67 issues in quires would cost him 67 shillings—the publisher doubting he could assemble a complete collection. Dodington wrote to Oldenburg that he had brought with him to Venice a complete collection of the *Transactions* "from March 11. 1666. no. 23. fol. 409 & ending in 1668/no. 43. fol. 876 [scarcely complete]. I would begg to have ye preceding & subsequent ones, if to be gott for the love of money." He added that the collection had been well bound probably in Venice.[29]

Selling usually at a nominal price—in quires or well bound— the *Philosophical Transactions* offered the scholar the most recent innovation in science. It remains one of the greatest achievements of the Restoration and vies with the writings of Newton, Hooke, Boyle, Evelyn, Wren, and others—all of whom contributed to its pages. The Journal reflects the intellectual ferment of England and the continent: the disputatious character of the age, its curiosity, research, observations. Interest in its publication stretched from the New World to the seats of learning in the Old. Above all it bespeaks the aspirations of man to inquire, to discern, to create. It endures as an invaluable repository of scientific experiment and achievement.

PART II

THE LIBRARY OF ROBERT HOOKE

9

The Collector

Robert Hooke displayed all the attributes of a true collector: a
relentless passion for books, a ceaseless search for those texts which
reflected his manifold interests, a loyalty to his booksellers, and
triumph at the detection of a sleeper. He relished his prowls in
Duck Lane and Moorfields on the trail of a rarity, visiting "the first
shop, second shop, third shop." In turn he was cosseted by his
dealers who appreciated his avidity for books, his readiness to buy,
his tremendous knowledge, and who permitted him to charge
books, take items 'on approval,' return and exchange them. The
bookseller occasionally indulged this capricious customer who was
often resistant to price. The dealer's premises became Hooke's
rendezvous where he read and copied texts, met friends, discussed
meetings of the Royal Society and curiosities of the day.

Hooke enjoyed the peripheral aspects of book collecting—
techniques of printing, binding, gilding. His "first and last Mistress
Mechanicks" lured him to the premises of the type-founder Joseph
Moxon to whom he explained his theory of "cutting borders and
letters for a press in copper." He frequently spent time in
Moorfields with the quasi-bookseller Philip Barret observing his
experiments in the manufacture of printer's black and varnish.
Hooke experimented with the marbling of paper and the gilding of
leather. He collected the histories of printing, the lives of notable
booksellers, catalogues of dealers and auctioneers. An inveterate
auction buff, he attended as many as four sales in one day. An
astute buyer, he viewed books prior to the sale, carefully analyzing
the contents of catalogues. He bought avidly although he criticized
prices. His memoranda of 56 auction sales held between August

1686 and August 1689 in the metropolitan area and the outskirts reflect his deep interest in the auction market and entitle him perhaps to be the progenitor of later editors of *Book Auction Records.*

Hooke cannot be called a fashionable collector. His library was primarily a working one—designed to answer his professional needs. Of his favorite author Euclid whose first three books he had mastered as a young man within a single week, he owned 27 editions. Although he imparted to his niece Grace the fundamental principles of bookbinding, there is no indication that he personally indulged in lavish bindings or visited the chic binding ateliers of the period. His was largely the library of the scholar-scientist who learned Dutch, wrote Portuguese, and studied Malabaric and Arabic characters.

According to Waller it was from his employment as city surveyor that Hooke derived the major portion of his income. "It was evident by a large Iron Chest of Money found after his Death, which had been lock'd down with the Key in it, with a date of the Time by which it appear'd to have been so shut up for above thirty years to the value of many thousands in gold and silver." There is no doubt that a considerable portion of this "gold and silver" was invested in books purchased by Hooke from Martyn, Pitt, Littlebury, Thompson, and the dealers of Duck Lane and Moorfields, Bunhill, Tower Ditch, and Fish Street Hill. The Curator of Experiments also bought books from nonprofessional sources frequently helping his impecunious friend, the antiquarian John Aubrey, ever in financial need. From Aubrey he purchased Descartes, *De Lumiere;* Hartlib, *Of Husbandy;* the *Conicks* of Apollonius Pergaeus; *De re navali* of the French scholar Baif; Galileo, *Tractatus de proportione Instumentuum* at 10sh.; the *Alchimia* of Geber; and numerous other titles. Diary entries also refer to book purchases from one Mr. Kite. The scientist cites the cost of these books as £6.0 "12sh. carriage, 2sh. porterage and 2sh. boxes." A Diary entry of 23 July 1686 alludes to the acquisition of several volumes from a Mr. Heyt totalling £3.10, carriage 6sh. A ramble through Cheapside resulted in the purchase of a French copy book at 4d.[1]

Although Hooke acquired the majority of his holdings in London he ordered a few directly from the continent possibly hoping to avoid the profit of an intermediary English dealer. From abroad he received "Felibien, P. Pardies, maps of starrs, Origine de fontaines, Eaux minerales, Influence de astros, Pappin, Machines, 8 Journalls." Apparently awaiting an overseas shipment, he visited Buttolf Wharf where he "received a bundle of books from Roan [Rouen]." Shortly thereafter he spent some time "about books in customs house." If the English customs of 1676 bore any resemblance to the bureaucracy of present-day customs, it is certain the Curator of Experiments had learned his lesson—let the dealer suffer and take the profit![2]

Hooke occasionally engaged an agent for the purchase of foreign books. Dr. Theodore Diodati, a cousin of Charles, the close friend of Milton, traveled abroad frequently. Apparently an admirer of Hooke, he presented him with an Italian psalter. Together they dined at the Dutch Ordinary or Garaway's, discussing books and politics. During February 1676/77 Hooke wrote: "News from Diodati of books," shortly thereafter paying him 6sh. for a run of the *Journal des Sçavans,* issues of which the London physician had apparently procured for him. Since the *Journal des Sçavans* rivalled to some extent the *Philosophical Transactions,* Hooke was a keen reader of its articles on chemistry and physics as well as its announcement of current and forthcoming scientific texts. Obviously the Curator of Experiments carefully scanned this column since he ordered several titles mentioned "through Diodati." Hooke's Diary entries refer to payment for issues of the *Journal:* "Paid Diodati 3sh.6d. for 7 Journall des Sçavans. Received from Dr. Diodati 11 Journalls."[3]

For the arrangement of his collection Hooke, the scientist, applied a systematic method. He owned and studied essential texts on library planning: *Instructions for the Erecting of a Library* by Gabriel Naudé, translated into English by Hooke's fellow bibliophile, Sir John Evelyn; *The Reformed Library Keeper* of John Durie; *Bibliotheca Bibliothecarum* of Père Labbé; *De Bibliothecis* of Johann Lomeier and the extremely uncommon *Traité des plus belles bibliothèques de l'Europe* of Père Gallois. Having met Daniel Elzevier at Aldersgate, Hooke naturally invested in a copy of the stout stock Elzevier Catalogue of 1674. His inquiring mind impelled him to bid 4d. at a Hussey sale for a copy of Richard Simon, *Critical enquiries into the various editions of the Bible* (London 1684). Hooke, the scientist and hypochondriac, owned two copies of Joannes van der Linden, *De scriptis medicis* (1686) from which compendium he might discern titles whose content might aid him in the distress and cure of phlegm, dizziness, catarrh of the nose and throat, headaches, and multitudinous complaints.[4]

Among Hooke's specialized bilbiographies and library catalogues were the *Bibliotheca chymica* of Pierre Borel, the *Bibliotheca Oizeliana,* the collection of Jacob Oisel, and the *Bibliothèque Françoise* of Charles Sorel. In addition, he owned two copies of Thomas Hyde, *Catalogus Impressorum Librorum Bibliothecae Bodleianae* and the *Catalogus Librorum in Bibliotheca Collegi Sioni.* As Curator of Experiments of the Royal Society, he naturally bought a copy of the *Catalogue of Rarities in Gresham College* by his fellow academician Nehemiah Grew. Bibliographical compilations by the Prussian Cornelis à Beughem included his *Bibliographia mathematica,* a tool for Hooke's extensive holdings in the field. The scientist acquired this volume in December 1689 "in quires for 2sh." from the science specialist Samuel Smith, "Printer to the Royal Society." At the time of this purchase it is possible that Hooke's credit was in question since "he spake of adjusting accounts."[5]

Allied with his library manuals and bibliographies were a few texts on the history of printing and biographies of publishers: Jean de la Caille, *Histoire de l'Imprimerie et de la Librairie;* and the lives of the Parisian scholar-publishers, the Estiennes, by Jansson ab Almeloveen. In January 1677/78 Hooke wrote: "Bought of Moxon his first monthly exercise 6d." This was a section of the celebrated *Mechanick Exercises,* a complete copy of which is found in the library.[6]

In order to keep pace with his fast developing collection, Hooke constantly ordered additional "boxes" or presses for the books. He was in frequent touch with the joiner Kettle who supplied him with cases and shelving. In December 1688 Hooke settled with Kettle for one box "4sh." and his Diary alludes subsequently to several orders for additional presses. He paid Kettle in September 1689 "9sh. for 3 boxes in full. Mr. Kettle for 2 more book boxes and bespoke more." The collector also alludes to a book chest.[7]

In his "boxes" Robert Hooke arranged his holdings in mathematics and astronomy, medicine and physics, mechanics, travel and discovery, botany, alchemy, witchcraft, surveying and philology. Numerous Diary entries refer to the care he devoted to his library. There is an indication that although he sought from Pitt "a catalogue-maker," he himself on several occasions catalogued his collection. "Kept in rangd and catalogued library. Mended shelves and ranged books." Like other contemporary collections, the Hooke Library was arranged according to format, folios, quartos, octavos, twelvemos, etc. "Rangd some folios." Irritated like most collectors by the elusive, erratic conduct of octavos and smaller books which slip and slide behind larger texts or tumble down to lower shelves, appearing to be irretrievably lost, Hooke "contrivd gliders" designed to prevent an unruly twelvemo from teetering into a dark corner. Diary entries refer to smaller books which were constantly being re-arranged. In January 1676/77 he wrote: "Setld books and numbered them. Cleared books and shelves. Markd A & B box."[8]

There is no indication that the Curator of Experiments purchased books for the elegance of binding. At home he occasionally stitched books remarking "stitcht Hugens...Siam." A Diary entry of June 1689 reads: "3.6 for my own 6 pieces bound at Kingsmill." This elusive bindery has not been identified. Upon occasion he did have a few texts bound well. In 1675 a copy of Vitruvius purchased from Oldenburg was bound at the cost of 5 shillings. For his set of Marot, *Recueil des Plans, Profils & Elevations des plusieurs Palais, Chasteaux,* acquired at 17sh., he spent 1sh.6d for the binding. Diary jottings note "binding 8 sh.," while the *Bibliotheca Hookiana* cites a copy of Evelyn, *Sculptura* "Bd Bl. Turkey and Gilt Leaves." The copy may have been presented to Hooke by Evelyn the majority of whose books were well bound.[9]

The Curator of Experiments instructed his niece Grace in binding technique having constructed for her a binding frame. Hooke refers to her bindings of the *Works* of the mathematician Oughtred, the "2nd volume of Kircher, China" and an alchemical treatise of Samuel Zimmerman.[10]

Trained in the scientific method, Hooke studied trade and auction catalogues, many of which he kept as part of his bibliographical holdings. Upon a visit to Martyn he picked up Cooper's catalogues, probably copies of the forthcoming auction sales of the libraries of Stephen Watkins and Dr. Thomas Shirley. Examining the stock of the French dealer Cailloue, he was presented with a copy of the proprietor's "French Catalogue."

Hooke, the enthusiastic auction buff, received copies of forthcoming sales from Millington. During a visit to Tom's coffee-house he studied the catalogue of the upcoming sale of the collections of his revered late friend Boyle to be sold with the holdings of the arms-painter Sylvanus Morgan. Like the most sophisticated collector, Hooke kept his auction catalogues. A Diary entry of 1 August 1689 states: "Rangd auction catalogs."[11-12]

Hooke, an astute and careful collector, collated his books. Having received a copy of Hevelius, *Machina coelestis,* he found it to be imperfect. His copy of Pietro della Valle, *Travels in India* is described as "deficient," while Zahn, *Oculus,* purchased at the Maitland Sale, 8 May 1689, was returned as "imperfect." The *Tartar Grammar* of Witsen was found "wanting" and also returned, but fortunately after collating a treatise by Salmasius, the collector noted "perfect."

Hooke the bookman was also Hooke the reader. Although many of the books he purchased were designed to assist him in his professional ventures, there is ample evidence that he spent much of his leisure reading: "Read Serlio, Bodley's life of his own writing, Poliphile and Thevet." During 1672 and 1673 he alludes to the reading of Hobbes's translation of the *History* of Thucydides and "Hobbs his life." Visiting Boyle, he passed part of the time perusing a French text and in July 1676 he read the "3 first propositions of Euclid to Tom," his young cousin. "Perus'd Schott's Technica Curiosa, Zwelfer's Pharmacopeia Augustana, Monardes and several editions of the Journals, Cassini Theoria Cometae, Halley and Dr. Cutter's Solution of Ellipses." He apparently tarried long enough at the Princes Arms, the shop of Robert Scott, to digest Moncony's *Voyages* while at home he read passages from Debes, *Description of the Island and Inhabitants of the Feroe,* a text he had picked up in Duck Lane. "Read Hacluit, Morhof, De methodo media." He spent time analyzing the articles in the different issues of the *Journal des Sçavans* procured for him by Dr. Diodati. In May 1693 he completed the reading of a treatise on river navigation with the comment "short but good."[13]

Gathered with his friends at one of the many London coffee-houses, he discussed Society meetings, the accession of William III, the birth of a two-headed child, and books. "With Sir J.Hoskins at Garaways and Jonathans till 11. Talkd much of the New Atlantis. Sir W. Turners rambld about books." On 23 September 1676

Hooke dined with Boyle and presented the renowned chemist with a "guilt calf copy of his treatise Lampas. He gave me his new book."[14]

Hooke was a generous collector who lent desired texts to his friends. Dr. Croon borrowed his copy of *La Science des forces mouvantes* of the Jesuit Ignace Pardies. Having read his copy of Hobbes's translation of the *History* of Thucydides, Hooke lent it to Mr. Godfrey. Sir John Hoskins, who had succeeded as President of the Royal Society, borrowed 3 *Journals des Sçavans* and Alpinus, *De plantis exoticis.* To Theodore Haux he lent some light reading, *Les Amours de la Duchesse de Savoie;* to Sir Peter Wyche "a book on the Nyle." Messrs. Hill and Blackburne borrowed a variety of texts including a work on the "Mogulls country, Le Febure Chymistry and the Racovian Catechism." He placed at the disposal of his niece Grace copies of Sherwood, *French tutor* and the *Rules of civility,* Bunworth, *Doctresse* in French, and doubtless to improve any knowledge of Latin, a copy of *Linguae Latinae Dictionarius quadripartitus,* a Latin-English dictionary. Tompion selected for reading from the Hooke Library a copy of Street, *Astronomy* and Foster, *Miscellanies.*[15]

In the quest of bibliophily Hooke did not accept the maxim of Polonius: "Neither a borrower nor a lender be." As he lent books, so he borrowed them. From Pitt he took on loan a copy of *A Description of Spitsberg* and from his friend Sir Edward Chamberlayne, *A Description of Ceylon.* "Borrowd from Mr. Hill Captain James Voyages . . . of Mr. Martin a foolish German book . . . from Llodowick Lloyd his new universall alphabet." On 31 July 1676 he noted: "Talkd long with Mr. Montague. He promisd and invited me to France. Borrowd French anatomy and measure of the earth." From his friend the art specialist Godfrey Richards he borrowed copies of *Principes de Geometrie* and *Les nouvelles pensées* of Galileo. It is of interest to observe that several of the titles of the books borrowed by Hooke are in his library. Did the Curator of Experiments fail to return these volumes? It is more likely that he gave them a trial run—reading them—before he decided to make an outright purchase. He owned *A Description of Spitsberg;* James, *Voyages;* and *Les nouvelles pensées* of Galileo.[16]

Several of the books in the Hooke Library had been gifts. Halley presented to him "his hemisphere and books . . . From Dr. Gale Burnets 2nd part of Telluris Historia." On 7 January 1692/93

Hooke wrote: "I was presented with Mr. Boyle's new book of the generall History of the Air 4^0 by Mr Churchill. With Tompion to Sir W. Pettys. He gave me his new book." The Hooke Collection lists a copy of Petty, *Use of duplicate proportion,* 1674. The physician Robert Pierce gave Hooke a copy of the chemical treatise *Cursus triumphalis* of Yonge, while from Italy Boccone sent him a copy of his *Icones et Descriptio Variorum Plantas Siciliae, Melitae, Galliae et Italiae.*[17]

A recipient of books, Hooke in turn presented his friends with copies of recent publications. "Presented Mr. Kendall with Mr Boyle's Book of Cold, Guilt." Dr. Jonathan Goddard received a copy of Boyle, *The Strange Subtility of Effluviums,* while Hooke gave the great chemist a copy of Elsholtz *On Earthquakes.*[18]

A copy of Boyle, *Some Considerations touching the stile of Scriptures,* 1690, is one of the few known extant works from the Hooke Library. An inscription on the flyleaf reads: "Sum ex libris R.Hooke pret. 2sh.8 & sum ex libris Thomae Birch ex dono R.Hooke, Thos Birche." The Curator of Experiments had presented this treatise of Boyle to the future historian of his beloved Royal Society. Another work, recently come to light, is *De Anima Brutorum . . . Exercitationes duae* of Dr. Thomas Willis. The copy bears a most interesting inscription: "Given me by ye Reverend Dr John Tillotson Dean of Canterbury. for a remembrance of John I. B.^{P} of Chester. R Hooke Oct.8. 1673."[19]

As a bibliophile Hooke naturally was interested in other collections. Entries allude to a visit to the Temple Library where he "viewd mathematical books." In 1680 he examined the remainder of the Henry Stubbs collection "to be yet sold." With enthusiasm he recorded a visit with Sir. J. Hoskins and Mr. Hill to Ashmole. "Dugdale there. Saw Tradescants rarities in the garret. Saw Dees and Kethes and many other books and manuscripts about chymistry, conjurations, magic, etc. made me exceeding welcome."[20]

The Curator of Experiments was also expected to add to the Royal Society library holdings at Arundel House, many of which had been purchased by Thomas Howard, Second Earl of Arundel, "the Father of Vertu" in England. As Earl Marshal he had been dispatched by Charles I to Vienna. Upon his return he stopped off at Nuremberg where he acquired the great collection of books originally owned by the partrician Willibald Pirckheimer. It had been at the suggestion of Evelyn that his son Henry Howard presented the collection to the Royal Society. Specific Hooke Diary entries refer to his purchases for the Arundel Library: "Bought of Mr. Martin for Royal Society Guericke Experimenta Magdeburgica 10sh., Malpighi 6d., lib. de ovo 2sh., Langelotti, Epistola 6d., Morhofi 10sh." A copy of Morland, *Arithmetica* was acquired from Pitt for 3sh. Not only were purchases made but donations received: "Ramus, Artihmetick, Hevelius of the comet, Hobbes, Animadversions, Horrocks, Astronomia." Among his duties as Arundel librarian Hooke "perfected a catalogue of the society's books," a task apparently ordered by the Council.[21]

Although Hooke was a loyal servitor to the Society—its Curator of Experiments, its book agent, its catalogue compiler—he suffered an occasional reprimand. A Journal entry of 26 January 1676/77 reads: "Lord Brouncker ordered me to return home books to Arundell Library. I returned to Arundell Library, Palace de Genoa 2 vol. Fabius Colunna 2 vol., Hortus Faernaesianus, Acosta, Linscoten, Palladio, Vasari 4 volumes, Le matre [sic], Cesare Ripa Iconologia, Vita de Titiano Aretinus, Morus, Ureses perspective and some mapps." This sizable loan from Arundel House reflects Robert Hooke's manifold interests.[22]

Hooke's "gold and silver from the iron chest" was well invested in the folios, quartos, and octavos he carefully selected. The question naturally arises how did the prices paid for books compare with the cost of daily necessities and luxuries. For a copy of Willughby, *Ornithologia* Hooke paid 24 shillings, far more than the salary earned by his charwoman Martha for a quarter period. The price of the second edition of Copernicus, *De revolutionibus orbium coelestium* (Basle 1566), was identical with that of a pair of gloves, 2 shillings. Martyn demanded 30 shillings for a copy of Baudrant, *Geographical Lexicon.* An overcoat ordered by Hooke from Mr. Bull of the Fox and Goose amounted to 36sh.6d. Today's collector avidly drools at the cost of Kepler, *Logarithms,* 2sh.; Galileo, *Dialogues of Motion,* 3sh.6d.; and a lot of 16 texts—many of scientific significance—acquired in Duck Lane for 2sh.6d. The average book generally cost less than a daily need or luxury: a hat, hatband and lining, 5sh.; a quarter pound of Virginia tobacco, 9d.; chocolate at 5d. A new periwig cost 28sh.; whereas a brace of pistols totaled £3; a velvet coat and lining £5 and 5 yards of lute string 5sh.6d. The reader remains slightly aghast that Hooke paid £8.15 for a copy of one of Aldrovandi's texts. Apparently the highest known price paid by Hooke was for the *Hortus Etitensis.* His Diary entry reveals no criticism of the price but rather the heartfelt appreciation of the book: "Inprised at £9. Well worth it at 3d a Leaf."[23]

Robert Hooke enjoyed his afternoon discussions at Man's, Garaway's, or Jonathan's coffee-houses, tippling ale, claret, or sack with his many friends. Above all, the bibliophile Hooke relished the hours spent with Martyn and Pitt, the rambles in Duck Lane and Moorfields, the purchases on Fish Street Hill, Cheapside, and Cornhill. What is more, the library developed by Robert Hooke mirrors the many facets of his agile, brilliant mind and reflects the attitudes of a notable seventeenth-century collector.

10

Analysis of the Library

Robert Hooke died intestate at Gresham College on 3 March 1702/03. The books which he had assembled with enthusiasm and care were purchased by the bookseller Richard Smith who put them up for public sale on 29 April 1703 at the Inner Walk, Exeter Exchange in the Strand. For the occasion Smith compiled a catalogue entitled *Bibliotheca Hookiana.* sive Catalogus Diversorum Librorum: "Mathematic. Philologicor. Philosophic. Hist. Natural. Medicorum, Navigat. &c. Plurimis Facultatibus Linguisque Insignium Quos Doct. R. Hooke, Mathem. Professor, & Regal. Societ. Londin. Socius, Magno Sumptu, & Summa Curâ, sibi congessit. Quorum Auctio habenda est Londini, in Edibus vulgo dictis *Inner Lower-Walk* in *Exeter-Exchange* in the *Strand,* the 29th of *April,* 1703. *Per* Edoardum Millington, *Bibliop. Londin.* Catalogues may be had at 6*d.* each of *R. Smith* at the Angel and Bible without *Temple-Bar,* of Mr. *Teo* at the General Post-Office at *Charing-Cross,* of Mr. *Hartley* near *Middle-Row, Holbourn,* and of Mr. *Strahan* over-against the *Royal Exchange.*"[1]

In a brief foreword Smith stated that Hooke, late fellow of the Royal Society in London, had collected for many years at home and "been assisted by his friends abroad." His efforts resulted in the diversity of material "visible in the ensuing pages." Assuring the reader that the late collector was not "a mere idle Professor," Smith declared that many of the books bore curious notes. He claimed that the library included considerable "M.S.S.," which assertion must be contradicted since there is only a single manuscript listed in the Auction Catalogue.[2]

The Conditions of Sale were standard advising that "Any Gentlemen who cannot be present" could have "their Commissions faithfully Executed by R. Smith."

The late Robert Hooke may have been casually acquainted with Richard Smith, but he well knew the gentleman who would auction his beloved collections, Mr. Edward Millington whose many sales he had attended and where he had liberally purchased. The *Bibliotheca Hookiana* consists of 3,380 items offered in 3,300 lots. An analysis of the auction catalogue indicates that certain titles cited by Hooke in his Diaries are not included. Since the late fellow of the Royal Society was a generous lender of his books, it is quite possible that the well-intentioned borrower occasionally failed to return a work. It is of course likely that Hooke, late in life, misplaced certain items or that books had been lost or stolen.

The Auction Catalogue includes an Appendix and is arranged in 9 major sections subdivided according to format and language: Latin books in folio, quarto, octavo, twelvemo, etc., English, Foreign, English Books in Quires, English Miscellaneous, Latin Miscellaneous, French, Italian, and Spanish. The imprints, of which more than half are scientific, are almost all of the sixteenth and seventeenth centuries, among them a variety of recently printed texts.

Hooke's Library included only four incunabula: Antonius Andreae, *Questiones super xii libros Metaphysicae Aristotelis,* (Vicenza 1477); Albumasar, *Introductorium in Astronomiam,* (Augsburg 1489); the so-called *Collections* of William Caxton actually *The Myrrour of the World,* printed by Caxton at Westminster in 1490; and Julius Firmicius, *Astronomicorum libri 8 de Nativitatibus,* (Venice 1499).[3]

The paucity of incunabula is not difficult to explain. The publications of that period were largely religious and hence of small interest to the scientist-bibliophile. Later in life, he may have developed some curiosity about early printing. A Diary entry of 11 January 1690 suggests that he wished to acquire incunabula or texts relating to the field: "Smith noe incunabula typographica."[4]

Hooke's intellectual pursuits may be discerned from an analysis of the contents of his library. A study of the *Bibliotheca Hookiana* indicates that the Curator of Experiments owned 331 books in medicine, pharmacy, and microscopy. Whether Hooke suffered actual maladies or a bad case of hypochondria is difficult to determine. His Journals refer to a variety of ailments, medicines, and quackeries. Waller describes him as a child "very infirm and weakly . . . being often sick; all which time his chief food was milk or things made thereof, and Fruits no Flesh in the least agreeing with his weak Constitution." This sickly child certainly overcame his dependence upon milk since in his prime he constantly visited taverns drinking sack, claret, and beer with his robust associates. His frequent headaches brought him to the Strand to seek out "one Fuller that pretends to cure the senses." In March 1676/77 he complained: "Feverish at night, but upon rising and putting on coats and hat and sleeping it recoyled upon my head and the feaver left me." This episode was followed by dinner which he declared he had digested well attributing his recovery "to change of air, partly to pleasant small beer, possibly to warmer weather, possibly to my drinking ale with tost and cheese in the morning." The brilliant Hooke dosed himself with iron and mercury, senna, aloes, wormwood, laudanum, Dulwich water. He accepted the theories of a Mr. Wilde that the blood of a black cat would cure chilblains and the dripping of a roasted eel dropped into the ears would heal deafness.[5]

Perhaps his own poor health induced him to undertake experiments in respiration, physiology, anatomy and dissection. His research was rewarded and in 1691 he became Robert Hooke, M.D.

In light of his physical complaints—real or imaginary—it is not at all surprising that his library covered a wide range of medical texts whose content may have offered some cures. Certainly his medical holdings satisfied his tremendous curiosity and preoccupation with the subject. He owned two copies of Regnier de Graaf, *De mulierum organis generatione . . . tractatus* which he had acquired from Martyn and *The woemans boke* purchased during a book jaunt in Moorfields for 8d., actually the English translation of Eucharius Roesslin, *The Birth of Mankind or the Womans Book,* (1613). The library boasted the writings of the French physician Jean Fernel, *De lue,* four copies of the *Aphorisms* of Hippocrates, one bought at a Hussey Sale for 6d. Other foreign medical texts comprised the *Works* of Paracelsus and his treatise on the China root, the *Opera* of Vesalius, the *Elementorum Myologiae Specimen* of the Dane, Niels Stensen, who fathered the foundation work in muscular mechanics, a subject of great interest to Hooke. He had purchased the volume from Pitt for "2sh. not paid." At the Maitland Sale he successfully bid on the *Works* of the German physician Johann Wecker for which he paid 4sh.6d.[6]

Hooke did not neglect the writings of the English medical authorities, adding to his collection the *Anatomia oculi* of Briggs which he had bought for 1sh. from Martyn; two works of Francis Glisson acquired at a Millington Sale for 6sh.; two treatises of the great Harvey including the 1649 edition of *De circulatione sanguine tractatus;* 8 medical works by his esteemed friend Boyle; the writings of Highmore, Sydenham, Thruston, the popular *Via recta ad vitam longam* of Thomas Venner purchased from Henry Brome for 22d. and three compositions by his friend Willis. His collection of pharmacopeia included those by foreign as well as English authors: Du Cerceau, Schroder, the *Pharmacopeiae Collegii Regalis Londini* and the *Pharmaceutice* of Willis.[7]

Associated with his medical holdings were his works on microscopy. Hooke's own work in the field, his *Micrographia,* is regarded by Sir Geoffrey Keynes among the most important books ever published in the history of science. The *Bibliotheca Hookiana* includes only one copy of the *Micrographia,* the writings of the great Dutch microscopist Leeuwenhoek, the *Microcosmicum* of Remmelin, and the *Microcosmographia* of the German, Stackmaier.[8]

Waller stated that Hooke during his stay at the Westminster School had mastered the first six books of Euclid within a week. Having grasped the principles of the Greek master he "thence proceeded orderly from that sure basis to other parts of Mathameticks." Diary entries allude to his reading algebra to his young cousin Tom and his niece Grace. During a visit to Pitt he "looked over his mathematicall books" and in September 1677, while at the Temple Library, he "viewd some mathematicall books."[9]

The Hooke Library included 316 works in mathematics. The collector's intensive interest in Euclid is revealed in his holdings which embraced 27 editions of the great geometer's writings. He owned several Latin, English, French, and Dutch editions of the *Elementa* and *Geometria.* Entries refer to the 1674 purchase of the Dee edition of Euclid from the bookseller Wynne "for which I am to pay him 5sh." From his friend Aubrey he acquired a Greek and Latin Euclid at 10sh., and at auction purchased the Clavius edition for 4sh.6d. The Library was rich in the mathematical texts of

English authors, foremost among them the first edition of the *Principia* of his great rival Newton. Other mathematicians represented comprised Collins, Digges, Horrocks, Kersey, Barrow, and Napier, as well as William Oughtred whose *Opuscula* he "Bought of Miller at the Star" in September 1677. The Catalogue also lists four treatises by Wallis and two editions of *Mathematical Magick* of John Wilkins.[10]

Hooke was regarded as one of the foremost astronomers of the Royal Society. He defended his theories about the greater advantage of telescopic sights over plain sights in his criticism of the Danzig astronomer Hevelius. His treatise *Animadversions on the first part of the Machina Coelestis* (by Hevelius) expostulates his astronomical theories. In his *Micrographia* Hooke refers to "vales" in the moon describing them as volcanic craters. Before the Royal Society he delivered his paper "On comets."

Hooke's deep interest in astronomy is apparent since his Library embraced 214 books in the field. They include two incunabula: Albumasar, *Introductorium in Astronomiam* and Julius Firmicius, *Astronomicorum libri 8 de navitatibus.* In addition he owned writings of the giants in the field: the Basle 1566 edition of Copernicus, *De revolutionibus orbium coelestium* purchased in February 1672/73 at Tower Hill for 2sh.; two works of Tycho Brahe and four of Galileo. Although he was eventually to clash with Hevelius, Hooke appreciated his achievements as an astronomer and owned twelve of his treatises. Familiar with the great reputation of Johann Kepler, Hooke acquired thirteen titles by this celebrated scientist: the *Harmonices mundi* "bought at Mr. Littleberry for 6sh.," his *Tabulae Rudolphinae* and *De motibus stellis martis* for which the same dealer demanded 35sh., a price questioned by Hooke. From Martyn he purchased Kepler *Epitome Astronomiae Copernicanae* for 6d. "not paid." A copy of Peuerbach, *Theoricae Novae Planetarum,* (Paris 1558) was bought for the same price. Among other texts are those of Ptolemy, the German sixteenth-century scientist Regiomontanus, Johann Schoener, and the treatises of the English authorities, Streete, Wing, and Wittie.[11]

Allied with his books on astronomy are those related to meteorology and horology of which Hooke owned fifty. The collector is regarded as "our first meteorologist," having invented eleven meteorological instruments. These include a weather clock and an instrument to measure wind velocity. On 20 December 1667 he presented before the Royal Society "A Farther Description of the Sea Barometer." He also designed a method for keeping weather records, the beginning of modern meteorology. Hence it is not surprising that among his specialized holdings Hooke owned two editions of Bacon, *On Winds* and Boyle, *Experiments upon the Icy Noctiluca.* Allied subjects include texts by foreign scientists: Barra, *L'Usage de la Glace de la Neige et du Froid,* (Lyons 1675). A Diary note of November 1668 refers to this treatise: "Bought of Littleberry a French book of snow 2sh. paid." Among his holdings were the *Experimenta Crystalli Islandici* of Erasmus Bartolinus; Fromond, *Meteorologicorum Libri 6* which he had acquired from Cooper for 2sh.[12]

Horological texts embraced those by the English authors: Hall, *Explicatio Horologii in Horto Regio Londini,* (London 1643); Foster, *Eliptical or Azimuthal Holologiography,* (London 1654); Holder, *Discourse concerning time,* (1694). In the collection were three texts by Clavius, notably his treatise, *De horologiis* purchased at the Bear Auction for 1sh. Tracking through Duck Lane he picked up the notable horological work by the French humanist Oronce Finé.[13]

Almanacs and ephemerides were an outgrowth of an interest in horology. The library included 22 works by Digges, Gadbury, Streete and Childrey, Hecker and Kepler.[14]

As a dabbler in physics, Hooke attempted "to shew the Force and Velocity of Bodies falling from several heights." He investigated the phenomena of heat and light. Over 100 texts in his collection demonstrate his preoccupation with all aspects of the subject. He owned two editions of Gilbert, *De magnete;* Keill, *Introductio ad veram Physicam;* the treatises of Borelli, Cabei, Gassendi and Grandami whose *De magnete* he had acquired from "Pitts 3sh." To these may be added the *Experimenta nova Magdeburgica* of Otto Guericke; *De Lumiere* of Grimaldi for which Martyn demanded 25sh.; Huygens, *De la Lumiere,* 3sh.; texts by Kircher, Marchetti and the Jesuit Pardies, *La Source des Forces mouvantes,* (1672). He also owned Viviani, *De maximis et minimis Tractatus* and Pascal, *Traité de l'Equilibre des Liqueurs* which he purchased from the book scout Scowen in June 1678. The Library housed at least seven treatises by Boyle: *Experimenta et observationes Physicae,* (1691); *Origine of Forme and Qualities,* (1667); *Experiments about Flame* and Aire, (1672); *Hydrostatical Paradoxes,* (1665); *Effects of Languid Motion,* (1690), and others.[15]

Waller stated that Hooke "made a proposition for perfecting all sorts of Optick Glasses, the secret of which was deliver'd in an anagram to my Lord Brouncker." Although the number of books in optics in the library is small—twenty-two—they represent the texts of leading authorities: Barrow, *Lectiones opticae;* several works by David Gregory, *Catoptricae & Dioptricae* and *Optica Promota;* the writings of foreign experts: Ango, the Arab Alhazan Haly, and the *Opticae et Catoptrica* of his favorite Euclid, a copy of which he had purchased at the Maitland Sale for 10d. At the same sale he purchased Porta, *De refractione Optices* for 1sh., while from Pitt he acquired Kepler, *Dioptricks* at 4sh.6d.[16]

Hooke referred to Mechanics as "his first and last Mistress." His early propensity for anything mechanical led, according to Waller, to his "Excellency in such Contrivances, and admirable Facility . . . in applying Mechanical Principles to the explication of the most difficult Phaenomena of Nature." The Hooke Library contained 53 books in mechanics and technology: texts by Hero of Alexandria, Galileo, La Hire; *De Mechanica* of his fellow academician John Wallis; the *Technometria* of William Ames; *An Account of New Inventions and Improvements* by Thomas Hall; a Spanish edition of Besson, *Teatro de los Instrumentos* bought in Moorfields; Boeckler, *Theatrum Machinarum* for which he paid 35sh. Other texts included Neri, *Art of Glass,* and Schott, *Technica Curiosa* which he eventually purchased from Martyn: "18sh. not paid."[17]

Hooke's multiple talents brought him his appointment as one of the city surveyors for the restoration of London after the Fire of 1666. "The rebuilding of the City . . . required an able Person. Mr. Hooke was pitch'd upon, and appointed City Surveyor for that difficult Work which being very great, took up a large proportion of his Time, to no small hindrance of his Philosophical Disquisitions." It is rather surprising that Hooke owned only 12 books relating to this field including Dary, *The Compleat Gauger;* Hunt, *Guide for the Practical Gauger;* Newton, *Art of Practical Gauging;* Stephen Primate, *The City and Country Purchaser and Builder;* and three works by his friend, the surveyor and mathematician, William Leybourne.[18]

No alchemical abracadabra helped Hooke rebuild the demolished metropolis. Nonetheless his Library reflects his interest in alchemy and chemistry since he owned 86 books by adepts in both fields: Roger Bacon, *De arte chymica;* William Badcock, *Touchstone for Gold and Silver;* texts by Digby and Henry Cornelius Agrippa; Barba, *Art of Metals;* Croll, *Basilica Chymica;* three treatises of Robert Fludd; *De Alchimia* of the Arab Geber; the *Works* of Raymond Lull; the *Lapis Bononiensis* of Menzel, a copy of which he had purchased from Martyn who had advertised for it in the *Philosophical Transactions* of 1670. Having bought a copy of Wedel, *De sale tartarii* he declared: "not what I wanted." Hooke's collection of alchemical texts is counterbalanced by his acquisition of the second English and Latin editions of *The Sceptical Chymist* of Boyle in which the great chemist inveighs against alchemy, helping to prepare the way for the chemical revolution of the eighteenth century.[19]

Hooke's curiosity led him to explore literature on magic and witchcraft. The 56 books in the field owned by the scientist comprise the writings of Henry More, Naudé, Reginald Scott, and Trithemius; Cardan, *On Dreams;* Fontenelle, *The History of Oracles;* Lavater, *De spectris;* Porta, *Magia naturalis* and his *Occulta Philosophia.*[20]

The scientist Hooke was absorbed in his surroundings and the many facets of nature. The collection comprises 44 books relating to natural history, zoology, ornithology, and herpetology. The library shelves housed the writings of Aldrovandi, Belon, the *Cochlea* of Bonnani acquired for 4sh.10d. at one of the Maitland Sales; Godaert, *On Insects;* and a *Treatise on Spiders* by the bibliophile's friend Lister. Other texts are by Lovell and Pitsfield whose *History of Animals* cost Hooke 10 shillings. Two works of significance, both Martyn imprints 1678 and 1679, are Francis Willughby, *Ornithology* and Moise Charas, *New Experiments upon Vipers.*[21]

Botany and horticulture had a special appeal to the Curator of Experiments, not at all a surprising fact since Hooke, an Englishman, may even have cultivated his own spot of earth! A group of 92 books represent the opinions of specialists in these closely related fields. Naturally Hooke owned the writings of his fellow academician Sir John Evelyn, the *Herball* of John Gerard acquired at 3sh.10d., several texts of Nehemiah Grew, the significant treatise by Samuel Hartlib, *The reformed Virginian silkworm* in which the author claimed that the production of silk in the colonies would prove more lucrative than the cultivation of tobacco. Additional texts relating to English horticulture and aboriculture are by Parkinson, Ray, and Hans Sloane. With enthusiasm Hooke wrote that he had seen and acquired from Pitt the *Hortus Etitensis* (Eichstadt). This handsome folio of Basil Besler contained 368 plates. According to Hooke it had been "imprised [priced] at £9. Well worth it at 3d a Leaf." At a shop in Turn-stile alley he purchased Cornutus, *On the plants of Canada* eventually presenting it to Sir John Hoskins. Of equal rarity is Francisco Herñandes, *Historia plantarum animalium . . . Mexicanarum* on which he bid 4sh.6d. at the Maitland Sale. The Library included two works of the distinguished botanist Charles L'Ecluse. A Diary entry of 14 April 1674 notes: "Bought next the Blew Anchor in Duck Lane Clusius rariorum plantarum historia 6s. and ejusdem exoticarum libri 10s."[22]

To glean further knowledge of experiments and observations conducted by foreign scientists Hooke owned 26 items including runs of their respective academic proceedings and works on their history and contributions. As Curator of Experiments of the Royal Society and, after Oldenburg's death, editor of the *Philosophical Transactions,* Hooke might have been expected to own every issue of the publication. Nonetheless, the *Bibliotheca Hookiana* lists only 180 *Philosophical Transactions,* a number which would account for a run of merely fifteen years and which is probably inaccurate. Missing issues of the periodical may of course have been lost, lent, or given away. Moreover, Hooke appears to have been forced to purchase certain issues of the *Philosophical Transactions,* since he notes in his Diary: "To Martins paid Journalls for 1674 18d; 26 July 1679, Took of Martin 142 Transactions; bought 81 Transactions 18sh." Only on one occasion does the scientist record that he had been given the *Transactions* by Oldenburg. It is indeed odd that the Curator of Experiments and future editor of the Journal was compelled to buy copies of a monthly to which he so richly contributed and even edited.[23]

It was through Dr. Diodati that Hooke received the majority of issues of the *Journal des Sçavans,* although upon occasion he purchased numbers from the French booksellers Cailloue and Behagel. His records indicate that he paid Diodati 3sh.7d. in October 1675 for seven issues of the French periodical and in July 1675 he received from him "15 Journals des Scavans 6sh.6d.

carriage 6d." Upon another occasion he acquired 16 issues from the book scout Scowen "not paid." In 1677 he lent Sir John Hoskins 63 *Journals des Sçavans*. From Diary entries there is evidence that he purchased issues of the *Journal des Sçavans* not listed in the *Bibliotheca Hookiana,* which cites *"Le Journall des Scavans pour les ann. 1675. 76. 77."* Since Hooke purchased in May 1689 volume 16 of the *Journal* from Cailloue at 2½sh. and in February 1692/93 a bound set from Behagel (for which he was to return his "sticht" issues), it appears again that there are lacunae in the *Bibliotheca Hookiana.*[24]

Among other French periodicals owned by Hooke were two issues of the *Mercure Savant* published briefly in Holland by Nicolas de Blegny and the far more prestigious *Nouvelles de la Republique des Lettres* edited by the eminent Pierre Bayle. While the name suggests a purely literary publication, Bayle's periodical consisted largely of popular scientific articles. The work also presented scientific experiments along with reviews of books by Boyle and Wallis.[25]

Hooke's later Diary refers to the purchase of the "13th Bibliotheque 2sh." from Cailloue. He notes in December 1688 that he read Bibliotheca. The scientist's references are to the *Bibliotheque Universelle et historique* to which Willughby and he contributed.[26]

The *Bibliotheca Hookiana* cites *"Acta Eruditorum Anno 1682, 83, 84, 85. 2 vols. Leipzig."* The bidder at the Hooke Sale was offered the opportunity to acquire the monthly issues of the German scientific journal issued at Leipzig and sponsored by the German scientific society Collegium Leipsicum edited by Otto Mencke, professor of moral and practical philosophy. Hooke made some laconic entries regarding his purchases of the *Acta.* "At littleberrys for Leipsicks; At Smiths 2 Leipsic Acta of September & August. Took of Smith Acta of November 1692 and 1st supplement with Jan. 1693."[27]

Among the other items bought at the Pitt auction of December 1678, Hooke referred to the *Saggi di Natvrali Esperienze,* the scientific publication edited by Lorenzo Magalotti for the Florentine Scientific Society, the Accademia del Cimento. The *Saggi* appeared in Florence in 1677, eagerly anticipated by the English academicians.[28]

Hooke owned four volumes of the *Acta Medica et Philosophorum Hafniae* [Copenhagen] edited by Thomas Bartholinus and acquired from Martyn for 8 shillings.[29] Among the histories of scientific societies are those by Sprat, Duhamel, Pellisson, and Sturm, works of great interest to the Curator of Experiments.[30]

Hooke's holdings in art and music, subjects tangential to science, reflect his association with both disciplines. Works in art, architecture, perspective and drawing books numbered approximately ninety including texts by Roger Bacon, *Perspectiva;* Boyle, *Experiments touching colours;* Dugdale, *History of St. Paul's Cathedral;* Salmon, *Polygraphice;* and Sanderson, *Use of the pen and pencil* which he had purchased at auction in September 1687. Among his foreign texts of significance were those by Alberti and Bosse whose *Maniere de graver en Taille-Douce* had been bought from Davis for 5sh.6d. He acquired the first edition of Leonardo da Vinci, *Trattato della Pitture* from Pitt in October 1673 paying him 15 shillings. He owned a set of Marot, *Recueil des Plans, Profils & Elevations des plusieurs Palais, Chasteau* acquired at 17sh., binding 1sh.6d. The Library included several editions of Vitruvius and the second edition but first illustrated version of Vasari, *Lives of the Painters.*[31]

The Hooke Library was embellished not only with books but also with prints. On 9 June 1677 the scientist wrote: "I made a table of my prints." An entry of the following day refers specifically to his print holdings with prices: "Separated prints. 7sh., of St. Peters, 10sh., Tarripan Jesuits church, 1s.8d., Piazza del popolo, 1s.3d., chiesu di St. Maria della pace. 1s.3d, two prospa [prospects] of the Louvre, 2s.3d., Berninis St. Pieter 5sh., Merchants hall at Paris 5sh., St. Peters chair 6s.3d., Fornesys Jesuits church at Rome 3s.4d., Scavans large sheets of the Jesuits church at Paris 10sh., Fifteen of Perill's [Perelle] prospects 3s. 1½d., eighteen chimneys and altars 4s.3d., 109 views of Israells 22s.8½d."[32]

Waller refers to Hooke's musical ability and inventions. The scientist notes a purchase of lute strings and it is quite possible that he played this instrument. Thirteen works in music include theory and texts on harmonics: Butler, *The Principle of Musick;* Holder, *Ground and Principles of Harmony;* Lock, *English Operas;* Simpson, *Compendium of Practical Musick.* Texts by foreign authors embrace Descartes, *Musicae Compendium;* Mersenne,

Harmonicks purchased from Littlebury for 30sh. as well as Wallis's translation of Ptolemy on the same subject.[33]

Hooke owned another treatise by the great Egyptian mathematician and geographer Ptolemy, the Italian translation of his *Geographia,* a text which had dominated the Christian and Muslim worlds for over 1300 years. From childhood Hooke had evinced an interest in marine science and terrestrial phenomena. In January 1666/67 he was ordered by the Council of the Royal Society "to prosecute his observations of the earth's parallax." The results are presented in *An Attempt to Prove the Motion of the Earth from Observations,* 1674. Hooke arrived at his conclusions not merely from his findings but also from reading some of the 350 volumes in his library relating to these subjects as well as geography, atlases and maps, exploration, discoveries and travel.[34]

Hooke's expertise in cartography was well known to his associates. By several he was consulted for technical assistance in map design and textual arrangement. Had he not been Pitt's principal adviser for his unfortunate *English Atlas?* Diary entries allude to his conferences with John Ogilby for the preparation of the atlas *Britannia.* Visiting with Ogilby at Garaway's coffee-house in October 1673 he "Shewd him the way of Letters for marking his map and also the way of shadowing."[35]

The *Bibliotheca Hookiana* counted among its holdings Burnet, *Telluris Theoria Sacra;* Evelyn, *Philosophical Discourse concerning Earth;* several treatises by Dr. Plot; Whiston, *New Theory of the Earth* and Woodward, *Natural History of the Earth.* In addition Hooke owned several relations on earthquakes and a work by "Higii," i.e., Ittig, *Lucubrationes de montium incendiis* which he picked up at the Bell for 2sh.6d. A work of considerable interest was Borelli's narrative of the eruption of Mt. Etna. A few works in the field of marine science were acquired from the widow of Dixy Page located at Fish Street Hill: Bushnell, *The Compleat Shipwright;* Sir Henry Manwayring, *The Sea-Grammar* and his *Seaman's dictionary;* Peter Perkins, *The Seaman's Tutor.* At the Oakes Sale of May 1689 he successfully bid 7d. for Blagrave, *The Art of Dialling.* Other works cover economic-maritime content: *Navigation and Commerce* by Evelyn and *Of Affairs Maritime and of Commerce* by Molloy. In the foreign field he purchased from the needy Aubrey a copy of "Baytins [Bayfius] de re navali for 2sh.," the *Cosmolabe* of the French scientist Besson stocked by Pitt for 7sh. and Galileo, *Le Operazione del Compasso.*[36]

Two Diary entries of January and March 1675/76 refer to the rarest geographical and typographical ephemera. "Mr. Brome gave me Geographicall cards. Bought cards of Moxon." The bookseller Henry Brome of Ludgate Street had apparently presented Hooke with a set of geographical playing cards. Published in 1675, the deck of 52 playing cards depicted the counties of England and Wales, each card bearing an engraved map in the center with space reserved for suit marks. The heads of Charles II and his consort Catherine of Braganza were used for the kings and queens. Hooke's friend Moxon issued three sets of cards: "Astronomical Playing cards; Astronomical Cards and Geographical Playing Cards wherein is exactly described all the kingdoms of the earth, curiously engraved. Price Plain 1s., coloured 2s., best coloured and gilt 5s. the Pack." Hooke's selection of a specific pack is not indicated.[37]

Not all of the scientist's holdings in geography are as ephemeral as the Brome and Moxon sets of cards. Hooke owned the geographies of Carpenter, Gordon, Gore, the *Geographical Lexicon* of Baudrant, purchased from Martyn for 30sh.; Labbé, *La Geographie royale;* several copies of *De situ orbis* of Pomponius Mela; the *Tractatus de globis* of Robert Hues cited by Hooke in March 1678/79 as "Huse;" *L'Introduction à la geographie* of Nicolas Sanson and two editions of Bernhard Varenius, *Geographia generalis.*[38]

In his bibliophilic migrations Hooke acquired a variety of maps and atlases: Sanson's Poland, a map of France and Germany "from Mr. Richards paid 1sh., a map of England not paid; a map of Sirrinam 6d." His atlas collection is highlighted by a three-volume set of one of Merian's topographies and the *Topographia Gallia* of Zeiller. Although Hooke had assisted Ogilby in his cartographical ventures, it appears that he, nonetheless, was compelled to purchase the various atlases of the former dancing master. For an unbound copy of the *Atlas Chinensis* he paid 12 shillings acquiring as well the *Atlas Japanensis, Asia, or Description of Persia, Africa, America* and *Britannia, or the Roads of England and Wales.*[39]

Hooke's collection of maps and atlases included a complimentary copy of the *Index Villaris, or a Register of all the Cities* by the geographer John Adams, the *Atlas Major* of Jan Jansson, the *Sea Atlas* of Pieter Goos, two copies of the *Novus Atlas Sinensis,* the first European atlas of China by the Jesuit missionary Martino Martini, the 8vo edition costing the collector 20½ shillings—as well as the sea charts of the bookseller and prolific map-maker John Seller, "Hydrographer to Charles II and James II."[40.]

Works relating to global navigation lined Hooke's shelves: the Latin edition of the *Voyages* of Drake, Cavendish, and Hawkins; Hakluyt, *Principal Navigations, Voyages, Traffiques and Discoveries of the English Nation;* the *Voyages* of Jean Mocquet, Keeper of the Cabinet of Rarities of the King of France. At Martyn's he acquired a copy of John Ray, *Collection of Curious Travels and Voyages.*[41]

Hooke's extensive collection of travel literature naturally included works relating to the motherland: texts by Camden, Stow and others. Of uncommon interest are Martin Martin, *Late Voyage to St. Kilda,* a work which is said to have inspired Johnson's voyage thither, and James Wallace, *A Description of the Orkney Islands.*[42]

Although Hooke seldom departed his London haunts, his interest in European and Eastern travel narratives and descriptions was keen. His curiosity roamed the continent and the far away. Such texts embraced Ray, *Travels through Holland,* 1sh.; Guicciardini, *Description of the Countries* was obtained at the Pitt Sale of December 1678 for 5 shillings. A variety of texts in the Hooke Library relate to France, Spain, Germany, Italy, and Switzerland: *An Historical Explication of Versailles;* Antoine de Brunel, *Journey into Spain;* William Fiston, *The Estate of the German Empire;* and English and French editions of Lassels, *Voyage of Italy.*[43]

Fourteen works relating to Scandinavia, Finland, and Russia were purchased by Hooke on various occasions. During a trip to Duck Lane he picked up the rare English translation of Debes, *Description of the Island and Inhabitants of the Feroe.* In January 1674/75 he acquired the English version of the standard *History of the Goths* by Olaus Magnus of which he owned three versions. In addition he successfully bid on a copy of Scheffer, *Lapland* at the 1678 Pitt Sale, buying from time to time several significant works on Russia: Albert Pighius, *De Muscovia,* (1542); Samuel Collins, *The Present State of Russia,* (1671); the English translation of Chevalier, *A Discourse of the Original Countrey, Manners of the Cossacks* and Witsen, *Tartary.*[44]

Aware of the English concern with the Turkish threat and power as well as the bizarre character of the country, Hooke owned several narratives treating the Ottoman empire: George Sandys,

ANALYSIS OF THE LIBRARY

Travels into Turkey; Paul Rycaut, *The Present State of the Ottoman Empire;* Robert Withers, *Description of the Grand Seignor's Seraglio;* Jean Thevenot, *Voyage de Levant;* Nicolay, *Le Navigationi . . . nella Turchia,* 1576. A handsome addition to the Library, treating the Aegean, was the English version of Vicenzo Maria Coronelli, *An Historical and Geographical Account of Morea, Negroponte* adorned with 42 maps and plates.[45]

In the *Philosophical Collections* edited by Hooke, Number 6 included "A Relation of a Voyage made towards the South Terra incognita; extracts from the Journal of Captain Abel Tasman." Hooke was acquainted not only with Tasman's narrative but also with other relations detailing the East and the more remote areas described in the texts he sought. Such texts include two editions of *The Travels into the East Indies and Persia* by John Fryer, a surgeon who spent eight years in the service of the East India Company. *The Historical Relation of the Island of Ceylon* apparently fascinated Hooke, since he owned three copies. The author Robert Knox had been a Scottish commander in the service of the East India Company and had been taken prisoner, languishing in India for twenty years.[46]

Hooke's curiosity extended to the various kingdoms of the African continent: Sir Thomas Herbert, *Travels into Africa, Asia,* (1667); the exciting tale entitled *Adventures of an English Merchant into Africa,* (1670); Richard Jobson, *Golden Trade or Discovery of the River Gambia;* John Greaves, *Description of the Pyramids in Aegypt,* (1646); Vattier, *State of Egypt;* Geronimo Lobo, *Relation of the sourse and current of the River Nile,* (1673). An item of special interest is the *Itinerarium* of the Spanish Hebrew traveler Benjamin of Tudela who, from 1160 to 1177, visited Asia and Africa observing throughout his journey the settlements and condition of his fellow faithful.[47]

The Library further embraced texts on China, Japan, and remote Siam; English translations of the histories of Juan Gonzalez de Mendoza and Alvarez Samedo; *Observations of China* of the missionaries Le Comte and Kircher as well as two editions of the German Varenius's text *On Japan.* Hooke owned the relations of the Frenchmen Chaumont, De La Loubère, and Tachard on the history and customs of Siam, having purchased Tachard's text from the French refugee book dealer Boudet for "3sh.6d."[48]

Two treatises in the Hooke Library examine the vast world of the South Seas: Sir Richard Hawkins, *Observations on the Voyage into the South Seas* which recounts the explorer's adventures on the "Dainty" and his daring sail through the Straits of Magellan. Reading the *Voyages and Discoveries in the South Seas,* Hooke took delight in the exploits of Sir John Narborough. One lot in the *Bibliotheca Hookiana* includes Fernando de Queiros, *New Southern Discovery,* 1617, the report of Queiros, the Portuguese explorer, who discovered the continent of Australia.[49]

The deep interest of Robert Hooke in the North American continent and the English overseas colonies is expressed in his conversation, readings, and acquisitions. With his fellow-academicians at Jonathan's coffee-house he engaged in "much discourse . . . about mountains in Virginia, about curing flesh, fish, oysters, bevers, etc." A Diary entry of 3 December 1688 refers to a letter from Carolina with allusion to "wild silk wormes, vines 8 metres in diameter, 500 feet long growing in Swamps coverd with [water], double crops thriving of silk wormes and Mulbe[rries]."[50]

Works in the Hooke Library relating to the New World comprise two copies of Simon Grynaeus, *Novus orbis regionum ac insularum veteribus incognitarum;* Petrus Martyr Anglerius, *De novo orbo;* Jan de Laet, *America descriptio;* two editions of Esquemeling, *Buccaneers of America,* and others.[51]

Regional works enhanced the collection. It is not surprising that Hooke took the keenest interest in those relations describing or emanating from New England. One of the earliest books depicting the English overseas homeland is Morton, *The New English Canaan or New Canaan,* 1617. The bibliophile owned two copies of Josselyn, *Voyages of New England* and while wandering through Moorfields Hooke picked up a copy of "Sr Gorges Description of New England," actually *America Painted to the Life* by Sir Ferdinand Gorges, "Father of English colonization in America." It is highly speculative whether the Curator of Experiments realized the significance of two works imported from Cambridge, Massachusetts. The *Bibliotheca Hookiana* cites two texts by John Eliot, "the apostle to the Indians:" his *New Testament in the Indian Language* and *The Indian Grammar.* Printed by Samuel Green and Marmaduke Johnson, *The New Testament* appeared in 1661 in an edition of one thousand or fifteen hundred copies. Forty copies were sent to England and of this number Hooke was fortunate to

ANALYSIS OF THE LIBRARY

own one. *The Indian Grammar* appeared at Cambridge in 1666 in an edition of 500 copies, one of which could be found in the library of Robert Hooke.[52]

Interest in the Virginia colony is indicated by the collector's acquisition of John Smith, *History of Virginia* and Edward Williams, *Virginia richly and truly valued.*[53]

Hooke's reading extended from books relating to colonial England to texts describing New France: "Tinets voyages" acquired from "old Pits" in January 1675/76 may be identified as André Thevet, *Les Singularitez de la France arctique.* At the Oakes Sale of May 1689 Hooke was the successful bidder for Creux, *Historia Canadiensis seu Nova Francia libri X,* a work which details the sufferings of the French missionaries at the hands of savages. A narrative of extreme significance is Marc Lescarbot, *Nova Francia or the description of that part of New France which is one continent with Virginia.* Two notable additions to Hooke's collection included the *Description de Louisianie* and *Voyages and Discoveries in America* by the Recollet missionary Louis Hennepin.[54]

Secure in Gresham College, the spirit of Robert Hooke roamed fearlessly from the wilds of Louisiana to the islands of the Caribbean. Among several interesting items relating to the West Indies, Hooke purchased *America or an exact Description of the West Indies* by Thomas Speake. At the Shelton Sale of February 1692/93 Hooke successfully knocked down, for the trifling sum of 5d., Edmund Hickeringill, *Jamaica view'd with all its Ports, Harbours.* Other pertinent texts are Rochfort, *Histoire des Isles de S. Christophe, de la Guadeloupe* and Thomas Gage, *The Survey of the West Indies* at 5 shillings.[55]

There are few works in the Hooke collection relating to the New World south of the Antilles. The *Bibliotheca Hookiana* lists Augustine Zarate, *The Strange and delectable History of the Discoverie and Conquest of the Province of Peru* which relates Pizarro's discoveries and brutal treatment of the Indians; Blaise Pagan, *Historical and Geographical Description of the great Country and River of the Amazons* and Francesco Hernandes, *Historia plantarum animalium et Mineralium Mexicanarum* purchased at the Maitland Sale for 4sh.3d.[56]

Travelling with Hooke, the researcher shares the sites and marvels of distant climes. Although the scientist seldom departed the alleys, squares, the familiar haunts of old and new London, his mind roamed far and wide and in the books he owned, his spirit ascended the highest peak in Darien.

The pedestrian listings of the books owned by the late Dr. Robert Hooke and offered for public sale by the bookseller Richard Smith on 29 April 1703 are invested with a new aura and vitality when identified as those texts so eagerly searched by the Curator of Experiments at the shops and stalls, the London "rooms." The *Bibliotheca Hookiana* —long neglected—becomes another index to the brilliant, inquiring mind of one of the greatest seventeenth-century virtuosi, Robert Hooke.

PART III*

THE *BIBLIOTHECA HOOKIANA*

* Permission to reprint the *Bibliotheca Hookiana,* courtesy of A.W. Purvey, Esq., Photographic Services Manager, The British Library. Faded markings appear in the margins of the auction catalogue reproduced in its entirety on the following pages. These markings are the prices paid for the various items and were entered by an unidentified individual who attended the auction in 1703. Other markings may be attributed to an enthusiastic scholar's pen or pencil, the continuing anathema of rare book custodians. As an example, on page 46 (original pagination) of the *Bibliotheca Hookiana,* the running head, "English Books in Quarto," should have read "English Books in Octavo." An intrepid scholar, sometime during the intervening centuries since 1703, crossed out the word "Quarto" and above it entered "8vo."

Bibliotheca Hookiana.

SIVE

CATALOGUS

Diverforum Librorum:

viz.

MATHEMATIC. PHILOLOGICOR.
PHILOSOPHIC. HIST. NATURAL.
MEDICORUM, NAVIGAT. &c.

Plurimis   Facultatibus   Linguifque

INSIGNIUM

Quos Doct. R. HOOKE,

Mathem. Profeffor, & Regal. Societ. Londin.
Socius, Magno Sumptu, & Summa Curâ, fibi congeffit.

Quorum Auctio habenda eft Londini, in Edibus vulgo dictis *Inner Lower-Walk* in *Exeter-Exchange* in the *Strand*, the 29th of *April*, 1703.

Per Edoardum Millington, *Bibliop. Londin.*

Catalogues may be had at 6 *d.* each of *R. Smith* at the Angel and Bible without *Temple-Bar*, of Mr. *Teo* at the General Poft-Office at *Charing-Crofs*, of Mr. *Hartley* near *Middle-Row, Holbourn*, and of Mr. *Strahan* over-againft the *Royal-Exchange.*

143

TO T^{HE}
READER.

*T*HIS *Catalogue contains the Library of Dr.* Rob. Hooke, *late Fellow of the* Royal Society *in* London; *which for many Years he hath been on all occasions Collecting at Home, and been assisted by his Friends Abroad. Hence arose that Large, if not Compleat Collection of his Mathematical Books in all Volumes and Languages; with the Physick, Phylosophy, Natural History, Voyages, Travels,* &c. *that are visible in the ensuing Pages: And that the World may be satisfied that he was not a bare Idle Possessor of them, he hath left behind him many curious Notes on some, considerable M.S.S. Improvements to others, not unworthy the View and Perusal of the Virtuosi of the Age; for whose Advantage, and better Information, he unquestionably at first design'd them; in Pursuit of which they are now expos'd to Sale by,*

Your Humble Servant,

RICH. SMITH.

Conditions of *SALE.*

I. That he who bids moſt is the Buyer, and if any difference ariſe which the Company cannot decide, the Book or Books in queſtion, to be expoſed to Sale again.

II. That all the Books in this Catalogue are perfect for ought we know; if any prove otherwiſe before taking away, the Buyer to have his choice of taking or leaving them.

III. That the Money for the Books ſo bought, is to be paid at the Place of Sale, within three Days after the Sale is over.

IV. That the Books ſhall be expos'd to view Two Days before the Sale begins.

V. That no Perſon advance leſs than Six Pence each bidding, after any Book ariſes to the Sum of Ten Shillings.

Any Gentlemen who cannot be preſent, may have their Commiſſions faithfully Executed by R. Smith.

Libri Latini, &c. in Folio.

1 Clement. Alexandr. Op. Gr. & Lat. á Frid. Sylburgio. *Colon.* 1687 0 - 8. 0
   2 Rich. Holdsworth Prælectiones Theologicæ   *Lond.* 1661 0 - 5. 0
3 Flavii Josephi Opera Latinè   *Franc.* 1580
4 Jo. Vicars Decapla in Psalmos   *Lond.* 1639
5 Ben. Pererii Comment. & Disputat. in Genesin.   *Colon. Agr.* 1622 0 - 5. 0
  Ben. Ariæ Montani communes & famil. Hebr. Ling. Idiotis.
  —— Liber Joseph five de arcano Sermone
  —— Liber Jeremiæ five de Actione
6 —— Thubal Cain five de Mensuris sacris   *Antv.*
  —— Phaleg five de Genitum sedibus Primis   *Plant.* 0. 8. 0
  —— Chaleb five de Terræ Promissæ partitione   1572
  —— Exemplar five de facris Fabrices
  Cum quibusd. aliis Tractatib. Ejusd. Authoris. & fig.
7 Ger. Jo. Vossius de Origine & Progressu Idololatriæ. 2 Vol. *Amst.* 1668 0 - 9. 0
8 Origenis Opera Latinè. 2 vol. —— *Apud. Ascens.* 1512 0. 2. 0
9 Pet. Ravanelli Bibliotheca Sacra. 2 vol. —— *Gen.* 1650 0. 4. 0
10 D. Jo. Chryfoftomi Operum, Tomus 6. Græcè   *Etona* 1612 0. 3. 6
11 Theatrum Orbis Terrarum five Atlas Novus á Guil. & Jo. Bleau 0. 12. 6
       cum Chart.   *Amst.* 1640
12 Ger. Mercator. & J.Hondii Atlas Nov. *cum Chartis.* 2 vol. ap. *Janf.* 1638 0. 13. 6
13 Jo. Janssonii Atlas Major five Cosmographia Universalis, *cum Chart.* 4. a. 6
   2 vol.   *Amst.* 1675
14 Mart. Martinii Novus Atlas Sinensio.   *cum Chart.* —— 0. 12. 0
15 Theatrum Civitatum & Admirandorum Italiæ, á Jo. Bleau. *cum Chart.*
   2 vol.   *Amst.* 1663 4. 0. 0
16 —— Urbium Belgii cum Tabul. Illuminatis —— 4. 0. 0
17 Pet. Kerii Germ. Inferior. cum Tab. & Descript. á P.Mont. *Amst.* 1617 0. 2. 0
18 Italia di Gio. Ant. Magini, *con Tabul.*   *Bonon.* 1620 0. 2. 0
19 Tabulæ Geogr. Illumminat. & Edit. á divers. Authorib. Gallic. in
   4 vol. compacto 0. 6. 6
20 *Nieur Groot Stuermans Zee-Spiegel.* with Caart.   *Amst.* 1644 0. 2. 0
21 *Spiegel der Zeervaerdt, vande Navigatie der Westersche zee, dor Lucas* 0. 2. 6
   Janss, Washenaer. cum Chart.   *Leyden* 1584
22 Mich. Ant. Baudrand Lexicon Geographicum —— *Par.* 1670 0. 8. 6
23 Seb. Munsteri Cosmographia Universalis, *cum Fig.*   *Baf.* 1559 0. 5. 6
24 Ant. de Herrera Descriptio Indiæ Occidentalis, *cum Tabul.* *Amst.* 1622 0. 8. 0
25 Novus Orbis Region. & Insular. Veteribus incognitarum, *Baf.* 1555 0. 4. 0
26 Jo. de Laet Americæ utriusque Descriptio, *cum Fig.* L. *Bat.* 1633 0. 0. 0
27 Strabonis Geographia Gr. Lat. cum Guil. Xylandri Notis & Tab. 0. 0. 0
   Geograph. —— *Baf.* 1571 0. 0. 0
28 *Relation de Divers Voyages curieux qui riont point estè publiees,* avec Fig.
   Par. 1663 0. 5. 0
29 *Les 3 & 4 Decade de T. Live en Francois par Jehan Hamalin, Par.* 1580 0. 2. 0
30 *Le Deche di T. Livio delle Historie Romane, tradotte da Jac. Nardi.* 0. 1. 7
   Ven. 1562
31 Historia & Antiquitates Universitatis Oxoniensis.   *Oxon.* 1674 0. 5. 0
   B   32. Mart.

2. 6. 0 32 Mart. Zeillori Topogr. Gallia cum Plurim. Tab. 3 Vol. *Franc.* 1655
5. 2. 33 { Lud. Guiciardini Belgii, sive Infer. Germ. Descr. *cum Tab. Amst.* 1613
        { Marq. Freheri Origines Palatinæ. in 2. part.   1613
J. J. 34 Pauli Freheri Theat. Viror. eruditione clarorum, *cum Fig. Nor.* 1688
12. 0 35 H. Hollandi Horologia Angl. *b.e.* Clariff. aliq. Anglor. Effig. Vitæ, &c. —
J. 9 36 Theod. Zuingeri Theatrum Vitæ Humanæ   *Basil.* 1565
4. 5 37 Plutarchi Opera Gr. Lat. á G. Xylandro, Tom. 2.   *Franc.* 1620
10. 038 Geo. Matth. Konigii Bibliothæca Vetus & Nova   *Altf.* 1678
10. 039 Jos. Simleri Epitome Bibliothecæ Gresneri   *Titulus deest.*
1. 13. 40 P. Aringhii Roma Subterran. Noviff. *quamplur. Fig.* 2 vol. *Romæ* 1651
3. 41 Athan. Kircheri China Monumentis illuft. & Fig. ornat.   *Ant.* 1667
2. 1042 ——— Idem   Gallicé. ———   *Amst.* 1670
6. 0 43 ——— Arca Noæ,   *cum Fig.* ———   *ibid.* 1675
6. 0 44 ——— Ars Magna Lucis & Umbræ.   *cum Fig.*   *ibid.* 1671
5. 5 45 ——— Ars Magna Sciendi sive Combinatoria, *cum Fig.* *ibid.* 1669
9. 0 46 ——— Mundus Subterraneus,   *cum Fig.*   *ibid.* 1658
12. 47 Belliff. Ovidii Theatr. seu P. Ovid. Hift. æri incif. á G. Bavern. *Nor.* 1687
J. 48 Tabulæ Partitionum Oratoriar. M. T. Ciceron. á J. Sturmio. *Arg.* 1547
1. 1. 49 *F. Vestigi del l'Antichita di Roma raccolti & ritratti in Perspittiva da Stef. du Perac.*   con molti Fig.   *Rom.* 1653
11. 0 50 Jac. Lauri Antiquæ Urbis (Romæ) Splendor. cum Figur. & Descrip. tione Imaginum, in Lat. Ital. & Gall. ———   *Ibid.* 1612
11. 0 51 Confucius Sinar. Philof. sive Scient. Sinensis Latinæ exposita *Par.* 1687
13. 52 Joh. Bapt. Riccioli Chronologia reformata   *Bonon.* 1669
10. 053 ——— Geographia & Hydrgraphia Reformata   *Ibid.* 1661
16. 054 ——— Almageft. Nov. Aftron. Veter. Novamq; compleft. 2 Vol.
                                           Ibid. 1665
12. 055 ——— Aftronomia Reformata, *cum Fig.*   *Ibid.* 1665
1. 6 56 Jos. Scaliger de Emendatione Temporum.   *Gen.* 1629
4. 0 57 Pallad. de Gent. Ind. & Bragm. Gr. Lat. ab Ed. Biffæo. *Lond.* 1665
10. 058 Olai Magn. Hiftor. de Gent. Septent. variis condit. *cum Fig. Baf.* 1567
1. 8 59 Chrift. Helvici Theatrum Hift. & Chronolog.   *Oxon.* 1651
1. 3 60 Franc. Bacon. Novum Organum   *Lond.* ———
10. 0 61 Jo. Hen. Alftedij Scient. Omn. Encyclop. 4 Tom. in 2 Vol. *Lug.* 1649
2. 1062 Abr. Callovij Encyclop. Difciplin. realium   *Lub.* 1652
2. 5 63 Herodoti Hiftor. Græcè á Joach Camerario edita.   *Baf.* 1557
2. 0 64 Diodori Siculi Bibliotheca Hiftor. Latinè. ———   *Ibib.* 1578
6. 0 65 Jamblichus de Myft. G. Lat. cum Notis, Tho. Gale   *Oxon.* 1678
1. 4 66 Luciani Opera Latinè á Jac. Micyllo ———   *Lugd.* 1549
1. 10 67 Angeli Politiani Opera   apud *Ascensium* ———
3. 10 68 Itinerarium, *ofte Voyage ende Schip. vaert van F. Huggen van Linschoten,*   *cum Fig.* ———   *Amst.* 1644
2. 2 69 Jo. Rofini Antiquitates Romanæ ———   *Baf.* 1583
10. 0 70 Alex. T. Petronius de Victu. Romanorum & de Sanitate tuenda.
                                           Rom. 1581
12. 5 71 Platonis Opera Gr. Lat. cum Comment. Marf. Ficini *Lugd.* 1590
10. 072 Plotini Opera Gr. Lat. cum Comment. Marf. Ficini.   *Baf.* 1580
5. 0 73 Marf. Ficini Opera Omnia, 2 Vol. ———   *Ibib.* 1576
8. 074 Cl. Salmafij. Plinianæ Exercitationes in C. Jul. Solini Polyhift. 2 Vol.
                                           Par. 1629
1. 075 Jo. Pici Mirandulæ Comment. de opere 6 Dierum Genefeos, &c.—
11. 676 Catalogus Impreffor. Libror. Bibliotheca Bodleianæ.   *Oxon.* 1674
                                        77 Mart.

77 Mart. Lipenij Bibliotheca realis Philofophia ——— *Franc.* 1682

78 Alph. Pandulphus de Fine Mundi ——— *Bonon.* 1658

79 Nichol. Cabeus in 4. Meteorologicor. Ariftot. ——— *Rom.* 1646

80 ———Philofophia Magnetica, *cum Fig.* ——— *Forrar.* 1629

81 Guil Gilbert de Magnete, Magneticifq; Corporib. *Lond.* 1600

82 Jo. Scharfij Methodus Philofophiæ Peripateticæ *Lipf.* 1631

83 Articella noviffime per Hier. de Saliis recognita. *Charaæt Vetuft, Ven.* 1523

84 Bartholom. Anglicus de rerum proprietatibus. *Charaæt. Antiquo. Norimb.* 1519

85 Anton. Andreas fuper 12 Liber. Metaph. *Charaæt pervet. Vicent.* 1477

86 Franc. Piccolomineus de rerum definitionibus. *Ven.* 1600

87 Æmyl. Parifanus de Microcof. Subtil. *pars Altera. Ibid.* 1635

88 Barth. Keckermanni Opera omnia 2 vol. ——— *Gen.* 1614

89 Hieron. Cardanus de Subtilitate *Baf.* 1582

90 ——— De rerum Varietate ——— — *Ibid.* 1557

91 Ariftotelis Opera G. L. ab If. Cafaub. 2 Tom. in 1 Vol. *Col. Al.* 1525

92 Lud. Septalij Com. in Ariftot. Probl. Gr. Lat. *Lugd.* 1632

93 Simplicij Com. in Ariftot. Phyfica. Græcè *Apud. Ald.* 1526

94 Ariftot. Hift. Anim. & Theophraft. Hift. Plantar. Lat. *Baf.* 1534

95 { Pet. Forefti. Obfervat. & Curationes Medicinales —— *Franc.* 1614
{ ——— Obfervationes Chirurgicæ ——— *Ibid.* 1610

96 Jo. Pierij Hierogl. five de Sacr. Ægypt. &c. Lit. *cum Fig. Baf.* 1567

97 Jul. Cafter Placent. de quinque feniibus *cum Fig. Franc.* 1610

98 De Morbo Gallico omnia quæ extant apud Omnes Med. *Ven.* 1566

99 Andr. Vefalius de human. Corpor. Fabr. *cum Fig. Ven* 1568

100 Jo. Jac. Weckeri Med. utr. Syntaxes ——— *Baf.* 1576

101 Leonh. Fuchfius de curandis Morbis ——— *Franc.* 1567

102 Pharmacopœia Collegij Regalis Londini ——— *Lond.* 1677

103 Jo. Guintherius de Med. Vet. & Nova ——— *Baf.* 1571

104 Andr. Libavia Alchym. recog. & auæta *cum. Fig. Franc.* 1606

105 Syntagma Arcanor. Chymicorum ——— *Ibib.* 1615

106 Hippocratis Op. Gr. Lat. cum Annot. Anut. Foefij *Franc.* 1595

107 Pet. Gaffendi Op. Omn. 6 Vol. ——— *Lugd.* 1685

108 Gul. Pifo de Indiæ utriufq; re Natur. & Med. &c. *cum Fig. Amft.* 1658

109 Pet. Penæ & Mat. de Lobel. Stirp. Adverf. Nova. *cum Fig. Lond.* 1571

110 Adam Lonicerus de Plant. *cum. Fig.* acced. Onomaft. Plant. *Franc.* —

111 Rob. Sibbaldi Prodromus Hift. Natural. Scot. *cum. Fig. Edinb.* 1684

112 Chrift. Montzelij Index Nom. Plant. Univerf. *Berol.* 1682

113 Tob. Aldini rariores Plantæ Hort. Farnefi. *cum. Fig. Rom.* 1625

114 Othon. Brunfelfij Herbar. *cum Fig.* ——— *Arg.* 1532

115 Jo. Raij Hiftor. Plantarum. 2 Vol. *Lond.* 1686

116 Jo. Bauhini & Jo. Hen. Cherleri Hiftor. Plantarum Univerf. *cum Fig.* ex recenfione D. Chubrei 3 Vol. ——— *Ebrod.* 1650

117 Franc. Hernander Hiftor. Plantar. Animalium & Mineralium Mexicanorum, cum Notis & Figuris ——— *Rom.* 1551

118 Car. Clufij rariorum Plantarum Hift. *cum Fig.* *Ant.* 1601

119 — Exoticorium Lib. X. item Pet. Bellonij Obfervat. *cum. Fig. Ibid.* 1605

120 Pedac. Diofcoridis Opera, Gr. Lat. á Jano Saraceno — *Franc.* 1598

121 *P. A. Matthioli Difcorfi ne i fei libri di Ped. Diofcorid. con fig. Ven.* 1621

122 Cafp. Bauhini Theatrum Botanicum *cum Fig.* ——— *Baf.* 1658

123 Marc. Malpighii Anatome Plantarum *cum Fig.* ——— *Iond.* 1675

B 2   123 Marc.

123 Marc. Malpiglii Anatom. Plantarum. *Cum Fig.* ——— *Lond.* 1675
124 Conr. Gesneri Historia Animalium. *Cum fig.* 3 Vol. *Franc.* 1603
125 Jo. Jonstoni Hist. Natur. de Quadr. de Avib.de Piscib.de ⎱ *Amst* 1657
     Exang. Aquat. de Insect. & de Serpentib. *Cum fig.*2 Vol. ⎰
126 ——Hist. Natural. de Arborib. & Fructicib. *Cum fig.*2 Vol. *Franc.* 1662
127 Th.Mouseti Insect. sive Minimor. Animal.Theat. *cum fig.* *Lond.* 1634
128 Jo. Ben. Sinibaldi Geneanthrop. sive de Hominis Generat. *Rom.* 1542
129 ⎰ Musæum Wormianum sive Histor. Rer. rarior. ab ⎱ *L. Bat.* 1655
     ⎱ Olao Worm. *cum fig.*·——— ⎰
130 ⎰ ——Franc. Calceolarii à B. Ceruto inceptum & ab ⎱ *Veron.* 1622
     ⎱ Andr. Chiocco perfectum. *cum fig.* ——— ⎰
131 C. Plinii Secundi Historia Natural. Notis J. Dalechampii *Ludg.* 1606
132 *Histoire du Monde de C. Plinæ Second traduite per A. du Pinit.*Par. 1622
133 *Dell' Historia Naturale di Ferrante Imperata* ———Ibid. 1599
134 Geo. Agricola de Ortu & Caulis Subterraneor, &c. ———*Bas.* 1546
135 ——de Mensur. & Ponderib. Romanor. & Græcorum———*Ibid.* 1550
136 Hieron. Cardanus de Sanitate tuenda ——— *Ibid.* 1582
137 ——de Subtilitate——— ———*Norimb.* 1550
138 Aula Subterr. Domina Dominantium,Subdita Subditorum *Franc.* 1672
139 Paracelsi Opera. *Linguâ Teutonicâ* ———*Strasb.* 1603
140 *Le Theatre d'Agriculture & Menage des Champs d'Ol de Serres* Par. 1600
141 Danielis Sennerti Opera. 4 Vol. *interfoliat*———*Ludg.* 1656
142 J. Schenckii Observationes Medicæ rariores———*Ibid.* 1694
143 ⎰ Pet. Foresti Observat. Medicinal. Lib. 29,30,31,32. *Franc.* 1671
     ⎱ ——Observat. Chirurgicæ ——— *Ibid.* 1634
144 *Les Euvres d' Ambroise Paré.* avec des Fig. *Paris* 1579
145 Conr. Gesneri Meditationes Physicæ ——— *Tig.* 1586
146 Jo. Remmelini Catoptrum Microcosmicum. *cum fig.* ·——*Ulmæ* 1639
147 ⎰ B. Besler fascicul. rarior. & aspectu dignor. varii Gener. æri ⎱ 1616
     ⎱ ad vivum incis. ——— ⎰
148 ——Continuatio rarior. & aspectu dignor. varii generis,&c. *Nor.* 1622
149 Mich. Rup. Besleri Gazophilac. Rer. Naturalium *cum fig. æneis* 1642
150 C. J. Hygini Fabulæ: nec non Palæphat. Phurnut. &c. Lat. *Bas.* 1570
151 *Saggi di Naturali Esperienze fatte nell' Acad. del Cimento.* in Fir. 1667
152 *Discours du Songe de Poliphile.* avec des fig. ———*Paris* 1554
153 Jac. W. Dobrzenski de admirando Fontium Genio. *cum fig. Fer.* 1658
154 Otton. de Guericke Experimenta de vacuo Spatio.*cum fig. Amst.* 1672
     ⎰ Onuphr. Panvinii XXVII. Pontif. Maxim. Elog. & Imag.*Rom.* 1568
     ⎰ Effigies XXIV. Romanor. Imperator. à C. Jul. Cæsare ———
155 ⎰ Illustrium Viror. ut exstant in Urbe Vultus *Rom.* 1569
     ⎱ Imag. & Elog. Vir. illust. e Lapid.& Numis expr.à F.Ursino *Ib.* 1570
     ⎱ Illust. Jurisconf.Imag. ex Museo M.Mant.Benav. formis Lafreri 1565
156 P. Rami Scholæ in Liberales Artes ———*Bas.* 1578
157 ⎰ Theatr. Ingenii seu Expos. Monum. erecti Jo. Baptistæ & ⎱ 1692
     ⎱ Albati Hippolyto Fratrib. à P. Verbio Neutro. *cum fig.* ⎰
158 Desid. Erasmi Adagia ——— *Hann.* 1617
159 J. A. Comerii Opera Didactica omnia———*Amst* 1657
160 ⎰ Ang. à S. Joseph Gazophylacium Linguæ Persarum, ⎱ *Ibid.* 1684
     ⎱ Clari Italicæ, Lat. & Gallicæ .Linguæ referatum ⎰
161 Jac. Golii Lexicon Arabico-Latinum ——— *L. Bat.* 1653
162 Jo. Buxtorfii Lexicon Chaldaic. Talmudic. & Rabbinicum. *Bas.* 1640
163 Jo. Scapulæ Lexicon Græco-Latinum——————*Gen.* 1628

                    164 Tho.

164 Tho. Cooperi Thefaurus Linguæ Romanæ & Britannicæ *Lond.* 1573
165 Guil. Morelli Verbor. Latinor. cum Græc. Anglicifq; conjunctor. Comment.──────────────────── *Ibid.* 1583
166 Steph. Skinner Etymolog. Linguæ Anglic. (Charta Majora) *Ibid.* 1671
167 Jo. David. Rhæfi. Cambro Brytannicæ Linguæ Inftitution. *Ibid.* 1592
168 Jo. Davies Antiq. Linguæ Britan. & Ling. Latinæ Diction. *Ibid.* 1632
169 *James Howell's* French and English Dictionary───────── *Ibid.* 1673
170 Gafp. Schotti Curfus Mathematicus. *cum fig.* ─────── *Bamb.* 1677
171 Cl.Fr. Milliet Dechales Curf.feu|Mund.Math.*cum fig.* 3 Vol. *Ludg.* 1674
172 Andr. Tacquet Opera Mathematica. *cum plurimis fig.* ── *Ant.* 1669
173 F. Vietæ Opera Mathem. recognita à Fr. à Schoot. *cum fig.* *L.B.* 1646
174 Euclidis Elem. Math. edita à Fr. Fluffate Candella, *cum fig.* *Par.* 1566
175 ──Elementa cum Animadverf. &c. Cl. Richardi. *cum fig. Ant.* 1645
176 { ──Elem. cum Schol. Gr. Theon. & Proch. Græce *cum fig.* } *Baf.* 1533
      { ──Elem. cum expof. Theon. Camp. & Hypf. Latine *fig.* } 1537
177 Euclides Aductus & Methodicus Guar. Guarini, *cum fig. A.Taur.* 1671
178 Diophanti Alexandr. Arithm. & de Numeris Multiangulis, Lat.
179 ──Idem, Gr. & Lat. cum Comment. Cl. Gafp. Sacheti *Paris* 1621
180 ──Idem iterum acceffit Doctrina Analytica D. de Fermart *Tolof.* 1670
181 *De Arifmetifc.en Geometrifc. fondamen van Lud. van Keulen* Leyd. 1615
182 Henr. Briggii Arithmetica Logarithmica ───────── *Lond.* 1624
183 Ifm. Bullialdi opus novum ad Arithmeticam Infinitor. ── *Paris* 1682
184 Franc. Vietæ in Artem Analyticam Ifagoge──────── *Turin.* 1591
185 Tho. Harrioti Artis Analyticæ Praxis ─── ────── *Lond.* 1631
186 ──Idem, Iterum ───────── ──────── *Ibid.*
187 Car. Renaldini Ars Analytica Mathematum, 2 Vol. *cum fig. Flor.* 1665
188 Phil. Lansbergii Tabulæ Motuum Cœleftium perpetuæ *Middl.* 1632
189 Pet. Apiani Inftrumentum primi Mobilis, &c. ──── *Norimb.* 1534
190 Jo. Ant. Magnini Primum Mobile in XII. Libris ──── *Bovon.* 1609
191 Laur. Eichftadii Tabulæ Harmonio Cœleftium Motuum *Stetin.* 1644
192 Vinc. Renerii Tabulæ Motuum Cœleftium Univerfales *Flor.* 1647
193 Oron. Fineus de Mundi Sphæra five Cofmographia─── *Paris* 1542
194 Maur. Breftii Metrices Aftronomicæ Libr. 4. ──── *Ibid.* 1581
195 { Chriftoph. Scheiner Rofa Urfina five Sol ex admirando Facularum &
      { Macular. Suar. Phænomino varius, *cum fig.* ── *Brac.* 1630
196 { Franc. Ofanaldi Schrecfenfuchhii Comment. in novas Theoricas Planetar. Geog. Purbachii ─── ────── *Baf.*
197 Jo. Hevelii Selenographia five Lunæ Defcriptio, *cum fig. Ged.* 1647
198 { ──Prodromus Cometicus five Hiftor. Cometæ 1664─────*Ibid.* 1665
      { ──Defcriptio Cometæ, 1665. ──── ─────── *Ibid.* 1665
      { ──Cometographia, cum figuris──── ──── *Ibid.* 1663
199 ──De Obfervatione Deliquii Solis Anno 1649, &c.────*Ibid.* 1654
200 ──Mercur.in Sole vifus 1661 & Venus in Sole 1639. à J.Horroccio 1662
201 ──Annus Climact. five Rer. Uranicar. Obferv. Annus 49us────1685
202 ──Machina Cœleftis, cum fig. 3 Vol.──── ───── *Ibid.* 1673-79
203 Ifm. Bullialdi Aftronomia Philolaica, *cum fig.* ─────── *Paris* 1645
204 Julii Firmici Aftronomicorum Libri 8, &c.──────*Venet.* 1499
205 Matth. Hirzgarteri Aftronomia Lansbergiana reftituta *Tig.* 1639
206 Cl.Ptolomæi Almag. feu magna Conftr. Lat. a G.Trapezunt.*Ven.* 1528
207 ────Almageftum cum Theonis Comment. Græce ────*Baf.* 1538
208 { Jo. de Monte Regio & Geo. Purbachii Epitome, &c. *Ibid.* 1543
      { D. Severini Boetii Arithmetica cum Comment *apud Colin.* 1521
                                                  209 Mariæ

151

257 Jo.

Libri Latini, &c. in Folio. 7

257 Jo. Caramuelis Mathefis Sicepo Vetus & Nova, 2 Vo!. *Campan.* 1670 0 · *11* ·
258 { Pappi Alexandrini Mathematicæ Collectiones cum Fod. } *Ven.* 1588 0 - 6 · 6
   { Commandini Comment. ————— }
259 ————Idem————Iterum———— ———— *Bonon.* 1660 0 · 9 ·
260 Sim. Stevini Hypomnemata Mathematica, 2 Vol. ———— *L. Bat.* 1608 0 · 5 · 0
261 ————Idem———— Gallicè, per Alb. Girard. ——— *Leyd.* 1634 0 · 3 · 6
262 ————Idem———— Belgice———— *Leyd.* 1608
263 Jo. de Regio Monte de Triangulis omnimodis ———— *Norimb.* 1533
264 A. Rom.Chord. arcub. circuli primariis Subtenf. refolutio *Wirtem.* 1602 0 · 4 · 0
265 Geo. Jo. Rhætici Magnus Canon Doctrinæ Triangulorum ———— · 1 · 6
266 —Opus Palatinum de Triangulis Edit. à Valent. Othone———— 1596 0 · 1 · 6
267 —Thefaur.Mathemat. five Canon Sinuum edit. à B. Pitifco-*Fran.* 1613
268 H. Gellibrand Trigonomet. Brit. five de Doct.Triangulor.-*Goud.*1633 0 · 2 · 10
269 Tabula Numerorum Quadrator. decies Millium *Lond.* 1672 0 · 0 ·
270 Alhazeni Opticæ Thefaurus, item Vitellian. Optica *Baf.* 1572 0 · 4 · 0
271 Franc. Aguilonii Opticorum, Libri 6.———— ————*Ant.* 16130 · 6 · 6
272 *L'Optique & la Catoptrique du R. P. Merfenne*-————-*Par.* 1651 0 · 2 · 2
273 Jo. Zahn Oculus Artificialis Teledioptricus, *Cum Fig.*---*Herbip.* 1685 0 · 12 - 6
274 *Profpettiva Prattica di Piet. Accolti, con Fig.* ——— *Finen.* 1625 0 · 3 ·
275 { Eman. Maignan Perfpectiva Horariæ five de Horogra- } *Rom.*1648 0 · 1 2 · 6
   { phia Gnomonica, cum Fig. }
276 Chrift. Hugen. Zulichemi Horolog. Ofcillatorium, *cum Fig.*-*Par.* 1673 0 · 12 · 0
277 Andr. Schoneri Gnomonice,*b.e.*Defcript.Horol. Sciotoricor.*Norib.*1562
278 Chriftoph. Clavii Gnomonices Libri Octo———— ——*Rom.* 1581 0 · 2 · 2
279 Archimedis Opera, Gr. Lat. cum Com. D. Rio. à Fluentia-*Par.* 1615 0 · 8 · 0
280 --Monumenta omnia Mathem. ex tradit. Fr. Maurolici *Panormi.* 1685 0 · 5 · 0
281 Adr. Romani in Archimedis circuli dimenfionem expofitio-*Gen.* 1597 0 · 1 · 0
282 Dav. Sanclari pro Archimede & Euclide Δικαιολογια———— *Par.* 1622 0 · 2 · 6
283 *De Seven Boecken van. de Groote Zeevaert,door Abr.de Graef.Amft.*1658 0 · 4 · 0
284 { Geo. Fournier Hidrographie,*conten. la Theorie & la Prati*- } *Par,* 1667 · 3 · 0
   { *que de la Navigation* }
285 Geo. Agricolæ de Re Metallica Lib. xii. &c. cum Fig. *Baf.* 1556 , 0 · 5 · 0
286 *Teatro de los Inftrum.y Fig.Math.y Mecanic.por D.Beffon,conFig.Leon.*1602 · 4 ·
287 *Regola delli 5 Ordini d'Arch. di M. Giac. Barozzio,&c. conFig.Amft.*1648 1 · 3 · 0
288 *I 4 Libri dell' Architettura di Andr. Palladio, con Fig.*-————*Ven.* 1601 0 · 2 · 0
289 *L'Architettura ai Andr. Palladio, con Fig.* ————*Ven.* 1642 1 · 5 · 4
290 Architectura per Windel. Dieterlin Pictorem Argent.*Belg.cumFig.*1598 0 · 7 · 0
291 Geo. Andr. Bocklern Architectura curiofa nova, *cum Fig.*-*Norimb.*1664 1 · 10 ·
292 M.Vitruvii Pollion.de Architectura lib.x. cum Com.&Fig.&c.*Ven.*1567 0 · 4 · 8
293 ————Idem *Belgicè*, per D. Gualtherum H. Rivium,*cum Fig. Baf.*1575 0 · 1 · 0
294 { *Les x Livres d'Architecture de Vitruve, Corrigez & Tra-* } *Par.* 1673 2 · 1 ·
   { *duits en Francois, avec des Notes & des Figures*———— }
295 *Scheep Bow en Befter door N. Witfen, cum Fig.* ——— *Amft.*1671 0 · 5 · 0
296 *Palazzi di Genoua, con multi Figuri* ———— ———— 0 · 11 · 6
297 *Lionardi di Vinci della Pittura, con Fig.* ——— *Parig.* 1651 1 · 4 · 0
298 { *Nouvelle Inventice de lever l'Eau plus haut que fa fource.* } ——— 0 · 3 · 0
   { *par Ifaac de Caus. avec des Fig.* }
299 { Geo. Andr. Bockleri Theatrum Machinar. exhibens } *Norimb.*1662 1 · 13 · 6
   { Opera Molaria & Aquatica, *cum Fig.* }
300 { Fl. Vegetius de Re Militari. — S. J. Frontinus de Stra- } *Par.* 1535 0 · 4 · 8
   { tagemat. &c. cum Fig. }
301 Cafim. Siemienowicz Art. Mag. Artilleria,Pars I. *cum Fig.*-*Amft.* 1650 · 2 · 6
                                                    302 — Idem

153

Libri Latini, &c. in Quarto.

C

89 Se-

223 Fab. Columnæ minus cognitar. Stirpium Ecphrasis cum Fig. Rom. 1616 C
224 Jac. Cornuti Conadentium Plantarum Hiftoria, cum Fig.   Par. 1635.
225 P. Boccon. Icones & Defcript. rarior. Plantar. Siciiæ, Melitæ, Galliæ
    & Italiæ.   ———   ———   Oxon. 1624
226 Liber Plantarum, figuris ornatus & in Ling Teutonica confcriptus, 2 vol.
                                        Nuremb. 1679
227 Cafp. Bauhini Pinax Theatri Botanici   ———   Baf. 1623
228 Jo. Coftæus de univerfali Stirpium Natura.   Aug. Taur. 1578
229 Tho. Fieni Lib. Chirurg. XII. editi ab Herm. Conring. Franc. 1602
230 Gebri Arabis Alchemia, Latine   ———   Nuremb. 1545
231 Andr. Libavij Alchemia   ———   ———   Franc. 1597
232 Chrift. Love Morley Colleft. Chymica Lydenfia   Lug. Bat. 1684
233 Mart. Rulandi Lexicon Alchemiæ   ———   1612
234 Theophraft. Paracelle fes Secrets admirables.   ———   Par. 1631
235 Ger. Dorneri Fafciculus Paracelliæ Medicinæ -   Franc. 1581
236 Mufæum Hermeticum reformatum & amplificatum   ibid. 1677
237 Franc. Mercur. van Helmont Opera   ———   Amft. 1652
238 Mercurius Triumphans & Hebdomas Eclogar. Harmet. Migdeb. 1600
239 Jo. Seger. Weidenfeld de Secretis Adeptorum   Lond. 1684
240 Ofualdi Crollij Bafilica Chymica   ———   Franc. 1609
241 Annib. Barlet, la Theotechine Ergocofmique. avec des Fig. Par. 1653
242 Jo. Stignier Magni Lapides Natural. Philof. & vera Ars. Bren. 1664
243 Frid. Lachmund de Admirand. Foffilib. in traft. Heldef. repertis
                                        Hidfh. 1669
244 J. Lud. Honnoman Methodus cognofc. fimplicia Vegetab. Kil. 1677
245 Andr. Cefalpini de Metallicis Lib. tres   ———   Rom. 1596
246 Tho. Eraftus de Oculis Pharmacor. Poteftatib   Baf. 1574
247 Ant. Mufæ Brafavoli examen. Pilular. quarum apud Pharmacopol.
ufus eft.   ———   ———   Froben. 1543
248 Jof. Quercetani Pharmacopœia Dogmat. reftituta   Franc. 1615
249 La Pharmacopée de Baudaron avec des Remarques par Fr.Verng.Lyon.1662
250 Jo. Schroderi Pharmacopœia Medico Chymica   Lugd. 1665
251 ——— Quercetan Redivivus h. e. Ars Medica Dogmatico Hermetica
    3 Vol.   ———   Franc. 1648
252 Jo. Jac. Weckeri Antidot. Generale & Speciale   Baf. 1617
253 Pharmacopœia Auguftana cum Animado. Jo. Zwelfer.   Dordr. 1672
254 Mof. Clares, Pharmacopée Royale Galenique & Chymique Par. 1676
255 Mart. Lifter de Araneis & Cochleis, cum Fig.   Lond. 1678
256 De Humani Corporis Fabrica ab Adr. Spigelio. cum Fig. Franc. 1632
257 Orbis ftans quomodo in duobus Hemifpherij planis Defcribatur,
    cum Tebl.
258 La Geographia di Claudio Ptolomeo tradotta du Gier. Rufcelli, cum Fig.
                                        Ven. 1574
259 Jo. Magini Geographia Vetus & Nova, cum Tabl.   Arnh. 1617
260 Pet. Appiani & Genmæ Trefij Cofmographia, cum Fig. Antw. 1584
261 Ph. Brietij Parallela Geographiæ Veteris & Novæ; cum Fig. Par.1648
262 Ph. Cluveri Introduftio in Univerfam Geograph.   L. Bat. 1624
263 ——— Idem cum Tabul. Geogr. per Jo. Bunonem Guelph. 1661
264 Jo. Laurenbergij Græcia antiqua edita à S. Pufendorf, cum Tabul.
                                        Amft. 1660
265 Sam. Bocharti Geographia Sacra, cum Fig.   Franc. 1681
                                        266 Cartes

266 *Cartes Generales des Royaumes*, &c. *de la haute & baſte Aliemagne,* *par le Sir Taſſin*   ——   ——   Par. 1633

267 Ægid. Tſchudus de Priſca & vera Alipina Rhælia   Baſ. 1538

268 Franc. Creuxii Hiſtoria Canadenſis ſeu Nov. Franc. *cum Fig. Par.* 1604

269 Legatio Batavica ad Magn. Tart. Cham. fig. ornat. 2 vol. Belgice—

270 *Hiſtor. Naturale & Morale delle Indie,* caret Titulo.   ——

271 ——*Des Iſles de S. Chriſtophe, de la Guadeloupe,* &c.   Par. 1664

272 *Le Navigationi,* &c. *nella Turchia, di Nicol. del Nichol. del Delfinato* *cum Fig.* —— —— *Antv.* 1576

273 Navigationes Fr. Drake, Tho. Candiſh, J. Haukens, &c. ad Indies, &c. *cum Fig.* Belgice —— *Amſt.* 1598

274 *Voyage fait au Levant par M. de Thevenot* —— *Rouen.* 1665

275 Adr. Romani Deſcript. Urbium Præcip. tot. Orb. *cum Fig. Franc.* 1595

276 Jo. Alph. Borelli Hiſtor. & Meteorolog Incendij Ætnæi, 1669. *cum Fig.* —— *Regio Julio.* 1670

277 ——De Motionib. Natural.á Gravitate Pendentib. *cum Fig.Ib.*1670

278 *Le Vitte de Pittori, Scultori & Architetti Moderni da Gio Piet. Bel-* *lori, cum Fig.* —— —— *Rom.* 1672

279 Raph. Fabrettus de Aquis & Aquæd. Vet. Rom, *cum. Fig. Rom.* 1680

280 And. Mulleri Hebdomas Obſervat. de Rebus Sinicio *Col. Br.* 1674

281 Fab. Columna de Purpura edit. à Jo. Dan. Majore,*cum Fig. Kil.* 1675

282 Rei Agrariæ Auctores Legeſq; var. cum Not. W. Goeſij & N. Regal-ti, *cum Fig.* —— —— *Amſt.* 1674

283 Jo. Schefferus de re Vehiculari Veterum, *cum Fig.* *Franc.* 1671

284 Caneparius de Atramentis cujuſcunque Generis *Lond.* 1660

285 Tho. Burnetij Archeologia Philoſophica *Ibid.* 1692

286 Jo. Henr. Alſtedij Curſus Philoſophici Encyclopedia *Herb.* 1620

287 Henr. Mori Enchiridion Metaphyſicum, *cum Fig.* *Lond.* 1671

288 Nichol. Steno de Solido intra Solidum contento, *cum Fig. Flor.* 1669

289 Bened. Mazzotta de triplici Philoſophia Naturali Aſtrologica & Mi-nerali, *cum Fig.* —— *Bonon.* 1653

290 Franc. Mar. Grimaldus de Lumine, Colorib. & Iride *Ibid.* 1665

291 Jo. Conr. Peyerus de Ruminantib. & Ruminatione *Baſ.* 1685

292 Fortun. Liceti Ariſtotelicum Ænigma enodatum, *Patav.* 1630

293 De Nuritione Fœtus in Utero Paradoxa —— *Dant.* 1655

294 Anton. Molinet. de Senſib. & eorum Organis *Patav.* 1655

295 *The Old and New Teſtament Tranſlated into Iriſh, by Biſhop Bedel.* 2 Vol. (in the Iriſh Character) —— *Lond.* 1685

296 *Het Nieuwe Teſtament ouſes Heeren Jeſu Chriſti.* *Amſt.* 1661

297 J. Buxtorf. de Punctor. Vocal. & Accent. Orig. &c. *Baſ.* 1648

298 Binæ Tabulæ Geographicæ Viz. Neceſſar. Eddini Perſæ & Ulug. Beigi Tatari Arab. & Lat. á Jo. Gravio *Lond.* 1648

299 Ulug Beighi Tabul. Stellar fixarum Perſ. & Lat. á T. Hyde *Oxon.* 1665

300 P. Colomeſij Gallia Orientalis ſive Gallor. qui Ling. Oriental. exco-luerunt Vitæ *Hajæ* 1665

301 Tho. Hangij Cœlum Orientis & Priſci Mundi *Hafn.* 1657

302 Proverbia Ben. Siræ, Hebr. & Lat. á Jo. Druſio *Franeck* 1597

303 J. Mich. Langius de Charactere Primævo Biblior. Ebraicor. *Altf.* 1689

304 Gul. Seamam Grammatica Linguæ Turcicæ *Oxon.* 1670

305 Alphabetum Arabiumc Arab. & Lat. *Rom.* 1592

306 { —Arab. cum Iſag. Scrib. legend. Arab. à J.Chriſtmanno *Necp.*1582 { F. Junij Orationes duæ ad Lect.V. Teſt. & ad lect. Lib.Moſis *Ib.*1582

307 Chriſt.

307 Chrift. Crinefij Grammat. & Lexicon Chaldaicum   *Norimb.* 1627
308 Ath. Kircheri Prodromus Coptus five Ægyptianus.   *Rom.* 1636
309 Jac. Wemmers Lexicon Æthiopicum ——   *Ibid.* 1638
310 *Jo. Elliot's Indian Grammar* ——   *Cambr.*——
311 —— *New Teftoment in the Indian Language*   *Ibid.* 1661
312 *Dialogues in the Englifh and Malaian Languages* ——
313 Dictionarium Malaico Latinum ——
314 N.Clenardi Inftit.in Ling.Græc.cum Scholiis P.Antefignani*Franc.* 1580
315 Wolf. Seberi Index Vocab. in Humeri Poematis   Gr.   *Com.* 1604
316 Olaus Borichius de varijs Latinæ Linguæ ætatibus   *Haf.* 1675
317 De Natura & ufu Literarum Difceptat. Philologica.   *Monaft.* 1638
318 Valer. Probus de interpret. Romanor. Literis, &c.   *Soræ.* 1647
319 *Franc. Gouldman's Eng. & Lat. Lat. & Eng. Diction.*   *Lond.* 1664
320 Diction. Latino Hifpan. & Hifpanico Latin. ab Æ. Anton. Nebrif-
    fenfi ———   *Ant.* 1560
321 —— German Lat. á Jofua Pictorio ———   *Tiguri.* 1561
322 ——Lufitanico Latinum ab Auguft. Barbofa.   *Brach.* 1611
323 Ol. Wormij Runica feu Danica Literat. Antiquif.   *Amft.* 1636
324 *Le Grand Dictionarie François Flamen par J. Louys D'Arfy*   1663
325 *Dictionarie Italienne & Francoife par Ant. Oudin.*   *Par.* 1653
326 *An Entrance to the Spanifh Tongue, by J. Sandford.*   *Lond.* 1611
327 *Teforo de las tres Languas Efpannola, Francefa y Italiana per H. Victor.*
       Gen. 1637
328 Greg. Cnapij Thefauri Polono Latino Græci Tomus 3. continens
    Adag. Polonica   *Cracov.* 1632
329 Jac. Catzij Silenus Alcibiadis, five Proteus cum Fig. Lat. Gall.
    &. Belgice   *Amft.*——
330 *Spiegel van der ouden nieuwen Tijd door J. Cats, cum Fig. Graven.* 1632
331 *Verhail van de Reis des Biffcops van Beryte vit Frankera naar China,*
    cum Fig. ———   *Amft.* 1683
332 Joh. Kunckeli Ars Vitraria experiment. *cum Fig.* Teutonice*Franc.* 1679
333 *De Wonderlyke Reizen van Ferd. Mend. Pinto cum Fig. Belgice*
       Amft. 1652
334 *Hieron. Welfchen Reis befchreibung,* Teutonice   *Nuren.* 1659
335 Euclidis Data G. & L. à Claudio Hardy, *cum Fig.*   *Par.* 1625
336 ——Optica & Catoptrica G. & L. á Jo. Pena   *Ibid.* 1557
337 —— Arithmet. in 2 Part. demonft. à C. Dibvadio.   *Arnh.* 1605
338 —— Geometria demonft. à C. Dibvadio   *L. Bat.* 1603
339 H. Savilij Prælectiones in Euclidis Elementa   *Oxon.* 1621
340 Ovid. Montalbani Speculum Euclidianum   *Bonon.* 1629
341 *Les 6 premieus Livres des Elem. d' Euclide trad. & commentez par*
    P. Forcadel ———   *Par.* 1554
342 Theonis Smynæi Mathemat. G. L. cum Not. Ifm. Bulliald. *Par.* 1644
343 Ptolomæi opus quadripart. Lat. ab Ant. Gogava.   *Lovan.* 1548
344 — De Analemmate Lat. cum Fod. Command. Comment. *Romæ* 1542
345 Ariftot. Mathemat. Lat. à Jof. Blancano   *Bonon.* 1615
346 Archimedis Opera Latine per Nic. Tartaleam   *Ven.* 1543
347 — De iis quæ vehunt. in aqua cum Com. F.Commandini. *Bonon.* 1565
348 ——Opera, Apol. Pergæi Conica & Theodofii Spherica par If.
    Barrow ——————————————— *Lond.* 1675
349 *Archimede Redevivo con la Stadera del Momento da Gio. Bat. Ho-*
    dierna ———————————————— *Paler.* 1644
            350 Theodofij

440 Willeb. Snellii Cœli & Siderum in eo errantium Obſervation. Haſ-
    liacæ————————————————————L. Bat. 1618
441 *Ant. Santucci, Trattato nuovo delle Comete*————*Firenʒi* 1619
442 Cometæ Ann. 1577. ad parentis deſcripti, à Barth. Sculteto. *Gorl.* 1578
443 Fortun. Licetus de Comet. Quiete,Loco Bor. ſine Occaſu,&c. *Ven.* 1625
444 *P. Petit ſur la Nature des Comètes*————— ————*Paris* 1665
445 Eraſm. Bartholin. de Cometis Anni 1664 & 1665.————*Hafn.* 1665
446 Ant. Mizaldi Cometographia ——————————*Paris* 1549
447 Ph. Lansbergii Epilogiſ. duar. Eclipſ. horribilium 1635—*Tigur.*
448 Eraſmi Reinhold iPrutenicæ Tabulæ Cœleſtium Motuum *Witteb.* 1585
449 Jo. Schoneri Tabulæ reſolutæ Aſtronomicæ ————*Ibid.* 1587
450 Jo. Heckeri Motuum Cœleſt. Ephem. ab An. 1666,ad 1680. *Ged.* 1662
451 Andr. Argoli Ephemerides ab Anno 1640. ad Ann. 1700.— *Pat.* 1648
452 {—Tabulæ primi Mobilis, 2 Vol.————————*Ibid.* 1645
     {—Pandoſion Sphæricum ——————————*Ibid.* 1644
453 Dav. Origani Motuum Cœleſt. Ephem. ab A. 1595. ad A. 1655. *Franc.* 1609
454 Mich. Meſtlini Ephemerides ab Anno 1577 ad 1590. ———*Tub.* 1580
455 Jo. Ant. Magini Tabulæ Secundor. Mobilium Cœleſtium —*Ven.* 1585
456 Chriſtoph. Clavii Aſtrolabium——————————*Rom.* 1593
457 Jo. Regiomontan. de Torqueto,de Aſtrolabio armill.&c. *Norimb.* 1544
458 Jo. de Roias Comment. in Aſtrolabium————*apud Vaſcoſan.* 1550
459 Pet. Pitat veræ Solar. & Lunar. Anni quantitatis, &c. ad Calendar.
    Roman. pertinent. explicatio ——————————*Baſ.* 1568
460 Ulug. Beigi Epochæ Celebriores. Arab. & Lat. cum Comment. Jo.
    Gravii————————————————————*Lond.* 1650
461 Mich. Meſtlini novi Gregor. Kalendarii Examen.————*Tub.* 1586
462 Geo. Germani Calendar. triplex,Gregor. antiquum & novum *Franc.*
463 {Oront Finæi Sphera Mundi ſive Coſmographia *apud Vaſcoſan.* 1551
     {—De Speculo Uſtorio ——————————*Ibid.* 1551
     {Euclidis Elementor. Lib. 10. Pet. Montaureo Interprete *Ibid.* 1552
464 Ric. Albii Hemiſpherium diſſectum ——————*Romæ* 1648
465 *Sfera del Mondo di M. Aliſendro Piccolomini*————*Vineg.* 1553
466 Ptolomæi Planiſphær. cum Fed. Commendi in Comm. *Ven. ap. Al.* 1558
467 Chriſt Clavii in Sphæram Jo. de Sacro-Boſco Comment.—*Ludg.* 1607
468 Iſ. Habrechti Planiglobium Cœleſte & Terreſtre ——*Norimb.* 1662
469 Joſ. Blancani Sphera Mundi ſeu Coſmographia——*Bonon.* 1620
470 Jac. Bartſchii Planiſphærium Stellatum ————*Norimb.*
471 {Mich. Neandri Elementa Spheric. Doctrin. ———*Baſil.* 1561
     {Pet. Pitat ſuper Annua Solar. & Lunar. Anni quantitate *Vern.* 1560
     {Ariſtoxeni Harmonic. Elementor. Lib. 3. Lat.——*Ven.* 1562
     {Theodoſii Sphericor. Lib. 3.————————*Paris* 1558
     {Cl. Darioti ad Aſtrorum judicia Introductio ——*Ludg.* 1557
472 Comment. in Ruzname Naurus ſive Tab. æquinoctiales novi Perſar.
    Anni ——————————————————*Aug. Vind.* 1576
473 *Il Saggiatore del Sig. Galilei*————————*Rom.* 1623
474 Gal. Galilei Opinion. de Cometis à M. Guiducio Examinent. *Per.* 1619
475 Diſſert. de Mediis quibuſd. ad Aſtronom. reſtituend. neceſſ. *Hafn.* 1642
476 Tho. Diggeſii Alæ ſeu Scalæ Mathematicæ————*Lond.* 1573
477 Eliæ Molerii Aſtronomicus Epilogiſmus ——————1607
478 Ph. Lansberg. in Motum Terræ diurnum & annuum——*Midd.* 1630
479 Jo. Bageri Uranometria ————————*Aug. Vind.* 1654
480 Tricaſſi Ceraſaricus. Mantuani Chyromantia——*Norimb.* 1560
                                       481 Jo.

481 Jo. Kepleri ad Vitellionem Paralipomena ———— ———— *Franc.* 1604
482 ————Chilias Logarithmorum ———— ———— *Marp.* 1624
483 ————De Aſtronomia Lunari. ———— 1634
484 ————Tychonis Hyperaſpiſtes adv. Claramont. ———— *Franc.* 1625
485 { —Prodromus Diſſertation. Coſmographicarum ——— *Tub.* 1596
     { —De Anno quo æternus Dei filius human. Natur.ſumpſit.*Fran.*1614
486 —De Stella nova in pede Serpentarii, &c.———— ————*Prag.* 1606
487 —Diſſertatio cum Nuncio Pidereo———— ————*Franc.* 1611
488 —Ephemeridum Tomi, pars 2,& 3. ———— ————*Sageni.* 1630
489 —De Cometis Libelli tres ———— ———— ————*Aug. Vind.* 1619
490 —Ephemerides novæ Motuum cœleſtium ———— *Lincii.* 1637
491 Mart. Hortenſis Reſponſio ad Additiuncul. Jo. Kepler.   *L. Bat.* 1671
492 Cl.Ptolomæus de Judicandi facultate.Lat.cumNot.J.Bullialdi*Hag.*1663
493 Jo. Goads Aſtro-Meteorologia Sana————————*Lond.* 1690
494 Jo. de Monte Regio Tab. Direction. Aſtrolog. judic. utiles.*Witt.*1584
495 Valent. Nebods Elementa Aſtrologiæ ———— ————*Col.* 1560
496 Libri novem Judicum in Judiciis Aſtrorum———— ————*Ven.* 1508
497 Nicol. Zacchii Optica Philoſophia, 2 Vol. ———— *Lugd.* 1652
498 Iſ. Barrow Lectiones Opticæ, *cum Fig.* ————*Lond.*1669
499 Chriſt. Scheiner Oculus, *h. e.* Fundamentum Opticum ——*Lond.*1652
500 { Heliodori Optica, Gr. Lat. ———— 1610
     { Heron. Cheſibii Belopocæca, Gr. Lat. ———— *Aug. Vind.* 1616
501 Hon. Fabri Synopſis Optica ———— ————*Lugd.* 1667
502 Jo.Adol. Taſſii Photicæ(quæ vulgo Optica dicitur) Compendium1678
503 Jo. Bapt. Porta de refractione Optices ———— *Neap.* 1593
504 Fr. Eſchinardi centuria Problematum Opticor. 2 Vol. ——*Rom.* 1666
505 Jac. Gregorii Optica promota ———— ———— *Lond.* 1663
506 Rog. Baconis Perſpectiva, edita à Jo. Combachio————*Franc.*1614
507 Jo. Archiepiſc. Cantuarienſ. Perſpectiva communis ——*Col.* 1592
508 *La Proſpittiva di Euclide tradotta dal P. Egnatio Danti*   *Fior.* 1573
509 *Il Teleſcopio over Iſpecillo celeſte di Nic. Ant. Stelliola* ——*Nap.* 1627
510 Franc. Maurolycus de Lumine & Umbra ———— *Lugd.* 1617
511 Franc. Fontana de Luna Obſervationib. (Titulus deeſt)————
512 Seth. Wardi Idea Trigonometria, &c. ———— *Oxon.* 1654
513 Will. Oughtred Trigonometria ———— *Lond.* 1657
514 Benj. Urſini Trigonometria cum magno Logarithm. canone *Col.* 1625
515 Ant. Maginus de Planis Triangulis ———— ————*Ven.* 1592
516 Adr. Romani Canon Triangulor. Sphæricorum ———— *Mogunt.* 1609
517 *M. Paſchal Traite du Triangle Arithmetique, &c.* *Par.* 1665
518 Pet. Courcier Triangularium figurar. menſuratio————*Muſſip.*1675
519 Barth. Pitiſci Canon Triangulor. emendatiſſimis ———— 1608
520 Job Ludolfi Tetragonometria Tabularia ————————*Franc.* 1690
521 Jo. Voell. de Horologiis Sciothericio ———— *Turn.* 1606
522 Oron. Finæus de Solarib. Horologiis ———— *Par.* 1560
523 *Domen. Martinelli Horologi Elementari*———— *Ven.* 1669
524 Chriſt. Clavii Horologiorum nova deſcriptio———— *Romæ* 1599
525 Pauli Caſati Mechanica ———— *Ludg.* 1684
526 Cunr. Daſypodii Heron Mathematicus ſeu de Mechanic. Artib.
                                                    Argent. 1580
527 Jo. Wallis Mechanica ſive de Motu, pars prima ———— *Lond.* 1670
528 Gaſp. Schotti Mechanica Hydraulico-Pneumatica————*Herbip.*1657
529 Levin. Aulſii Inſtrumenta Mechanica ———— *Franc.*1605
                 D 2   530 *Projet*

577 Steph. de Angelis de infinitis Parabolis ——— *Ven.* 1659:

578 ———De infinitar. Cochlearum Menſuris ——— *Ibid.* 1661

579 ———Miſcellaneum Hyperbolicum & Parabolicum———*Ibid.* 1659

580 ———De Infinitis Spiralibus inverſis ——— ———*Patav.* 1667

581 ———De Superficie Ungulæ ——— *Ven.* 1661

582 Athan. Kircheri Magnes ſive de Arte Magnetica ——— *Col. Agr.* 1643

583 Guil. Gilbertus de Magnete, Magneticisq; Corporib. &c. *Sed.* 1633

584 Vincent. Leotandi Magnetologia ——— *Lugd.* 1668

585 Tho. Hobbes Operum, Tomus prior ———

586 Jo. Camilli Exercitationes Mathematicæ, in 2 Decad. *Neap.* 1627

587 Jac. Grandamici nova demonſtratio Immobilitatis Terræ, *cum Figur.*
Flex. 1645

588 Galil. Galilæi Dialog. de Syſtemate Mundi ——— *Lugd.* 1641

589 Eraſmi Bartholini Dioriſtice ſeu Æquationum determinat. *Hann.* 1663

590 Rob. Flud Monochordum Mundi Symphoniacum ———*Franc.* 1622

591 Philolaus ſive de vero Syſtemate Mundi ——— *Amſt.* 1639

592 Chriſt.Sever. Longomontani Inventio Quadraturæ Circuli.-*Hafn.*1634

593 Foder. Commandin. de centro Gravitatis Solidorum— } *Bonon.* 1565 *C*
—cum 3bus, aliis Lib. de Re Mathem.conjunct compact }

594 *Pyrotechnia, Libri X. campoſti per Vannuc.Biringucciæ,con Fig.Vineg.*1550

595 *Documenti Militari del Colloñelo Nic. Volo Cretienſe* ——— *Pad.*1667

596 Jo. Bapt. Porta de Munctione ——— *Neap.*1608

597 Vincent. Viviani Enodatio Problematum Gallicor. ———*Florent.*1677

598 Pauli Caſati Terra Machinis Mota ——— *Rom.* 1658

599 Lib. Fromondi Labyrinthus ſive de Compoſitione Continui *Ant.* 1631

600 *De Beghinſelendor Weeghconſt beſchreven duer Sim. Stevit.* *Leyd.*1686

601 Ludov. à Ceulen de Circulo & Adſcriptis——— ———*L. Bat.* 1619

602 ⎧ Hieron. Sirturi Teleſcopium ——— *Franc.* 1618
   ⎪ Nicol. Cheſnecopheri Iſagoge Optica——— *Ibid.* 1593
   ⎨ Jo. Marc. Marci Thaumantia, de Arcu cœleſti, &c. *Frag.* 1648
   ⎩ Pet. Borellus de vero Teleſcopii Inventore *Hag.* 1655

603 Jo.Haftman. Beyeri Stereometriæ inanium nova ratio. *Franc.*1603

604 Jo. Bapt. Balian. de motu Naturali gravium Solid.& Liquid.*Gen.* 1646

605 Corn. Gemma de Arte Cyclognomica *Apud Plant.*1569

606 Ren. Franc. Sluſii Meſolabum. ——— ——— *Leod.* 1668

607 Franc. Maurolyci Coſmographia ——— *Ven.* 1570

608 *Faques Beſſon, le Coſmolabie ou Inſtrument Univerſel* ——— *Par.* 1567

609 ⎧ Wilebr. Snellii Apollonius Batavus ——— *Lugd.*1608
   ⎨ ———Tiphys Batavus ſive de Navium curſib. ———*L.Bat.*1624
   ⎩ ———Cyclometricus, de Circuli dimenſione ———*Ibid.*1621

610 ———Eratoſthenes Batavus de Terra ambitus quantitate *Ibid.* 1617

611 *Delle Vite de i Filoſofi tratte de Laertio, con Fig.* ——— *Ven.* 1598

612 Jo. Mich. Moſcheroſch Imago Reipub. Argentinenſis *Argent.*1648

613 Catalogus Libror. in Bibliotheca Colleg. Sionii ——— *Lond.* 1650

614 ———Libror. in Bibliotheca Bodleiana ——— *Oxon.*1620

Libri

Libri Latini, &c. *in Octavo.*

1   VEtus Teftamentum, Hebraicè cum punctis *Amft.* 1635
  Novum Teftamentum, Græcè ——— *Ibid.* 1635
2 Biblia S. Latinè uná cum Apocrypha, (Titulus Deeft.)
3 ——— Idem, nec non Liturgia & Pfalmi Metr. in Lingua Cambro-
 Britannico   *Lond.* 1674
4 ——— Idem in Sermone Belgico *Leyd.* 1637
5 Vet. Teftam. & Apocrypha Græcè ex verf. LXX. Interpr. cum Schol.
 apud Daniel   1653
6 Nov. Teftam. Gr. & Lat. *apud H. Steph.* 1567
7 ———in Lingua Belgica *Dord.* 1606
8 Pfalmi Proverbia, &c. Hebr. & Lat. interlin.
9 *The Pfal.and Lament.in Hebr.and its reading in Eng.Let.byW.R.Lond.*1655
10 H. Grotius de Veritate Relig. Chriftianæ Arabicè
11 Libr. M.S. Arabice, pulcherrime exaratus in nitidiffimam Chartam.—
12 Chrift. Sandij Interpret. Paradoxa in 4. Evangelift. 167c
13——— Nucleus Hift. Ecclefiaft, in 3 partib. . 1569
14 D. Auguftinus de Civit. Dei cum Lud. Vivis Com. 2 Vol. *Gen.* 1622
15 Franc. Potteri Interpretatio Numeri 666 *Amft.* 1677
16 Tho. Smith de Græc. Ecclef. hodierno Statu *Lond.* 1578
17 T. Tullie præcipuor. Theol. capit. Enchirid. Dedicat. *Lond.* 1668
18 *Wol. Geriften und gefchnidten figuren Aufz. der Bibel.* *Lyon.* 1564
19 *Impiete des Deifts & Libertiens renverfée & refutée* *Par.* 1630
20 Rob. Sharrock de Officijs fecundum Naturæ Jus *Oxon.* 1660
21 Tho. Lydiat de variis Annorum formis *Lond.* 1609
22 Ifr. Spacci Nomenclat. Script. Philof. & Philol. *Argent.* 1598
23 Henneng. Witten. Memor. Philof. Orat. &c. Decad. 4. *Fr.* 1672
24 Tho. Lydiat de var. Ann. form. contr. Jof. Scaligerum. *Lond.* 1607
25 Jo. Henr. Alftedii Thefaurus Chronologicus ——— *Herb.* 1650
26 *G. Marcel, Tablettes Chronologiques* *Amft.* 1687
27 Tho. Rivii Hiftoria Navalis *Lond.* 1629
28 Tho. Gore Nomenclator Geographicus *Oxon.* 1667
29 Pii 2. Pon. Max. Afiæ Europæq; Defcriptio *Par.* 1534
30 Chrift. Adrichomii urbis Hierofolymæ Defcript. *Col. Agr.* 1583
31 Jo. Leonis totius Africæ Defcriptio. *Antv.* 1556
32 Pet. Martyr de Orbe Novo cum Annot. R. Hakluyti *Par.* 1587
33 Nova novi Orbis Hiftoria 1578
34 Bernh. Venenii defcript. Saponiæ & Siam *Cantab* 1673
35 Tho. Stanleii Hiftor. Philof. Oriental. cum Not. Jo. Clerici. *Amft.* 1690
36 Levin. Apollonius de Peruviæ intentione *Ant.* 1567
37 *Hiftoire des Indes de Jean Pierne Maftée* *Lyon* 1604
38 *Recueil de Voyages de Mr. Thevenot* *Pan.* 1681
39 *Voyage de Siam des Peres Jefuites, avec des Fig.* *Amft.* 1688
40 *Viage de Pedro Teixeria de la India bafta Italia*
41 Itinerarium Benjamini. Lat. per Ben. Ar. Montanum *C. Plant.* 1575
42 *Voyages de Jean Mocquet,* *avec des Fig.*
43 *Relation de la Nouvelle France en* 1636, 1638, 1644, & 45, *par B. Vimont.*
 3 Vol.   *Par.* 1646
44 *Hiftoria de la Guerra de Tartaria* *Madr.* 1665
45 Jul. Cæf. Recupitus de Vefuviano Incendio *Neap.* 1633
          46 Ph.

46 Ph. Jac. Hartmann Succini Pruffici Hift. ——— Franc. 1677
47 Mart. Martinij Hift. Sinica ——— Amft. 1659
48 *Voyage faict par Terre jufques à la China* ——— Par. 1630
49 *Journal du Voyage de Siam* ——— Amft. 1687
50 *Viaggia da Venetia ab Santo Sepolcro* ——— Ven. 1606 o
51 { Albert. Compenfis de Mofcovia — Ibid. 1543
   { *Hiftoria della du Samatie di Matth. di Micheovo* — Vineg. 1561
52 Guil. Camdeni Britannica ——— Lond. 1587
53 Geo. Hornius de Originib. Americanis Haga 1652 o
54 { Jo. de Laet Notæ ad Diff. H.Grotij de orig. Gent. Amer. Amft. 1643
   { ——— Refponf. ad Differt. fecundam H. Grotij ——— Ibib. 1644
55 N. Trigantij Literæ Societ. Jefu è regno Sinarum Aug. Vind. 1615
56 *Anticitta della Citta di Puzzuolo, cum Fig.* Nap. 1606 o
57 Dan. á Goes Reb. Hifpanic. Luft. Aragon. & Æthiop. Col. Agr. 1602 o
58 Herodoti Hiftor. Lat. á Laur Valla ——— o
59 Leon. Allatij Apes Urbanæ fivæ de Viris illuftrib. Rom. 1633
60 Infignium aliquot Virorum Icones. Apud Tornæf. 1559 o
61 *Les Memoirs de la Roime Marguerite* ——— Pan. 1628 o o
62 Melch. Adami Vitæ Germanor. Medicor. ——— Heidelb. 1620 o
63 ——— Vitæ Theologor. exterorum ——— Franc. 1680 o
64 Hadn. Valefij Vita Henrici Valefii ——— Lipf. 1680 o
65 Pauli Jovii Elogia Doctor. Virorum Baf. 1571 o
66 Mich. Maierus de Legib. Fraternitatis Franc. 1618 o
67 Rob. Sharrock de variis Incontinentiæ Specieb. Oxon. 1662 o
68 Homeri Ilias & Odyffea Gr. Lat. 2 Vol. ——— Cantab. 1664 o
69 ——— Nepanthes feu de abolendo Luctu Lugd. ——— o o o
70 Poetæ Minores Gr. Lat.   (Caret Titulo) o
71 Heftiadi Opera Gr. Lat. Notis Melanchthonis Witteb. 1623
72 Ex Veter. Comicor. Fabulis Sententiæ Gr. Lat. apud Morel. 1553 o
73 Ifocratis Orationes Græce ——— Baf. ——— o o
74 Opera Gr. Lat. caret Titulo. o o
75 Æfopi, Babriæ, &c. Fabulæ Gr. Lat. cum Not. & Figuris Franc. 1610 o
76 Xenophon de Cyri Vita & Difciplina, Gr. Lat. Ingolft. 1600
77 Dionyf. Longinus Gr. Dat. cum Notis Ger. Langbait Oxon. 1638 o o
78 P. Ovidii Metamorphofis cum Notis Tho. Farnabij. Lond. 1636
79 —Metamorphof. Hiftorica,Natur.Moral. Ecphraf. cum Fig. Franc.1619 o
80 *Metamorphofes en Rondeaux enrichis de figuris* ——— Amft. 1679 o
81 ——— Metamorphof. Belgice cum Fig. ——— Ant. 1608
82 Gabr. Faerni Centum Fabulæ Lond. 1672
83 Marcel Palingenij Zodiachus Vitæ Lond. 1639
84 An. Marl. Sever. Boetij Confol. Philof. cum Not. Varior. L.'Bat. 1671
85 Fabij Quintiliani Opera Gr. 1625
86 C. Julij Cæfaris Commentarij Apud. Gryph. 1551 o o
87 M. T. Ciceronis Opera, 2 Vol. è Dion. Lambina Aurel. 1608 o
88 ——— Epiftolæ ad Atticum Hannov. 1609
89 ——— Epiftolæ ad Familiares, apud R. Steph. 1543 o
90 Amiani Marcellini Hiftoria apud R. Steph. 1544 o
91 T. Pomponius Atticus five de Tranquilitate Vitæ Hannov. 1598 o o
92 Natal. Comitis Mythologia Gen. 1653 o
93 Terrent. Varror de Ling. Lat. & de Re Ruft. cum Scaligeri Notis 1581 o
94 M.Porc. Cato de Re Ruft. cum Not.A. Popmæ & J.Meurfij Franc. 1620
95 Conr. Heresbachii Rei Ruftiæ Libri 4, ——— Spicæ 1594 o

95 Nic.

144 ————Epitome Radicum Hebraicar. & Chaldaicar.————Baſ. 1607
145 Jo. Henr. Hottingeri Cippi Hebraici.——— Heidelb. 1662
146 *Jo. Vdall's Key to the Holy Tongue* ———— —— Leyd. 1593
147 { *Jo. Buxtorfs ſhort Introduct. to the Hebrew Tongue*——Lond. 1656
{ Wilh. Schickardi Rota Hebræa pro facilitate conjugandi Lipſ.1636
148 Jac. Welleri Grammatica Græca nova ———— Ibid. 1663
149 Theod. Gazæ Inſtitutiones Grammaticæ ———— —— Par. 1539
150 Othon. Gualtperii Grammatica Græca——— ——Marp. 1606
151 Mart. Rulandi Synonymia Latino-Græca——— ——Gen. 1646
152 Matth. Martinii Cadmus Græco-Phænix ———— Brem. 1625
153 Balt. Garthii Lexicon Latino-Græcum —— Franc. 1613
154 Busbeii Rudim. Anglo-Latin. Gram. Literalis & Numeral. Lond.1688
155 ————Rudiment. Grammaticæ Græco Latinæ Metricum—Ibid. 1689
156 Wilh. Baxter de Analogia ſive Arte Lat. Ling. —— Ibid. 1679
157 J. A. Comenii Janua Linguar.reſerata. Lat. Gall. & Belg. —Amſt.1638
158 ————Idem, Latine & Anglice——— ——Lond. 1673
159 ————Latinæ Ling. Janua reſerata. cum Fig. Lat. & Angl. Ibid.1658
160 ————Orbis Senſualium Pictus, Lat. & Angl. cum Fig.—Lond.1659
161 Chriſt. Becman. de Originib. Lat. Ling. ———— 1613
162 Sethi Calviſii Thaſaurus Latini Sermonis ——Lipſ. 1634
163 Tho. Draxe Bibliotheca Scholaſtica——— Lond. 1633
164 Promptuarium Latin. Ling. Apud Plant. 1571
165 A. Lovel Index Univerſalis —— Lond. 1679
166 Schol. Wintonienſ. Phraſes Latin. Ibid. 1654
167 Jo. Wallis Grammatica Ling. Anglicana Oxf.1674
168 Jo. Davies Linguæ Cambro-Britannicæ rudimenta —— Lond. 1621
169 *Grammaire Francoiſe de Claude Mauger* —— Ibid. 1679
170 *Dialogues Francoiſes, par J. N. Parival.* —— Leyd. 1659
171 *Dictionaire Francois-Latin, par Charles Pajot* ——Lyon. 1655
172 *Oudin, Grammaire Eſpagnole* Bruxel.1639
173 Henr. Doerganck Inſtitutiones in Linguam Hiſpanic. — Colon. 1614
174 *Loven. Francioſini, Grammatica Spagnuola & Italiana* —— Gen. 1648
175 *M. de la Molliere, Portuguez Grammar.* ——Lond. 1662
176 *Gio. Torriano, Introduction to the Italian Tongue* Ibid. 1657
177 *Gio. Molino, Dittionaria della Lingua Italiano, Turchaſι* — Rom. 1641
178 *Nomenclatura Italiana, Franceſe & Spagnuola* — Ven. 1629
179 *The Dutch-Tutor, or, A New Book of Dutch and Engliſh* — Lond.
180 Dueſii Compend. Grammaticæ Germanicæ ——Amſt. 1668
181 *Hen. Oſſelen, German and Engliſh Grammar* ——Lond. 1687
182 Corn. Kiliani Dusſlei Etymologicum Teutonica Ling. Alem. 1613
183 Pet. Daſypodii Dictionarium Latino-Germanicum——Argent.
184 *Rog. William's Key into the Language of America* —— 1643
185 Logica ſive Ars Cogitandi Lond. 1677
186 Rob. Sanderſoni Logicæ & Phyſicæ Artis Compendium — Oxon. 1672
187 Aug. Nunnæi Dialectica —— C. Plant. 1573
188 Joh. Chriſt. Sturmii Philoſophia Eclectica, h. e. Exercitat. Academ. Altd. 1686
189 { Gilb. Clerke de reſtitutione Corporum —— Lond. 1662
{ Nonnus in S. Joannem, Gr.——
190 Joh. Phocylidis Holvardæ Philoſophia Naturalis—Franek. 1651
91 Othon. Caſmanni Scholæ Philoſophicæ——— —— Han. 1596
92 Ant. le Grand Inſtitutio Philoſophiæ ——— Lond. 1672
F.   193 Giordano

E 2   290 Hieron:

340 Erhardi Weigelii Philofophia Mathematica, &c. ——— Jenæ 1691.
341 Barth. Keckermanni Syftema compendiof.totius Mathemat. Oxon.1661
342 P. Rami Proæmium Mathematicum ——— ——— Par. 1567
343 Jof. Langii Elementale Mathematicum ——— ———Frib. 1612
344 Jo. Jac. Heinlini Synoplis Mathematica Univerfalis———Tubin. 1663
345 P. Horigonis Curfus Mathematicus, Lat. Gall. 5 Vol.———Par.
346 Maur. Steinmatz Arithmeticæ præcepta ——— ———Lipf.1575
347 Jac. Peletarii Arithmetica practica ——— ——— Par.
348 Hudubr. Regii utriufque Arithmeticæ Epitome ——— ——— 1536
349 Chr. Clavii Epitome Arithmeticæ practicæ——— ——— Rom. 1585
350 Cl. Buxerii Ludus Pythagoreas(qui Rythmomachia nominat.)Pan.1556
351 { Jo. Camerar. de Græcis Latinifque Numeror. Notis———
    { Arn. Delens in Geometrica Elementa Eifagoge---Apud C. Plant.1565
352 Adr. Metii Manuale Arithmeticæ & Geometriæ practicæ Franek. 1646
353 D. Henriom, Sommaire de l'Algebre.——— ———Par. 1623
354 Andr. Tacquet Arithmeticæ Theoria & Praxis———Ant.1665
355 ———Elementa Geomet. plan. & folid. ——— ——— Ant. 1665
356 Jod. Willichii Arithmeticæ Libri tres ——— ——— Argent. 1640
357 L'Arithmetique de Gemme Phifon ——— Anv. 1582
358 Hier. Cardani Arithmetica practica ——— ———Mediol.1539
359 L'Arithmetique de Simon Stevin avec des Annot. par Alb. Girard.
                                                    Leiden 1625
360 Jo. Tho. Fregii Quæftiones Geometricæ & Stereometricæ—Baf. 1583
361 La Geometrie reduite en une facile practique. ——— ———Par. 1626
362 Car. Bovilli Geometricum opus ——— ·——— Apud Morell. 1557
363 Jo. Vogelin Elementa Geometriæ ——— ———
364 Jo. Wallis Elenchus Geometriæ Hobbianæ——— —Oxon. 1655
365 Guil. Bleau Inftitutio Aftronomica ——— Amft. 1668
366 Eberh. Welperi Compendium Aftronomiæ ——— Argent. 1634
367 { Erh. Weigelii Aftronomiæ pars Sphærica ——— Jenæ. 1657
    { Wilh. Schickardi Aftrofcopium ——— Nordl. 659
368 Setqi Wardi Aftronomia Geometrica ——— ——— Lond. 1656
369 Pet. Crugeri Doctrina Aftronomiæ Spherica ——— Dant. 1635
370 Nicol. Mercatoris Inftitutiones Aftronom.——— ———Lond. 1676
371 Annulus Aftronomicus, una cum Meteorofcopio ——— Lutet. 1558
372 Muham. Alfragani Chronolog. & Aftronomica Elementa per J. Chrift-
    mannum———————Franc. 1590
373 Rob. Dodonæus de Aftron. & Geograp. principis —Apud Plant.1584.
374 Mich. Mæftlini Epitome Aftronomiæ ——— Tub.1624
375 Jo. Kepleri Epitome Aftronomiæ Copernicano ——— Franc. 1635
376 Sidereus Nuncius ——— ——— Lond. 1653
377 Adr. Metii Univerf. Aftronom. Inftitutio. ——— Franek. 1605
378 ———De Genuino ufu utriufque Globi ——— —Amft. 1626
379 Jo. Ant. Magini novæ Cœleftium Orbium Theor. Mog. 1608
380 Proclus de Sphæra, Cleomedes de Mundo & Dionyfii Defcr. Orbis,
    Gr. Lat. · ——— Ant. 1553
381 Rob. Hues de Globis & eorum ufu——— · ——— Lond. 1594
382 Jo. de Sacro Bofco Sphæra emendata ——— Col. 1594
383 Tho. Lydiat de Anni Solaris Menfura——— ——— Lond. 1621
384 Cunr. Aflach. de natura Cœli triplicis ——— ——Sigen. 1597
385 Guidi Ubaldi Planifpherior. Univerfalium Theoria——— Col. 1581
386 Jo. Stoflerin, de ufu Aftrolabii ——— ——— Par. 1585
                                                    387 Geo.

431 Lib. Fromondi Meteorologicor. Libri 6.——— ———*Oxon.* 1639
432 { Fab. Sommer. de inventione, defcriptione, &c. Thermar. Car. 4.
     Imper. ————————————————*Lipf.* 1571
     Jo. Bokelius de Catarrho febrili————————*Helmft.* 1580
433 Lud. Septelius de Nævis—————————————*Patav.* 1628
434 Andr. Lucanæ Method. Cognofcendi, & Excrefcentes in Veſica collo
     Carunculas————————————————*Oliſip.* 1560
435 Jo. Fernelius de Luis Venereæ curatione——— ———.*apud Plant.* 1579
436 Ant. Mizaldi Hiftoria Hortenfium—————————*Col. Agr.* 1577
437 *Recueil de diverfes pieces touchant quelques nouvelles Machines. Caft.* 1695
438 *Lovis Savot l'Architecture Francoife*——————————*Paris* 1624
439 *Reigles des 5 Ordres d'Architect de Vinole, revenes par le Muet. Amft.*
440 M. Vitruvius de Architectura, *cum Fig. Titulus deeft*———————
441 *La Pratique du Trait à preuves de M. Defargies par A. Bofte. Paris* 1643
442 *Gugl. Chovi fopro la Caftremat.& Bagni antichi de i Gr. & Rom.* ———1559
443 *Architecture de Vitruve en Abrege par M. Porault*—————*Amft.* 1681
444 *Des Manieres de graver en Taille Douce par A.Bofte. avec Fig. Paris* 1645
445 { Iſagogos Mufic. Libr. duo per M. Cyriac. Snegaffium————1596
     Cum XI. aliis ad eand. Scientiam Spectantib. ———————
446 Jo. Wigandi vera Hiftor. de Succino Boruffico————— *Jena*
447 Lexicon Januale h. e. Latin. Linguæ Sylva, 2 Vol.———————1650
448 Raymundi Lullii Opera————————————*Argent.* 1598
449 Viror. Clariffim. Epiſt. circa aliquot Chymica Experim. *Hamb.* 1673
450 Domin. Maffarius de ponderibus. & menfuris medicinalib.—*Tig.* 1584
451 Andr. Reyheri Synopfis totius Philofophiæ———————*Gothæ* 1669
452 Tho. Lydiat de Natura Cœli & conditionib. Elementor.—*Lond.* 1605
453 Franc. Baroccii Cofmographia in 4 Libris——————*Ven.* 1585
454 Franc. Maurolyci Cofmographia ————————*Paris* 1558
455 Nath. Carpentarii Philofophia Libera————————*Oxon.* 1622
456 J. Swammerdam, De Uteri Muliebris fabrica cum Not. J. van Horn
     Lond. 1680
457 *Cæf. D'Arcons du Flux & Reflux de la Mer.*———— ———*Rouen* 1655
458 *M. de Froidur fes Travaux qui fe font en Languedoc pour la communicat.*
     des deux Meus ——— ——— ———*Touloufe* 1672
459 Gafp. Schotti Anatomia Phyfico-Hydroftat.Font.& Flum. *Herbip.* 1663
460 Chr. Franc. Paullini Lagographia feu Leporis Defcript. *Aug.Vind.*1691
461 Henr. Crolach. Gotthanus de Cultura Herb. Ifatidis————*Tig.*
462 Nic. Dortomannus de caufis & effectib.Thermar. Belilucan.*Lugd.* 1579
463 D. Becheri Novum Organon Philologicum ——————*Franc.* 1674
464 Tho. Hobbes Elementa Philofophiæ de Corpore ——— *Lond.* 1655
465 *Beroerde Oceaan door* Arnoldus Montenus, cum Fig.———*Amft.* 1655
466 Femiani Stradæ de Bello Belgico Decas prima————*Ant.* 1649
467 Ger. J. Voffius de Rhetorices Natura & antiquis Rhetorib. *L.Bat.* 1622
468 Tho. Bartholin. de Bibliothecæ Incendio——— ———*Hafn.* 1670
469 A. Janffonii Mundus furiofus ——— ————*Col. Agr.* 1598
470 Mich. Neandri Orbis Terræ partium explicatio ——*Lipf.* 1586
471 Jo. Filefacus de Idololatria Magica———————*Paris* 1609
472 Jo. Bapt. Porta de Occultis Literar. Notis ———*Argent.* 1606
473 ———De Humana Phyfiognomia————————*Franc.* 1618
474 Jo. Henr. Alftedii Clavis Artis Lullianæ——————*Argent.* 1652
475 Jo. Keil Introductio ad veran Phyficam——————*Oxon.* 1702
476 Rob. Plott de Origine Fontium ——— ————*Oxon.* 1685
                                 477 *Bern.*

Libri Latini, &c. in Duodecimo.

33 *Viaggi*

33 *Viaggio Pittorefco d'Italia da Giac Barri* —————————— *Ven.* 1671
34 ——*Di Pietro della Valle il Peregrino,* 4 *Vol.* ———— *Bolog.* 1672
35 *Voyages de l'Empereur de la Chine, dans la Tartarie* ——— *Par.* 1695
36 ——*De M. le Marquis de Ville au Levant* ———— *Amft.* 1671
37 ————*Du Chev. Chardin en Perfe & aux Ind. Orient. avec Fig. Ibid.* 1685
38 ————*On divers Etats d'Europe & d'Afie, avec Fig.* ——— *Par.* 1693
39 ————*En Angleterre, par M. Sorbiera* ——— *Col.* 1666
40 *Rel. de l'Amb. du Chev. de Chaumont à du Roy de Siam, avec Fig. Amft.* 1685
41 Vitæ Philofophor. à Diog. Laert. Eunapio & Hefychio. *Apud Raph.* 1595
42 *La Vie de Jean Bapt. Colbert, Miniftra d'Etat* ———— *Col.* 1695
43 ————*De M. Des Cartes, contenant l'Hift. de la Philefphie*——*Par.* 1693
44 Leon. Cozzand. de Magifterio Antiquor. Philofophor. —— *Gen.* 1684
45 L. Feneftella de Magiftratibus Sace, dotiifque Romanum — *Rothom.* 1606
46 Homeri Ilias, Gr. — *Gen.* 1622
47 Luciani Dialogi Selecti, Gr. & Lat. ———— *Lond.* 1649
48 Theognidis, Phocylididis, Pyrhag. &c. Poemata Gromica, G. L. *Ultraj.* 1602
49 Æfopi Fabulæ, Gr. & Lat. *cum Fig.* ————— *Ludg.* 1609
50 Ant. Liberalis Metamorpho'eos, Gr. Lat. ab Abr. Berkeiio. *L. B at.* 1674
51 Æliani Variæ Hiftoriæ Libri xiiii. Gr. Lat. ————*Col. All.* 1625
52 L. Ann. Senecæ Epiftolæ ex recentione Lipfii & Gronovii *L. Bat.* 1649
53 —Op. omnia ex rec. Lipfii & Gronovii, cum pofterior notis, 4V. *Amft.* 1659
54 C. Plinii Cæc. Sec. Epiftolæ & Panegyric. cum Not. If. Cafauboni 1605
55 L. Apuleii Opera omnia, recognita & emendata ———— *Rapheling.* 1610
56 Juftini Hiftoria, cum Not. If. Voffi ——— *Oxon.* 1669
57 Auli Gellii Noctes Atticæ ———*Aur. Allob.* 1609
58 Macrobii Opera, recognita & aucta ————————1607
59 M. T. Cicero de Philofophia, 2 Tom. in uno Vol. ——— *Ludg.* 1562
60 ——Opera Rhetorica, 2 Tom. in uno Vol. ——— *Ibid.* 1578
61 Jo. Barclaii Argenis, cum Clave ————*Apud Elziv.* 1627
62 ——Euphormionis Satyricon ———— *Amft.* 1628
63 Pub. Virgilii Opera, cum Notis Tho. Farnabii ——— *Ibid.* 1642
64 P. Ovidii Metamorphofis, cum Not. Tho. Farnabii ——— *Ibid.* 1650
65 M. Accii Plauti Comœdiæ ex recentione Doulica ——*L. Bat.* 1589
66 Br. Waltoni Introd. ad Lectionem Linguam Orientalium —*Lond.* 1655
67 Jo. Claii Grammatica Germ. Ling. ——— *Ifleb.* 1604
68 Synonyma five Copia Vocum Hebraicar. ——— *Lond.* 1647
69 Syllabus Ling. Latin. & Suav. ——— *Holm.* 1649
70 Franc. Pomey Indicul. Univerfalis Latino-Germanicus *Norimb.* 1671
71 Geo. Paforis Manuale Gr. N. Teftamenti Vocum ——— *Herb.* 1624
72 ——Syllabus Gr. Lat. omnium N. Teftam. Vocum——*Amft.* 1650
73 Bon. Hepburni Lexicon S. Ling. fuccinctum
74 Ger. Jo. Voffii, & alior. de Studior. ratione opufcula—*Ultraj.* 1651
75 Jof. Webb Carmen Hexametrum & Pentametrum ——*Lond.* 1626
76 Tho. Farnabii Index Rhetoricus & Oratorius ——— *Lond.*
77 Chrift. Helvici familiaria Colloquia —— ——— *Lond.* 1652
78 Adagiorum D. Erafmi Epitome ——— *Amft.* 1650
79 Bibliotheca Heinfiana five Catalog. Libror. Nic. Henfii —*L. Bat.*
80 ——Chymica à Pet. Borellio. ——— *Par.* 1654
81 Corn. à Beughem Bibliographia Medica & Phyfica ——— *Amft.* 1681
82 Catalog. Libr. qui in Bibliopolio Van Elfevirii venales extant-*Ibid.* 1674
83 Fr. Baconi de Verulamio Sermones fideles Ethici, Politici, &c.-*Ibid.* 1662
84 ————De Augmentis Scientiarum, Lib. 9.——— ———*Ibid.* 1662

F   85 ——— Novum

85 ———Novum Organum Scientiar. ——— ——— *L. Bat.* 1650
86 ———De Sapientia Veterum ——— *Lond.* 1617
87 ———Scripta in Naturali & Universali Philosophia ——— *Amst.* 1653
88 *Recueil des Conferences publiques du Bureau d'Adresse,* 5 Vol.—*Par.* 1666
89 *La Poverta, Contenta, descritta da Dan. Bartoli.* ——— *Milan.* 1657
90 David. Abercrombii Fur Academicus ——— ——— *Amst.* 1689
91 Tho. White Sciri, sive Sceptices a jure Disputationis exclusio-*Lond.*1663
92 E. Leichneri Gymnasiosophia, *h. e.* viva Idea Gymnasii———*Franc.*1687
93 Jo. Meursii Theophrastus sive de illius Libris qui injuria Tempor. inter-
cider. ——— ——— ——— *L. Bat.* 1640
94 *Instruction pour la Teinture des Laines & Manufact. de Laine* 1671
94 Jani Cæc. Freg. Via ad Scientias discendas ——— ——— *Par.* 1628
96 *Juizo Historico, Juridico, Politico sobre, a Par entre a Cor. de Franca*
& Castella ——— ——— ——— *Lisb.* 1666
97 Mer. Casaubon de Verborum usu ——— ——— *Lond.* 1647
98 Ant. Nerus de Arte Vitraria cum notis Chr. Merretti *Amst.* 1686
99 Thom. Bartholini de Unicornu observationes, *cum Fig.* *Ibid.* 1678
100 Hier. Cardanus de propria Vita ——— ——— *Amst.* 1654
101 Mich. Radau Orator extemporaneus sive Artis Orator. Brev. *Ibid.*1673
102 Ant. Mezaldi Memorabilium sive Arcanor. omnis generis, Cent9. *Col.* 1574
103 Sardi Venales Satyra Menippea, à P. Cunæo ——— *Jen.* 1617
104 Ger. Jo. Vossius de cognitione sui *Amst.* 1654
105 Literæ Pseudo-Senatus Angl. Cromwellii, &c. script. a J. Miltono—1676
106 Jamblichus de Mysterii Ægyptiorum *Ludg.* 1571
107 { *La Legende du Gascon, ou la Let. de C. Drelincourt, à M Porrée-lb.* 1674
{ Car. Drelincurtii Apologio Medica *L. Bat.* 1672
108 ———Libitinæ Trophæa, pro Concione computata———*Ibid.* 1680
109 *L'Escole des Filles ou la Philosophie des Dames* ——— 1668
110 Eccard. Leichneri Schediasma de Intelligentia vera & enormo 1687
111 Hug. Grotii Tragœdia Sophampæneas, &c. *Amst.* 1635
112 Martialis Epigrammata in usum Schol. Westmonas. *Lond.* 1655
113 Nugæ Venales sive Thesaurus Ridendi & Jocandi — 1644
114 Manuale Rer. admirabilium & Abstrusarum — *Hamb.* 1610
115 *Le Journal des Scavans de l'Ann.* 1665. *jusque a l'Ann.* 1694. *inclusive,*
in 24 Vol. *Amst.*
116 *Jugemens des Scavans sur les principaux Ouvrages des Autures,* 9 Vol.
Par. 1685
117 *Memoirs concernants les Acts & les Sciences de l'Ann.* 1672. 1672
118 *Histoire des Ouvrages des Scavans, Sept.*1687. *Juin, Juillet, Aoust* 1691.
Dec. 1692. *Jan. Febr. Juin, Juillet, Aoust, Dec.* 1693. *Jan. Feb.*
Mars, Avril, Mai, Sept. Octob, Novemb. 1694. *Mars, Avril, Mai,*
Juin, Juillet, Aoust 1695. ——— *Roter.*
119 *Mercure Scavant, Jan. Febr.* 1684. *Amst.*
120 *Bibliotheque Universelle, pour les Ann.* 1688. 89, 93. *Amst.*
121 *Nouvelles de la Repub. des Lettres pour les Annees* 1684, 85, 86, 87.
& Octob. 1702. *Amst.*
122 *La Fr. Scavante, i. e.* Gallia erudita, &c. à Corn. â Beughem—*Amst.*1683
123 Chr. Juncker. de Ephemeridib. sive Diariis Eruditor. in Europa *Lips.*1692
124 Acta Philosophica Societ. Reg. in Anglia, *Ann.*1665.66. 69. 3 Vol.
125 *La Logique ou l'Art de penser* ——— *Amst.*1675
126 Tho. White Institutiones Peripatetice *Lond.* 1647
127 Jo. Jonstoni Enchiridion Ethicum ——— *Bregæ.* 1658
120 Antoni

Libri Latini, &c. *in* 16°. 18°. 24°. 32°.

15 M.

English Books in Folio.

29 The

29 The 3d Univerfity of Engl. or Foundat. of all the Colleg. &c. in and
near London. —————— ——— ———— 1615
30 W. Dugdale's Hift. of St. Paul's Cath. of Lond. with Fig.   Ibid. 1658
31 Inigo Jones's Stoneheng reftored, with Fig.   Ibid. 1655
32 P Rycaut's pref. State of the Ottom. Empire, with Fig.   Ibid. 1668
33 The Heroick Acts of P. Maurice of Naffaw   —————
34 Rob. Knox's Hift. Rel. of the I. of Ceylon in the E. Ind, with Fig. Ib. 1681
35 R. Ligon's Hift. of the Ifland of Barbary, with Fig.   Ibid. 1673
36 Tho. Gage's Survey of the Weft-Indies   ———— Ibid. 1648
37 Jo. Smith's Hift. of Virgin. N. Engl. and the Sum. Ifles, with Maps Ib. 1672
38 Hiftor. Relat. of the Kingdom of Siam, with Fig.   Ibid. 1693
39 G. Wheeler's Journey into Greece, with Fig.   Ibid. 1682
40 Trav. of Piet. del. Valle in E. India or Arabia Deferta   Ibid. 1665
41 —of G. Sandy's into Turkey, Ægypt, Hol. Land, &c. with Fig. Ibid. 1627
42 —of Vin. le Blanc into the E. and W. Indies, &c.   Ibid. 1560
43 —of Sr. T. Herbert into Africa and Afia the Great, with Fig. Ibid. 1667
44 —of Sir J. Chardin into Perfia and the E. Ind. with Fig.   Ibid. 1684
45 —of J. Fryer into E. India and Perfia, with Fig. interleav'd. Ibid. 1698
46 Voyages and Travels of the Ambaffad. of the D. of Holftein, into
Mufcovy and Perfia, with Fig.   ———— Ibid. 1662
47 — J. Bapt. Tavernier thro' Turk. into Perf. and the E. In. with Fig. Ib. 1678
48 — of Fern. Mendez Pinto into Ethiop. China, Tartaria, &c.   Ibid. 1653
49 —of Sir. R. Hawkins into the South Sea   ———— Ibid. 1622
50 —Trafficks and Difcoveries of the Eng. Nation, Publifh'd by Richard
Hackluyt, 3 Toms, 2 Vol.   ———— Ibid. 1599
51 Sam. Purchas's Pilgrims and Pilgrimage, 5 Vol.   — Ibid. 1625
52 The Eng. Atlas, with Mapps. pnblifh. by Mont. Pitt. Vol. 1,2,and 3, Oxm.
53 Abrah. Ortelius's Theatre of the whole World, with Mapps Ibid. 1675
54 Jo. Seller's Sea-Charts, with Mapps   ———— Ibid. 1657
55 The Sea Atlas or the Water-World, with Mapps   Amft. 1669
56 Lewis Roberts's Merchant's Mapp of Commerce   Lond. 1671
57 Plutarch's Lives of the Noble Grecians and Romans, &c. Cambr. 1675
58 Morals Tranflated by Philem. Holland   ———— Lond. 1657
59 Thucydides Hift. of the Pelopon. War, Tranf. by T. Hobbes Ibid. 1629
60 Xenophon's Hift. of the Afcent of Cyrus, Tranf. by J. Bingham Ibid. 1623
61 Homer's Iliads Tranf. into Verfe, by G. Chapman,
62 L. Ann. Seneca's Works, Tranf. by Tho. Lodge   Ibid. 1620
63 Corn. Tacitus's Hift. with Annotat. by H. Savile   ———— 1591
64 Ovid's Metamorphof. in Verfe, by G. Sandys, with Fig.   Oxf. 1632
65 Juvenal and Perfius Tranf. and Illuft. with S. and N. by B. Holiday Oxf. 1673
66 M. Manilius's Sph. made an Engl. P. An. & Fig. by Sr. Ed. Serb. Lond. 1675
67 Æfop's Fab. with his L. in E. F and Lat. with Sculp. by F. Barlow Ib. 1666
68 Fr. Beaumont and J. Fletcher's Comedies and Tragedies   Ibid. 1647
69 Tho. Killigrew's Comedies and Tragedies   ———— Ibid. 1664
70 Edm. Spencer's Works, wants the Title.   ———— Ibid. 1611
71 Abraham Cowley's Poems   ———— Ibid. 1656
72 Tho. Stanley's Hiftory of Philofophy, 3 Vol.   ———— Ibid. 1660
73 Dutches of Newcaftle's Philofoph. & Phyfical Opinions   Ibid. 1663
74 —Obfervations upon Experimental Philofophy.   Ibid. 1666
75 Franc. L. Bacon's Natural Hiftory, &c.   Ibid. 1664
76 —of the Advancement and Proficiency of Learning   Oxf. 1640
77 — Works Civil, Hiftorical, Philofophical and Theological. Lond. 1657
78 Bp.

78 Bp. Wilkin's Essay tow. the real Charact. large Pap. with Cutts *Ib.*1668
79 Sir K. Digby, of the Nature of Bodies and of Man's Soul. L. P. *Par.* 1644
80 N. Grew's Catal. of the Rarit. in Gresh. College, with Fig. *Ibid.* 1681
81 — Anatomy of Plants, with Fig. large Paper   *Ibid.* 1682
82 Os. Gabelhover's Book of Physick, Transf. out of H. Dutch. *Dort* 1599
83 Ch. Wiltzun's Pract. of Physick Transf. and Enl. by J. Mosham, wants Tit.
84 Helk Crook's Descript. of the Body of Man, with Fig.   *Lond.* 1615
85 S. Collin's System of Anat. with Fig. 2 Vol.   *Ibid.* 1685
86 Alex. Pitfield's Natural Hist. of Animals, with Fig.   *Ibid.* 1688
87 Fr. Willughby's Ornithology or Descript. of Birds, with Fig. *Ibid.*1678
88 J. Parkinson's Gard. of Flowers and of Herbs and Orch. with Fig. *Ib.*1629
89 — Theatre of Plants, or Compleat Herbal, with Fig.   *Ibid.* 1640
90 Rich Wiseman's Chirurgical Treatises   *Ibid.* 1676
91 M. Choras's Royal Pharmacop. Galenical and Chymical   *Ibid.* 1578
92 Sr. Jo. Pettus Fodinæ Regalis   *Ibid.* 1670
93 — Laws of Art and Nat. in knowing, &c. of Metals, with Fig. *Ibid.* 1683
94 Euclid's Elem. with Annotat. and a Pref. by Jo. Dee, with Fig. *Ib.* 1570
95 Dr. Jo. Wallis's Algebra, Historical and Practical. with Fig. *Ibid.* 1685
96 Jo. Kersey's Elements of Algebra, Vol. 2.   *Ibid.* 1673
97 W. Leybourn's Dialling, Plain, Concave, Convex, &c. with Fig. *Ib.*1682
98 T. Salisbury's Mathemat Collect. and Translations.   *Ibid.* 1661
99 T. Morlay's Introduct. to Practical Musick   *Ibid.* 1597
100 J. Blagrave's Mathematical Jewel   *Ibid.* ——
101 Tho. Digger's Pantometra, with Fig.   *Ibid.* 1591
102 Vinc. Wing's Harmonicon Cœleste   *Ibid* 1651
103 J. Goad's Aphorisms of the Bodies Cœlest. their Nat. &c. *Ibid.* 1686
104 Edw. Hayward's Sizes and Lengths of Riggions for Ships *Ibid.* 1660
105 Alex. Brown, of Drawing, Paint Limn. and Etch. with Fig. *Ib.* 1669
106 Will. Sanderson's Use of the Pen and Pencil   — *Ibid.* 1658
107 A Book of Drawing, Limn. Wash. &c. of Mapps and Prints *Ib.* 1666
108 Jos. Moxon's Practical Perspective, with Fig. wants the Tit. ——
109 F. Freart's Paral. of Ancient. Arch. with the M. by J. Evelyn, with C. *Ib.*1694
110 Bardon's Tables and Accomps
111 Jo. Babington of Artificial Fireworks, with Fig.   *Ibid.* 1635
112 Nic. Tartaglia of shooting in Pieces of Artillery   *Ibid.* 1588
113 Alex. Francine's Architecture Publish. by R. Prick, with Fig. *Ib.* 1669
114 Jacob de Gheyn's Exercise of Arms for Cavaleers, Muskets and
    Pikes, adorn'd with curious Cutts   *Hague* 1680
115 Stat. at large, from M. Chart. till the 29 of Q. Elizabeth. *Lond.* 1587
116 F. Pulton's Stat. now in Use, continued by T. Manby   *Ibid.* 1670
117 T. Blount's Law Dictionary   *Ibid.* 1670
118 Mic. Dalton's Country Justice   *Ibib.* 1677
119 Will. Sheppard's Law of Common Assucances   — *Ibid.* 1669
120 T. Fuller's Hist. of the Holy War   *Cambr.* 1639
121 — Holy and Profane State, with Fig.   . *Ibid.* 1642
122 Dr. Cudworth's True Intellect. Syst. of the World   *Lond.* 1678
123 Philip's New World of Words, or Engl. Dictionary   *Ibid.* 1678
124 Gr. Malynes's Lex Mercatoria, or the Anc. Law-Merch. *Ibid.* 1622
125 The Merchant's Mapp of Com. by L. Roberts with Mapps *Ib.* 1677
126 Philostratus's Life of Apol. Tyanæus with Notes by C. Blount, *Ibid.* 1680
127 Burton's Anatomy of Melancholy   — *Ibid.* 1699
128 Mich. de Montaign's Essays, with an Index   *Ibid.* 1632
                        229 Jo.

128 John Lockers Effay concerning Human Underftanding *Lond.* 1690
129 John Evelyns Dif. of Forreft Trees and Propag. of Timber 1670
130 Relat. of what paffed between Dr. Dee and fome Spirits, by
    M. Cafaubon   *Lond.* 1659
131 Traj. Boccalins Advertifements from Parneffus   *ibid.* 1656
132 ———— Idem ———— the 3d. Edit. corrected   *ibid.* 1674
133 Dr. Thomas Burnets Theory of the Earth, the Two firft Books
    with Fig.   *London* 1684
134 The Sizes and Lengths of Riggigns for Ships and Frigats *ibid.* 1660
135 Wings cœleftial Harmony of the vifible World   *ibid.* 1651
136 Book of Phyfick tranflat. out of High-dutch by C. Bates *Dort.* 1599
137 A Geographical Table of all the Towns, Parifhes, *&c.* in *England*
    and *Wales*
138 Abraham Bloëmaerts Book of Drawings
139 A New Hiftorical Relation of the Kingdom of Siam———wants the
    Title, *&c.*
140 John Ogilbys Affrica or Defcription of Ægypt, Barbary, *&c.*
    with Maps (in Quires)   *Lond.* 1670
141 ——— Afia or Defcription of Perfia, *&c.* with Maps in (Quires)
                                                    Lond. 1673
142 ——— America or Defcription of the New World, with Maps
    (in Quires)   *ibid.* 1671
143 ——— Embaffy of the Dutch Eaft India Company to China, with
    Maps   *ibid.* 1669
144 ——— Atlas Chinenfis or the fecond part of the Embaffy to China,
    with Maps   *ibid.* 1671
145 ——— Atlas Japannenfis or Embaffy of the Dutch Eaft India Com-
    pany to the Emperor of Japan with Maps   *ibid.* 1670
146 ——— Britannia, or the Roads of Eng. and Wales with Maps *ib.* 1675
147 Homers Iliads and Odyffes with Sculpt. and Annot. 2 vol. *ib.* 1669

English Books in QUARTO.

1 Simons Critic. Enquir. into the var. Edit. of the Bible *Lond.* 1674
2 Edw. Leighs *Critica Sacra* or Philol. and Theol. Obferv. of the
    N. T.   *ibid.* 1648
3 Ph. Fletchers way to Bleffednefs or Comment. on the 1 Pfal. *ib.* 1632
4 Rich. Turnbulls Expofit. on the Epift. of St. James   *ib.* 1606
5 John Boys's Expofit. of the Feftival Epiftles and Gofpels *ib* 1613
6 John Calvins Serm. on the Epift. of the Galathians   *ib.* 1574
7 P. Haufteds 10 Serm. upon Sundays and Saints days   *ib.* 1636
8 John Gregorys Works   *ib.* 1671
9 John Daille of the right ufe of the Fathers   *ib.* 1651
10 Tho. Swadlin, the Jefuit the chief if not the only State Heretic 1647
11 Dr. Geo. Abbot againft Dr. Hill   *Oxf.* 1604
12 John Pocklintons dead Vicars Plea   *Lond.* 1637
13 A. Cades Juftificat. of the Church of England   1630
14 Rich. Rogers his 7 Treatifes   *Lond.* 1630
15 Sam. Gareys Great Britains little Calendar   *ibid.* 1618
16 Th. James of the Corrupt. of the Fathers, *&c.* by the Ch. of Rome 1611
17 John Crellius of one God the Father   1655
18 The Faith of One God affected and defended in feveral Tracts 1691

G

G 2

                                      153 *Musæ*

English Books in Octavo.

49 of

91 Journal

143 Auc.

296 Elements

English Books in *Duodecimo.*

57 *Tho.*

57 *Tho. Hobbes* of Liberty and Neceſſity, with Obſervations — 1677
58 *Forges's* Catalogue of Rarities
59 *W. Cocke's* foreſeeing the Alteration of the Weather — 1671
60 Sir *William Petty's* Uſe of duplicate Proportion — 1674,
61 Curing of Fevers and Agues by Jeſuit's Powder — 1681
62 *T. Hale's* Account of new Inventions and Improvements — 1691
63 Manner of making Coffee, Tea, and Chocolate — 1685
64 *Rob. Lovell's* compleat Herbal — *Oxf* 1659
65 Right Courſe of preſerving Health — *Cambr.* 1636
66 *Harvey's* Family Phyſician and Houſe Apothecary — *Lond.* 1676
67 The Deaf and Dumb Man's Friend — 1648
68 *Du Clas's* Obſervations on the Mineral Waters of *France* — 1684
69 *Medicina Statica*, or the Rules of Health — 1676
70 Diſſection of the Muſcles of the Affections — 1649
71 *Amman's Iccking's* deaf Man — 1694
72 *J. Cooke's* Obſervation on English Bodies — 1657
73 *R. Raniſter* of the Diſeaſes of the Eyes — 1622
74 Cure of Diſeaſes by Signature
75 Frier *Bacon* of the Miracles of Art, Nature, and Magick 1659
76 *Dunworth's* Doctreſs, or curing of Womens Diſeaſes 1656
77 *Tho. Lawrence* of Subterranean Cockle, Muſcle, &c. 1664
78 The Marrow of Chymical Phyſick — 1669
79 *Franc.* Lord *Bacon's* Hiſtory of Life and Death — 1638
80 — Natur. and Experient. Hiſtory of Winds — 1653
81 *Sam. Gilbert's* Floriſts Vade Mecum 1682
82 *Will. Huges* Flower-Garden and Compleat Vineyard — 1683
83 — *America* Phyſician — 1672
84 *Rob. Boyles* Collect. of choice Remedies in 2 parts — 1693
85 — Heads for a Natural Hiſtory of a Country — 1692
86 *Tho. Houghtons* compleat Miners — 1681
87 Deſcription of a Numerical Table of Proportion — 1681
88 *Rich. Belams* Algebra — 1653
89 *Nepair's* Table of Logarithms, by *H. Bridges* — 1618
90 *Edm. Wingates* uſe of the Logarithmetical Tables — 1648

Libri in Albiis, in Folio.

1 *Loyſii Ferdin. Comit. Marſigli Danubial operis* *Prodrom.* 1700
2 *Gronden en Afbeel dſelo der voornaemſte Gebowen, van*
  alle die Phil. Vingboon's } *Amſt.* 1665
3 Horticus Indicus Malabaricus, *cum Fig.* 4 primi Tomi *Amſt.* 1677
4 Jo. Bapt. Nicoloſii Hercules Siculus, *cum Tab.* Geogr. *Rom.* 1670
5 Jac. Breynii Exoticar. Plantar. Centuriar, *cum Fig.* *Ged.* 1678
6 Kircheri, Collegii Rom. Soc. Jeſu Muſeum, *cum Fig.* *Amſt.* 1678
7 *Maniere de Baſtir par P. le Muet, avec Fig.* *Par.* 1623
8 Marc. Malpighii Anatome Plantan, *cum Fig.* *Lond.* 1675
9 — Opera Poſthuma, *cum Fig.* *Lond.* 1697
10 Jo. Hevelii Prodromus Aſtronomiæ, *cum Fig.* *Ged.* 1690
11 — Annus Climactericus, *cum Fig.* *ibid.* 1685
12 — De Motu Lunæ Libratorio, *cum Fig.* *ibid.* 1654

13 De—

Libri in Albiis in Quarto.

28 Jo. Jouſius de Scriptorib. Hiſtoriæ Philoſophicæ——— *Franc.* 1659
29 Exercitatio Theoricon Copernico Cœleſtium ——— 1689
30 Vander Linden de Scriptis Medicis continuat. à G. A. Merch-
lino. ——— ——— *Nor.* 1686
31 Gaſp. Schotti Iter Exſtaticum Kircherianum ——— *Herbip.* 1671
32 *De Americaonſche Zee Roovers,* cum Fig. ——— 1678
33 Jo. Gabr. Schmidt de Valvulis ——— · ——— 1681
34 Jo. Chr. Sturuii ad Henn. Morum Epiſtolæ ——— *Norimb.* 1685
35 Eraſm. Bartholin. de Naturæ Mirabilib. ——— *Hafn.* 1674
36 *Naeuve Keurige Beſchrivingi van Oud & Nieum Greonland.* ——— 1678
37 Lothar Zumbach Planeto labium. ——— ——— *L. Bat.* 1691
38 Caſp. Bartholin. de Fontium Fluviorumque Origine ex Pluviis.
Hafn. 1689
39 Euclides reſtitutus à Jo. Alph. Borellio ——— *Piſis* 1658
40 *Swammerdam Hiſt. Generale des Inſectes* ——— *Utr.* 1685
41 Ol. Borichius de uſu Plantar. indigena in Medicina ——— *Hafn.* 1690
42 Ragnetani Specimen Problemat. Hercoteſtonico Geometric. *Am.* 1646
43 Jo. Prætorii Elucidarium Uraniæ ——— *Norib.*
44 Exercitatio de Antipathia Nationum ——— ——— *Lipſ.* 1661
45 Jo. Schuler de Cometis. ——— *Hage* 1665
46 Fr. Halli explicatio Horologii in ·Horto Regio *Londini* *Leod.* 1673
47 Dan. Geo. Morhof. de Scypho Viorio ——— *Kilon.* 1682
48 Jo. Marci Othoſophia ſeu Philoſophia Impulſus ——— *Prage* 1682
49 Excerpta ex Literis ad Jo. Herelium de Reb. Aſtronomic. *Ged.* 1683
50 Epiſtola ad Jo. Ott. Halbigium à Duumviris Hermeticis *Ged.* 1681
51 Jo. Jac. Zimmerman Prodomus Biceps ——— *Stutg.* 1679
52 Cometica Obſervationes habitæ ab Acad. Romana ——— *Rom.* 1681
53 Salem. Reiſelii Sipho Wurtemburgicus ——— *Stutg.*
54 Azikus Neſephæus de Cognitione Dei & Hominis ——— *Col.* 1665
55 De voc. de Beck. de Eclipſe Solis Futura, 1684——— *Hamb.* 1683
56 Mich. Eogoni ClavisMed. ad Chinar. doſtr. de pulſib. ——— 1686
57 Jo. Chr. Sturmii Collegii Experimentalis, *Pars 2da.* *Norimb.* 1685

Libri in Albis in Octavo.

1 Iberii de Sancto Amore Epiſt. Theologicæ ——— *Iren.* 1679
2 *I Salme di David in Rime Italiane de Gio. Diodate* ——— *Hael.* 1664
3 *La Geographie Royale par Ph. Labbe* ——— ——— *Gren.* 1658
4 Th. J. ab Almeloveen Bibliotheca promiſſa & latens *Gaudæ* 1692
5 Jo. Groningii Bibliotheca Univerſalis -——— *Hamb.* 1701
6 Ant. Van Dalen de Oraculis, *cum Fig.* ——— *Amſt.* 1683
7 Sam. Dieſt. Clavis Linguæ Sanctæ ——— *Amſt.* 1669
8 Ehren. Hagendorn de Catechu ſive Terra Japonica——— *Jenæ* 1679
9 Ph. Jac. Hartmann Succini i ruſſici Hiſtoria ——— *Franc.* 1677
10 Bibl. Pickeimeri Deſcr. Germaniæ utriuſque ——— *C. Plant.* 1585
11 *La Morale de Confucius* ——— *Amſt.* 1688
12 *N. Sanſon, Introduction à la Geographie* ——— *Utr.* 1692
13 Fr. Arioſt. de Oleo Montio Zibini *Hafn.* 1690
14 Jo. Helf Junken Chymia Experimentalis *Franc.* 1681
15 Jo. Geo. Greulichius de Bile ſana & ægra ——— *Franc.* 1682
16 Obſervat. Phyſ. & Mathemat. par l' Acad. Royale ——— *Par.* 1688
17 Jac. Bernoull. de gravitate Ætheris *Amſt.*
18 Sethi Wardi Aſtronomia Geometrica ——— *Lond.* 1656
19 *Bened.*

Libri in Albiis, &c.

Engliſh Books in Quires in *Folio*.

Engliſh Books in Quires in *Quarto*.

FINIS.

APPENDIX,

TO

Dr. HOOKE's *Catalogue.*

English *Miscellanies*, *in* Folio.

1 Ogilby's (*John*) *Africa*, with Cuts and Maps, Tit. —*Lond.* 1670
2 Burnet's (Bp. *Gilb.*) History of the Reformation, Part I.—1681
3 *Boccace*'s Tales, Old and Imperfect ——— ——— ———
4 *Cabala* : Or Mysteries of State, Third Edition ——————1691
5 *Coke's* (*Edw.*) Institutes, Part I. Seventh Edition ———1670
6 *Knox's* (*Rob.*) History of *Ceylon*, with Cuts ———1681
7 *Cornelius Tacitus*, in *English* ——— ———1591
8 *Tyrrel's* History of *England*, G. B.————
9 Lord *Bacon's* History of King *Henry* VII. ——— ———1622
10 *Caxton's* (*Will.*) Collections, &c. ———1490
11 *Rushworth's* (*Jo.*) Tryal of *Thomas* Earl of *Strafford*——1680
12 *Sandford's* (*Fran.*) Genealogical History of the Kings of *England*, with Fig. ——— ——— ———1677

English *Miscellanies*, &c. *in* Quarto.

1 Staunforde's Pleas of the Crown, with the King's Prerogative 1583
2 *Thomas's* (*Will.*) History of *Italy*——— ———1549
3 *Mascal*, (*Leon.*) Of Planting and Grafting, Stitcht——— ———1582
4 *Markham's* (*Geo.*) Soldiers Exercise ——— ———1643
5 *Peacham's* (*Hen.*) Compleat Gentleman ——— ———1661
6 *Selden's* (*John*) History of Tythes ——— ———1618
7 *Godwin's* (*Tho.*) *Roman* and *Jewish*; and *Rouse's* Attick Antiqities, Compleat, G. B.——— ———1674

English *Miscellanies*, *in* Octavo *and* Duodecimo.

1 Theory of Sciences ——— ———
2 *Salmon's* (Dr. *Will.*) Polygraphice, with Fig.——— ———1675
3 *Wingate's* (*Edw.*) and *Kersey's* Arithmetick——— ———1673
4 *Gaffarel's* (*James*) Unheard of Curiosities ——— ———1550
5 Terms of the Law——— ——— ———1636
6 *Osborn's* (Sir *Fr.*) Works ——— ———1673
7 *Plutarch's* Lives, Vol. II. with Cuts, G. B.——— ———1684
8 *Gage's* (*Tho.*) Survey of the *West-Indies* ——— ———1677
9 *Lucas's* (*Rich.*) Duty of Servants, Old——— ———1685
10 *Oughtred's* (*W.*) Circles of Proportion——— *Oxford* 1660
11 *Fuller's* Worthies ——— ———
12 *Jones*, Of Opium ——— ———
13 *Wilkins's* (*Jo.*) Mathematical Magick——— ———1680
14 *Torriano's* (*Geo.*) *Italian* and *English* Grammar ——— ———1673
15 *Casaubon*, (*Mer.*) Of Credulity and Incredulity——— ———1670
16 *Britannia Languens*: Or, a Discourse of Trade——— ———1680
17 *Boyle's* (*Rob.*) Christian Virtuoso, Tom. I. ——— ———1690
18 *Evelin's* (*J.*) *Sculptura*: Or History of Chalcography, with Figures, Bd. Bl. Turky and Gilt Leaves ——— ———1662
19 *Mackenzy's* (Sir *Geo.*) Moral History of Frugality——— ———1691
20 Memoirs of *France* ———

A   21 *Blount's*

Libri Miscellanei in Folio.

17 Durerus (Alb.) de Symetria partium humanar.————
18 Budæus (Guil.) de Affe & partibus ejus ——————*Baf.* 1556
19 Stephani (Car.) Dictionarum Hiftor. Geogr. Poeticum cum addition.
    Nic. Lloydii——— ——— ———*Oxon.* 1670
20 Euclidis Elementa Gr. Lat. Tit.—————————*Lond.* 1620
21 Poggii Opera —— ——— ————————1513
22 Hiftoriæ Romanæ Scriptores Græci Minores, Gr. Lat. cum Not. Frid.
    Sylburgii——— *Franc.* 1590

Libri Miscellanei, &c. *in* Quarto.

1 IGnatii Martyris Epift. Genuinæ, &c. cum Notis If. Voffii, Gr. Lat.
       \ *Lond.* 1680.
2 Sparavierii (Fr.) Caftigationes ad Apologiam,Th. Mazzæ,&c. Tit. 1676
3 Gaffendi (Pet.) Vita Piereskii ——— ——— *H. Com.* 1655
4 Grapaldus (Fr. Mar.) de Partibus Ædium, &c. & Platina de Honefta
    Voluptate——— ——— ——— ———*Parm.* 1516
5 Marianæ (Jo.) Hiftoria de Rebus Hifpaniæ——————*Mog.* 1605
6 Niphii (Aug.) Opufcula Moralia & Politica————*Paris* 1645
7 Naudæi (Gab.) Syntagma de Studio Militari————*Romæ* 1637
8 Bembi (Pet.) Rerum Venetarum Hiftoria——— ——— *Lut.* 1551
9 Bonifacii Rhodigini (Balt.) Hiftoria Ludicra————*Brux.* 1656
10 Virgilii (Pub.) Opera cum Servii Comment.————*C. Allob.* 1620
11 Antoninus de Seipfo cum Comment. Th. Gatakeri Gr. Lat. D. D.
       Cant. 1652
12 Boetii de Boodt (Anf.) Gemmarum & Lapidum Hiftoria — *Han.* 1609
13 Crackanthorpi (Ri.) Logica Quarta Edit. D. D.———*Oxon.* 1677
14 Batefii (Guil.) Vitæ Selectorum aliquot Virorum charta Maj. Tit.
       Lond. 1681
15 Fracaftorii (Hen.) Opera omnia ——— ——— *Ven.* 1584
16 Stephani (Hen.) Lexicon Græc. Lat. Epitom.— ——————*Ol.* 1607
17 Politani (Aug.) Sylva feu Rufticus cum Beraldi Interp.——*Baf.* 1518
18 Gaffendus (Pet.) de Vita & Moribus Epicuri—————*H.Com.* 1656
19 Beveregii (Guil.) Inftitut. Chronologicæ——— ——— *Lond.* 1669
20 Ennii (Q.) Annales & Fragmenta a P. Merula———————*L.Bat.*1595
21 Plinii (Caii) Hiftoria Naturalis in Uf. Delph. 5 Vol. D. D. *Paris* 1685
22 Gratianus (Ant. Mar.) de Vita Jo. Francifci Commendoni Cardinalis
       Paris 1669
23 Lucilii (C.) Satyrarum Reliqüiæ cum F. Doufa Notis ——*L. Bat.* 1597
24 Junius (Fr.) de Pictura Veterum——— ——————*Amft.* 1635
25 Jo. Camilli Exercitationos Mathematicæ——— ——————*Neap.* 1627
26 Alex. Marchettus de Refiftentia Solidorum ——— ——— *Flor.* 1669
27 Ren. Franc. Slufii Mefolabium——— ——————*Leod.* 1668
28 Jo. Kepleri ad Vitellionem Paralipomena —————*Franc.* 1624
29 Joan. Trithemii Steganographia—————————*Darmbft.* 1621
30 Franc. Maurolyci Mathematica——— ————————*Ven.* 1575
31 Euclidis Data Gr. Lat. cum Claudii Hardy Notis ——— *Paris* 1625
32 Geor. Germanni Calendarium Triplex——— ——— *Franc.*
33 Erafm. Bartholin. de Cometis Ann. 1664,65.———————*Hafn.* 1665
34 Jo. Bapt. Porta de Refractione Optices——————*Neap.* 1593
35 Steph. de Angelis de Superficie Ungulæ—————*Ven.* 1661

Libri Miscellanei in Octavo & Duodecimo.

46 Macrobii (A. Theod.) Opera, cum Notis ——— ——*L. Bat.* 1597
47 Palearii (Aon-) Epiftolæ, Orationes & de animorum Immortalitate.
——————————————*Gryph.* 1552
48 Camdeni, (Guil.) Annales Rerum Anglic. &c. ———— *Amft.* 1677
49 Labbe (Phil.) Bibliotheca Bibliothecarum ——— *Roth.* 1678
50 Græca Gramat. ad ufum Scholæ Weftmonaft. ——— *Lond.* 1671
51 Biblia Sacra ——————————————*Gen.* 1583
52 Leflæi (Jo.) afflicti animi confolat. & animi tranquilli Muniment. &
confervatio ——— ——— *Par.* 1574
53 Orationes Funebres in Morte Principum, Imperatorum, &c.*Han.* 1613
54 Rapinus (Ren.) de Hortis, Meurfii Arboretum Sacrum & Politiani
Rufticus——— ——— ——— *Ultr.* 1672
55 Grammatica Oxonienf. ——— ——————*Oxon.* 1675
56 Guagnini (Alex.) Res Polonicæ ——— ——— *Franc.* 1584
57 Hues (Rob.) Tract. de Globis ——— ———*Oxon.* 1663
58 Mantuani Bucolica, cum J. Badii Comment. ———*Ant.* 1559
59 Caftilio (Balth.) de Curiali five Aulico ——— ——*Lond.* 1603
60 Doctiffim. noftra ætate Italorum Epigram. ——— 1547
61 Cardanus (Hier.) de Sapientia & Confolat ——— ——*Aur.* 1624
62 Clementis Epiftolæ duæ ad Corinthios. Gr. Lat. ——— *Lond.* 1687
63 Lactantii (Cæl.) Opera——— ——— *Aldus* 1535
64 Batei (Geo.) Elenchus Motuum nuper. in Anglia & Skynneri Elenchus, &c. compact. ——— ——— *Lond.* 1676
65 Biblia Sacra ——— ——— ——— *Amft.* 1648
66 Saleii (And.) Ethica——— ——— ———*Oxon.* 1680
67 Jo. Sarisberienfis Policraticus——— ——— *L. Bat.* 1595
68 Bonfinius (Aut.) de Pudicitia conjugali ——— *Baf.*
69 Tho. Mori Opera ——— ——— *Baf.* 1563
70 Whear (Deg.) Methodus Legendi Hiftorias——— ——*Cant.* 1684
71 Cato (Porc.) de Agricultura ——— ——— 1598
72 Bruti (Jo. Mich.) Epiftolæ Selectæ——— ——*Crac.* 1583
73 Sanderfonus (Rob.) de Obligat. Confcientiæ ——— *Lond.* 1682
74 Goreccii (Loon.) Defcriptio Belli Juonicæ, &c. ——— *Franc.* 1578
75 Garnerii (Phil.) Gemulæ Gall. Lat. & Germ. Linguar.—*Arg.* 1628
76 Janfonii ab Almeloveen, (Theod.) de Vitis Stephanorum.*Amft.* 1683
77 Lomeier (Jo.) de Bibliothecis ——— *Ultr.* 1680
78 Perroniana five Excerpta ex Ore Perronii ——— *Gen.* 1667
79 Eutropii Hift. Romanæ cum Diaconi Addit. ——— *L. Bat.* 1592
80 Schefferus (Jo.) de Arte Pingendi ——— *Nor.* 1669
81 Arifteneti Epiftolæ, Gr. Lat. cum Notis ——— *Par.* 1596
82 Euftachii (Fr.) Ethica ——— ——— *Lond.* 1677
83 Grotii (Hug.) Catechifmus in Ang. Lat. & Græc. Carm. ——— 1650
84 Longolii (Chrift.) Epiftolæ ——— *Baf.* 1570
85 Faria (Tho. de) Lufiadum, lib. 10. ——— *Ulyff.* 1622
86 Phalaridis Tyranni Epiftolæ, Gr. Lat. ——— ———*Baf.* 1558
87 Cowleii (Abr.) Poemata Latina ——— *Lond.* 1678
88 Anthologia feu Poemata Italorum ——— ———1584
89 Epicteti Enchiridion, Gr. Lat. ——— ———*Oxon.* 1680
90 Ifocratis Orationes 2. ad Demonic. & ad Nicocleu, G. L. ———1677
91 Scaligerana ——— ——— ———*C. Agr.* 1657
92 Heereboord (Adr.) Philofophia Naturalis ——— *Oxon.* 1679
93 J. Lucretius de Rerum Natura cum Tan. Fabri Notis———*Cant.* 1675
94 Val.

Vigesim

Vigesimo Quarto.

142 Donzellini (Hier.) Remedinm serendarum Injuriarum L. Bat. 1635
143 Bacon (Franc.) de Sapientia Veterum ——— ———1633
144 Salluftius Philof. de Diis & Mundo ——— ———1639
145 Nov. Teftament. Græc. ——— ——— Elʒ. Amft. 1670
146 Buchanani (Geo.) Poemata, Tit. ——— 1676
147 Busbequii (Gifl.) Epiftolæ ——— ———1660
148 Pap. Statii Opera, cum Fr. Gronovij Not. 1653
149 Cardanis (Hier.) de Prudentia Civili ——Elʒ. L. Bat. 1635
150 Terentii Comediæ——— ——— ——Cant.——
151 Apuleii Madaur. Platonicus——— Amft. 1624
152 Silius Italicus de Bello Punice ——— 1631
153 Comicorum Græcorum Sententiæ, Gr. Lat.——H. Steph. 1569
154 Refpublica Italiæ——— L. Bat.
155 ———Hifpaniæ——— ———1629
156 ———Arabiæ ——— Amft. 1633
157 ——— Conftantinopoleos ——— —L. Bat. 1632
158 Dictus Cretenfis de Bello Trojano, &c. ——— Amft. 1631
159 T. Petronii Arbitri Satyricon, cum J. Bofchii Notis ——1677
160 Lipfius de Conftantia ——— 1652
161 Oweni (Jo.) Epigrammata ———Elʒ. L. Bat. 1628
162 Benjaminis Itinerarium ——— Ibid. 1633

8vo, 120, & 240.

163 Ciceronis (M. T.) Philofophica, 2 Tom. 1 Vol. ——Arg. 1574
164 ———de Officiis, Cato Major de Senect. &c.——— ———1669
165 ———de Officiis, &c. 240. ——Roth. 1665
166 Barclaii (Jo.) Icon Animorum, fol. deaur.——— Franc. 1625
167 ———Argenis ——— Elʒ. L. Bat. 1630
168 Baconi (Fran.) Sermones Fideles ——— Amft. 1662
169 ———de Augmentis Scientiarum ——— L. Bat. 1652
170 ———Novum Organum ——— 1650
171 Fr. Sylvii De le Boe Opera, 2 Tom. 1 Vol. Par. 1671
172 Auli Gellii Noctes Atticæ ——Amft. 1666
173 Erafmus (Def.) de Linguæ ufu atque abufu ——L. Bat. 1641
174 ———Enchiridion Militis Chriftiani ——— ———1641
175 ———de Confcribendis Epiftolis——— ——Amft. 1670
176 T. Lucretius de Rerum Natura, cum T. Creech Notis—Oxon. 1695
177 Cardanus (Hier.) de Utilitate ——— ——Amft. 1672
178 Petavii (Dion.) Rationarium ——— ——Par. 1688
179 Virgilii (Pub.) Opera——— ——Ex Offic. Elʒiv. Amft. 1676
180 Sannazarii (Act. Sync.) Opera, cum Notis ——Amft. 1689
181 M. T. Ciceronis de Officiis, lib. 3.——Ex Offic. Elʒev. Amft. 1656
182 ———Opera, in 10 Tom. & 8 Vol.——Elʒ. L. Bat. 1642
183 Grotius (Hug.) de Veritate Relig. Chriftianæ, cum ejufd. Annotat.
——— Ex Offic. Elʒiv. Amft. 1675
184 Dan. Heinfii in Q. Horatii Opera Animadv. & Notæ. Tit. L. Bat. 1629
185 Pfalterium Davidis ad Exemplar Vaticanum 1592.——Elʒv. Iugd. 1653
186 Terentii (Pub.) Comediæ Sex ——— ——I. Bat. 1635

187 Corn.

186 Corn. Taciti Opera ——— ——— ——— *Eliz. L. Bat.* 1634
187 Merlini Cocai Macaronicorum Opus ——— ——— *Ven.* 1573
188 Ovidii (P.) Gpera ——— 24°. ——— *Tit. Eliz. Amst.* 1664
189 Catullus Tibullus Propertius ——— 24° *Eliz. Amst.* 1651
190 Erasmi Moriæ Enconmium ——— 24° ——— *L. Bat.* 1624

Libri Gallici in Folio.

1 Bude (Guil.) de l'Institution du Prince ——— ——— 1547
2 B Cl. Irson Methode pour bien dresser toutes Sortes de Comptes——— ——— ——— ——— *Par.* 178

Libri Gallici in Quarto.

1 LA Nove (Seign. de) Discours Politiques & Militaires ---*Baf.* 1597
2 L Neufville Sr. de Villeroy (Nic. de) Memoires &c. ——— *Par.* 1622
3 Frangidelphe (M.) Hist. de la Mappe Monde Papistique———1567
4 Serre (Sr. de la) le Miroir qui ne Flate point — Fol. deaur. — 1632
5 Belon (Pier.) les observat. de plusieur Singularitez &c. ——— 1555
6 De Tristan les Amours ——— le Mariane Tragedie———*Par.* } 1638
     Le Cid Tragi-Comedie— les Visionaires Comediæ— } —37
7 Perefixe (Hard. de) Histoire du Roy Henry le Grand———1662

Libri Gallici in Octavo & Duodecimo.

1 DE Ville (Ant.) les Fortifications avec Fig. ——— *Par.* 1656
2 D De Malherbe (M.) les Poesies avec les observat. } *Par.* 1666
    de Monsr. Menage ——— ——— }
3 Marolles (M. de) Catalogue de livres D'Estampes } *Par.* 1666
    & de Figures en Taille Douce——— }
4 Houssaie (Amel. de la) Hist. du Governem. de Venise——— *Par.* 1677
5 Nouvelle Maniére de Fortifier les Places &c, ——— 1689
6 Mattheu (P.) de la Mort de Hen. IV, Roy de France ——— 1613
7 La Liturgie de L'Eglise Anglicane ——— 1665
8 Gelee (Theorph.) l'Anatomie Francoise——— 1939
9 La Bible ——— ——— *Gen.* 1605
10 Du Vair (du Sr.) les Oeuvres ——— *Rov.* 1636
11 Abraham (Jean) l'Arithmetique ——— ——— *Rov.* 1628
12 De Seneque les Authoritez Sentences &c. Lat. Franc. ———
13 Quevedo Villegas (Dom. Fr. de) les Oeuvres ——— *Rou.* 1645
14 Belley Mr. de) les Evenemens Singuliers ——— 1643
15 De Mellin de S. Gelais les Oeuvres Poetiques——— *Lyon* 1574
16 Wicquefort (Mr. de) Memoires touchant les Am- } *la Haye*—1677
    bassadeurs & les Ministers Publics ——— }
17 Coeffeateau (F. N.) Tableau des Passions humaines—— *Par.* 1630
18 Sr. Theophile les Oeuvres ——— *Rov.* 1648
19 Aubery (Lovis) Memoires de Hollande ——— *Par.* 1687
20 De Aristophane Comedies Grecques Trad. par Mad. Dacier *Par.* 1692

                                       22 Maurice

21 Maurice *(de S.)* le Guide fidele les Etrangers dans le Voyage de France ——— *Par.* 1672

22 Dialogues de la Sante ——— *Par.* 1683

23 Hiftoire de Theodofe le Grand par Mr. Flechier ——— 1681

24 Sr. de la Croix Memoires ——— en 2 Tom. 1 Vol. — 1684

25 Bernier *(F.)* Abrege de la Philofophie de Mr. Gaffendi ——— 1677

26 Quinte-Curce de laVie d'Alexandre le Grand. Trad. par fer Monfr. de Ryer —1668

27 Laffels (Rich.) Voyage d' Italie ——— 1671

28 Chevræana ou diverfes Renfees par Mr. Chevreau ——— 1700

29 Hire *(Mr. de la)* l' Art de Tracer des Cardans ——— *Par.* 1682

30 Picard (M.) Traito du Nivellement ——— 1684

31 Le Chev. de Mere de la Converfation ——— —1677

32 D'Anacreon & de Sapho Franc. Græc. avec des Remarques par Madam le Fevre —1681

33 Sr. de Varillus Hift. Secrete de la Maifon de Medicis ——— *Hage* 1685

34 D'Anacreon & de Sapho les Oeuvres Franc. & Græc. par Mr. de Longepierre ——— *Par.* 1692

35 De Mr. Conrard a Mr. Felibien Lettres Familieres ——— 1681

36 Gracian (Balt.) l' homine de trompe ou le Criticon ——— 1696

37 De Mr. L. C. D. Rocfort les Memoires &c. ——— *Col.* 1687

38 Mr. Efprit la Fauffete des Vertus humaines ——— *Par.* 1693

39 Le Chevalier de Mere de l' Efprit ——— 1677

40 Mr. de Vaugelas Remarques fur la langue Francoife ——— 1672

41 Bourfault (des Monfr.) Lettres de Refpect &c. ——— 1683

42 Les Converfations D. M. D. C. E. D. C. D. M. ——— *Par.* 1671

43 Le Chev. le Mere Difcours des Agremens ——— 1677

44 Le Divorce de l' Amour & de l' Hymenée — Voyage de Bachaumont & la Chapelle ——— les Noyers &c. —

45 Bouhours (P.) Ponfées Ingenieufes des anciens & des Mod. — 1692

46 Eutretiens Galans en 2 Tom. 1 Vol. ——— 1681

47 Noms des Pointres les plus celebres & les plus connus &c. ———1679

48 Hiftoire de Henry Duc de Rohan Pair de France ——— 1656

49 Petit (Monfr. Dialogues Satyriques & Moraux ——— *Amft.* 1688

50 Hiftoire des plus illuftres Favoris anciens & Modernes———*Leyd.*1661

51 Traite de l' Arinan ——— avec Fig. *Amft.* 1687

52 Sorel (M. C.) la Bibliotheque Francoife ——— *Par.* 1667

53 Gallois (Sr. le) Traitte des plus Belles Bibliotheques de l' Europe —1680

54 D' Eftrées Memoires de la Regne Marie de Medicis ———*Par.* 1673

55 Monfr. Blondel Nouvelle Maniere de Fortifier les Places *Hage* 1685

56 Bonair *(Sr. de)* de l' Hiftoire de France avec Fig. ——— *Par.* 6?60

57 Critique du 9. livre de l' Hift. de M. Varillas &c. ———*Amft.* 1686

58 De le Duc de Bovillon les Memoires ——— *Par.* 1666

59 Rome Ancienne & Moderne ——— *Par.* 1671

60 Glafer (Chrift.) Traite de la Chymie avec Fig. ——— 1678

61 Le Traite du Sublime & Oeuvres diverfes — *Par.* 1674

62 Nouvelles Reflexions fur l' Art Poetique ——— 1668

63 Le Nouveau Teftament — *Cha.* 1668

64 Le Parfoit Capitaine avec l' Interoft des Princes ——— 1667

B 65 Teftament

213

111 Le

B 2   152 De

152 De Monf. le Chevalier de Mere les Lettres en 2 Vol.———*Paris* 1682

153 Perrault, M. Parallelle des anciens & des Modernes en 2 Vol. *Ibid.* 1693

154 Thomas, A. Hiftoire des plus illuftres & Scavans Hommes de Leurs Series en 8 Vol. ——— ——— ———*Ibid.* 1671

155 Olon, Monf. de S. Relat. de l'Empire de Maroc. avec Fig. *Paris* 1695

156 Rofs, Sir Alex. les Religions du Monde avec Fig. en 3 Vol. *Amft.* 1569

157 De Bethune Duc de Sully les Memoirs en 7 Vol.———*Paris* 1663

158 Petrarque Sur la Bonne & Mauvaife fortune, en 4 Vol.——— 1673

159 Montlue, Blaife de, les Commentaires, en 2 Vol. ——— 1661

160 Du Val, P. la Geographie univerf. en 2 Vol. avec Cartes & Fig. 1670

161 Du Duc de Rohan les Memoirs, en 2 Vol. ——— ——— 1661

162 De M. de Voiture les Oeuvres, en 2 Vol.——— ———1660

163 Monf. de Fontenelles les Dialogues des Morts, en 2 Vol. *Lyon* 1683

164 Moliere les Oeuvres, en 5 Vol. ——— ———*Amft.* 1675

165 Du Sr. de Balzac les Oeuvres Diverfes, en 5 Vol. ——— 1664

166 J. Spon & G. Wheler Voyage d'Italie, &c. en 2 Vol———*Amft.* 1679

167 Monf. de Cheverny les Memories d'Eftat, en 2 Vol.——*La Haye* 1669

168 de Beftompiere les Memoires, en 2 Vol. ——— *Col.* 1692

169 Bernier, Sr. F. les Memoires Sur l'Empire du Grand Mogol, en 2 Vol.——— ——— ———*Paris* 1671

Libri Italici in Folio.

1 COrio (Bern) Hiftoria de Milan ——— ——— ——— }
    Ad Pag. 27. ———

2 La Sacra Biblia da Giov. Diodati fol. deaur. cart. Maj. Reg. & con medef. Comment. ——— ———1640

3 Davila, Hen. Cat. Hiftoria delle Guerre Civili de Francia ———1646

4 Bentivoglio, Card. della Guerra di Fiandra——— ———*Paris* 1648

5 P. Paolo Hiftoria del Concilio Tridentino——— ———*Lond.* 1619

6 Boccatio, Jo. il Philocolo ———

7 Vita di Caffino de Medici Gran Duca di Tufcana——— ———1586

8 Guiftiniano, Agoft. Caftigatiff. Annali di Genoa——— *Gen.* 1537

9 Silva de Varia Lecion, car. Tit.

10 Alunno de Ferrara, Franc. della Fabrica del Mondo ———*Ven.* 1600

11 Franc. de les Santos Defcription del Monafterio de S. Lorenzo *Mad.* 1657

12 Coftanzo, Aug. di, Hiftoria del Regno di Napoli ——— ——— 1582

Libri

Libri Italici in Quarto.

1 PAruta (Paolo) Hiftoria Vinetiana——— ———Ven. 1645
2 P Le Finezze de Pennelli Italiani di Luig. Searamuccia Perugino
   Pittore ——— ——Pav.
3 Paruta (Paolo) Difcorfi Politici——— ———Ven. 1599
4 Mafcardi (Agoft.) dell' Arte Hiftorica——— ———Rom.1636
5 Borghini (Vinc.) dell' Origine di Firenze, &c.——— Fior. 1584
6 Di Dante Aligièri de la Comedia con la Efpofitione di Aleffandro
   Vellutello———
7 Sanfovino (Franc.) Origine & fatti delle Famiglie illuftri d' Italia,
                                                      Ven. 1670
8 Machiavelli (Nic.) Tutte le Opere ——— - ———1550
9 Vafari (Giorg.) le Vite de Pittori, in 3 Vol. con figur.——Bol. 1647
10 ———Ragionamenti——— ———Fir. 1588
11 Lomazzo (G. P.) Trattato dell'Arte de la Pittura ——— Mil. 1584
12 ———Rime, &c. ——— ———1587
13 Varchi (Ben.) Lezzioni Sopra diverfe Malerie Poetiche e Filofofiche.
                                                      Fior. 1590
14 Armenino da Faenza (Giorg. Bat.) de Veri Precetti della Pittura
                                                      Rav. 1587
15 Ubaldino (Petr.) le Vite delle Donne illuftri del Regno d'Ingilterra
   & del Regno di Scotia ———1591
16 Boccalini (Traj.) Pietra del Paragone Politico, &c.——— ———1615
17 Catari (Vincenzo) le Imagini de i Dei de gli Antichi ——1625
18 Razzi (Sil.) Vite di Cinque Huomini illuftri, &c.———Fir. 1602
19 Campano (Gio. Ant.) Vite di Braccio Fortebraccio & di Nicolo Pici-
   nino——— ———Per. 1636
20 Gallo (Agoft.) le Vinti Giornate dell' Agricoltura ———Tur. 1579
21 Guiccardini (Lod.) Commentarii, &c. ——— ———Anv. 1565
22 Il Petrarcha con la Spofitione di M. G. A. Gefpaldo———Ven. 1553
23 Andreini (d'Ifab.) Lettere ——— ———Ven. 1612
24 Petrarcha (Franc.) le Vite dell' Imperatori & Pontef.———Rom.1625
25 Corio (Bern.) l'Hiftoria di Milano——— ———Pad. 1646
26 Gofelini (Givl.) Vita del Prencipe den Ferrando Gonzaga—Mil. 1574
27 Malefpini (Ricord.) Storia Anticha di Fiorenza——— —Fior. 1598
28 Capra (Aleff.) la Nuova Architettura famigliare ———Bol. 1678
29 Biondi (G. Fr.) l'Hiftoria delle guerre civili d'Inghilterra Vol. 1. & 2.
                                                      Ven. 1637
30 Alberti (Leand.) Defcrittione di tutta Italia——— —Vin. 1553
31 Sanfovino (Franc.) della Venetia citta Nobiliff.———Ven. 1604
32 Ammirato (Scip.) Opufculi, in 2 Vol.——— ———Fior. 1640
33 Cefare (Giv.) I Commentarii——— ———Ven. 1575
34 Cini (Giov. Bat.) Vita del Cofimo de Medici——— —Fior. 1611
35 Caro (Annib.) dele Lettere familiari, 1 Vol.——— —Ven. 1581
36 Lettere di Principi, Lib. 2. & 3.——— ———Ibid. 1575-7
37 Facio (Bart.) Fatti d'Alfonfo d'Arragona——— ———Vin. 1580
38 Sanfovino (Fran.) diverfe Orationi de Molti huomini illuftri de tempi
   noftri——— ———Ven.
                                                      39 Lomazzo

39 Lomazzo (Gio. Paolo) Idea del Tempo della Pittura —— *Mil.* ——
40 Speroni (Speron) Dialoghi—— —— —— *Ven.* 1596
41 D'Oratio l'Opere da Gio. Fabrini, &c. —— —— 1581
42 Piccolomini (Aleff.) della Inftitur. Morale —— — 1569
43 D'Ariftotele l'Ethica —— —*Fir.* 1550
44 Boccacci (Giov.) Annot. Sopra il Decameron —— *Fior.* 1574
45 Varchi (Bened.) l'Hercolano Dialogo, &c.—— ——*Vin.* 1570
46 Relat. delle Stato Torca Richeffa e Grandezza del Gran Duca di
Tofcana, &c. —— *In Manufcript.*
47 Nardi (Jac.) le Hiftorie della Citta di Fiorenza —— *Lion.* 1582
48 Bartoli (Col.) del Modo di Mifurare, &c. —— *Ven.* 1564
49 Guarini (Bat.) il Segretario Dialogo —— —*Ven.* 1600
50 Boccacio (Giov.) il Decamerone —— — *Vin.* 1552
51 Torq. Taffo Aminta Favola Bofchereccia —— *Ven.* 1590
52 ——delle Opere, &c. in 3 Tom. 1 Vol. —— *Rom.* 1666
53 Difciplina Univerfale dell' Arte Militare, e P. Sardi Capo de Bombar-
dieri —— —— —— *Ven.* 1641
54 Rime del Commendatore Annibal Caro —— ——1584
55 Di Cl. Achillini Poefie —— —— —*Bol.* 1632
56 Nani (Bat.) Hiftoria della Republ. Veneta, in 2 Vol.——*Ven.* 1676
57 Bellori (Gio. Piet.) le Vite de Pittori, Scultori & Architetti Moderni.
—*Rom.* 1672
58 Lettere di Principi—— ——*Ven.* 1570
59 Di Vinc. Martelli Lettere —— *Fir.* 1606
60 Di Bart. Cavalcanti Trattati overo Difcorfi —— *Ven.* 1571
61 J. Marmi del Doni, in 4 Tom. 1 Vol. —— —*Vin.* 1552

Libri Italici in Octavo & Duodecimo.

1 DI Eureta Mifofcolo la Lucerna e Rime—— ——*Ver.*
2 D Arefino (Piet.) Lettere, en 6 Tom. 3 Vol. ——*Par.* 1609
3 Lancelotti (Sec.) l'Hoggidi Difinganno, in 2 Vol. ——*Ven.* 1675
4 ——la Prudenza humana falaciffima, lib. 8.—— ——1662
5 Contarini (Gafp.) della Republ. & Magiftrati di Venetia——1591
6 Pino (di M. Bern.) Nuova Scielta di Lettere di diverfi nobiliff. Huomini —— —— ——*Ven.* 1574
7 Bocchi (Fran.) le Belezze della Citta di Firenze —— *Fir.* 1677
8 Mormile (Giuf.) Defcrittione della Citta di Napoli e dell' Antich. della
Citta di Pozzuolo, con Fig. —— *Nap.* 1670
9 Chiabrera (Gab.) Alcane Poefie Bofchereccio ——*Fior.* 1608
Borghini (Raf.) Diana pietofa Comedia paftorale —— 1587
Villifranchi (Giov.) Altamoro Tragedia —— ——1595
Buonfanti (Piet.) Errori incogniti Comedia—— 1587
10 Garimberto (Hier.) Problemi naturali & morali ——*Ven.* 1549
11 Lancelotti (Sec.) Farfalloni di gli Antichi Hiftor. —— 1668
12 Politi (Adr.) Lettere —— *Ven.* 1624
13 Di Monf. Giov. della Cafa Profe *Imperfect* ——*Par.* 1667
14 ——Rime con le Annotat. del Ægid. Menagio— *Par.* 1667
15 Platina della Vite de Pontefici —— —*Vin.* 1552
16 Menavino (Gio. Ant.) della Vita & Legge Turchefea——*Fior.* 1551

17 Fedini

17 Fedini (Giov.) delle due Perule Comedia

Da Bibiena (Bern.) Calandra Comedia ——— *Fior.* 1558

.Polifila Comedia Piacevole e nuova ——— ——— 1556

Piftoia (Giov. da) la Gioia Comedia ——— ———*Ven.* 1586

18 Nuovo Libro di Lettere de I piu rari autori, &c. ——— *Vin.* 1545

19 Piccolomini (d'Aleff.) della inftitut. di tutta la Vita dell' huomo nato nobili & in Citta libera ——— ——— ———*Vin.* 1559

20 Ariofto (Lod.) la Caffaria, la Lena, il Negromante la Scolaftica Comedia & Comedia Intit. Sive nomine ——— *Ven.* 1587

21 Rofmunda Tragedia di Gio. Rucellai ——— ——— *Fior.* 1568

22 Tarducci (Ach.) il Turco Vincibile in Unguria ——— *Fer.* 1600

23 Cecherelli (d'Afeff.) delle Azzioni & Sentenze, dell' S. Aleffandro de Medici 1ma. Duca di Firenze ——— *Fir.* 1602

24 Lettere Amorofe di Madonna Celia Gentildonna Rom. — *Ven.* 1572

25 Buonamico (Mat.) della Servitu Volontaria ——— *Ven.* 1590

26 Tolomei (M. Claud.) Lettere, lib. 6. ——— *Ven.* 1589

27 Bembo (Piet.) Gliafolani ——— *Vin.* 1515

28 Ficino (Marf.) Orazione Sopra l'Amore ——— *Fir.* 1594

29 Taffo (Bern.) le Lettere · ——— *Vin.* 1553

30 Lottini (G. Fr.) Auvedimenti Civili ——— —*Ven.* 1582

31 Collenuccio (Pand.) Compend. delle Hift. del regno di Napoli. *Ven.* 1543

32 Leti (Greg.) il Teatro Britannico, in 5 Vol. ——— *Amft.* 1684

33 Birago Avogaro (Gio. Bat.) Hiftoria della difumone del Regno di Portogallo, &c. ——— *Amft.* 1647

34 Savonarola (Hier.) Predicke ——— 1544

35 Garimberto (Gir.) della Fortuna———

36 Atanagi (M. Dion.) de la Ruine di diverfi Nobili Poeti Tofcani. *Ven.* 1565

37 La Cofe Maravigliofe di Roma Cive, Chiefe, & Luoghi Pii, con Fig. le Antichita dell' Alma Citta di Roma, con Fig ———*Rom.* 1644

38 Capella (Gal.) l'Authropologia ——— *Ald.* 1533

39 Sanfovino (Fran.) della Origine de Cavalieri ——— *Ven.* 1570

40 Rime diverfe di molte Excell. Auttori ·——— ———*Vin.* 1546

41 Atauagi (Dion.) Raccolt. de le Lettere facete & Piacevoli di diverfi grandi huomini ——— *Ven.* 1581

42 J. Sette Salmi della Penitentia de David ———

43 Guazzo (Stef.) la Civil Converfatione ——— ——— *Ven.* 1593

44 Paradoffi cioe Sententie Fuori del commun parere ——— 1563

45 Torelli (Pomp.) la Merope & il Tancredi Tragedie———*Par.* 1598

46 Di Xenophonte Opere trad. per Lod. Domenichi ——— *Vin.* 1548

47 Filoftrato Lemnio della Vita di Apollon. Tianeo, &c.———*Fior.* 1549

48 Il Libro delle Preghiere publiche 2do. l'ufo della Chiefa Anglic. *Lond.* 1684

49 Il Libro del Cortegiano del Conte Baldef. Caftiglione, nitid. compact. & deaur. ——— ——— ———*Ald.* 1547

50 Cofe de Turchi, nitid. compact. ——— 1541

51 Vieri (Fran. de) Difcorfo delle Bellezze ——— *Fir.* 1588

52 Atanagi (Dion.) delle Lettere facete, &c. ——— *Vin.* 1591

53 Gatti (Aleff.) la Caccia Poema Heroico——— ———*Lond.* 1619

54 Difegno del Doni partito in piu Ragionam——— ———*Vin.* 1549

5 Euftachio

c   55 Euftathio de Gli Amori d'Ifmenio ———— Ven. 1560
f   c   56 Tizenzouala (Agn.) le Belezze de Lodi, gli Amori, & i coftami delle
        Donne ————————————————Ven. 1622
c   .3 57 Domenichi (Lod.) Raccolt. di Facetie Motti & Barbe di diverfi fign. &
        perfone private——— ————————Ven. 1574
        58 Bembo (Piet.) Lettere, in 3 Tom. 2 Vol. ——— —Vin. 1552
        59 Lettere Volgari di diverfi huomini nobiliff. ——— ————1558
6 . 8   60 Ariftofane le Comedie ——————————1545
7   .   61 Terracina (Laur.) Rime & Arcadia del Sannazario——— { Vin. 1548
                                                                { Ald. 1534
1 . 11 62 Dante di Purgatorio, Paradifo & Inferno ————— Ald. 1515
c 4   63 Gerardo (Piet.) Vita & Gefti d'Ezzelino Tezzo da Romano Vin. 1552
        64 Scoto (And.) Itinerario d'Italia ——————Ven. 1610
1 . c   65 De Graia (Giov.) Regina d'Inghilterra Hift. de la Vita———1607
6 . c   66 De Doni la Filofofia Morale ————— ——— Ven. 1567
f . 7   67 Di N. Machiavelli Hiftorie——————————Ald. 1546
        68 Del Card. Bentivoglio Memorie overo Diario— ———Amft. 1648
1 . c   69 Aretino (Piet.) de Ragionamenti ———— —— — —1589
c   70 Sannazaro (Jac.) Sonetti Canzoni —— —— ——
        71 Loredano (Gio. Fran.) le Lettere, in 2 Vol. — — Ven. 1676
        72 Zatta (Aleff.) la 2da, Barca da Padoa —— — Ib. 1666
c . .   73 Lanci (Corn.) Meftola Comedia— & Borgheri (Raff.) la Donna
        Coftante Comedia —— —— Fior. 1583
        74 Scogli del Chriftiano Naufragio, &c. ————————1618
6 . c   75 Il Puttanifmo Romano ——————— Col. 1668
c . c   76 Modena (Leon.) Hiftoria de Gli Riti Hebraici ———— Par. 1637
c - 1   77 Boccalini (Traj.) de Ragguagli di Parnaffo, in 2 Vol.—Amft. 1669
        78 Boccacio (Giov.) Laberinto d'Amore——— ———Vin. 1535
2   79 Leti (Greg.) li Tefori della Corte di Roma, in 3 Vol.——Bruf. 1672
        80 Marino (Del Cav.) la Galeria —— ———— —Ven. 1536
c . c   81 Alamanni (Luigi) della Coltivatione ——— ———Fior. 1549
c . c   82 Boccacio (Gio.) Ameto Comedia delle Ninfe Fiorentine—Ven. 1592
c . c   83 Franco (Nic.) Dialogi piacevoli, (Printed on blue Paper.)—Vin. 1554
c . .   84 Titi (Fil.) Studio di Pittura, Scoltura & Architett. —— Rom. 1674
i . c   85 Ariofto (Lod.) Comedie, cioe, i Suppofiti, la Caffaria, la Lena, il
        Negromante & la Scolaftica ———— ————Vin. 1562
1 . .   86 Del Doni la Lucca, con figur. ——— ————Vin. 1551
        87 Marino (Cav.) il Tempio Panegirico ——— ———Lion. 1615
c   88 Bembo (Piet.) le Profe nelle quali fi ragiona della volgar Lingua
        Scritte al Card. de Medici, &c. ——— ——Vin. 1561
        89 Gabrieli (Ang) Lettere di Complimenti Semplici———Bol. 1649
        90 Il Garreggiamento Poetico del contufo Academ. Ordito in 8 Part.
        1 Vol. (Wants one Leaf) ——— ————Ven. 1611
1 . c   91 Tefti (Fulv.) Poefie Liriche——————Bol. 1672
c . .   92 Mafcardi (Agoft.) Profe Vulgari ——— ——Ven. 1653
c . c   93 Marino (Del Cav.) la Sampogna ——— ————1652
f . f   94 Tomafii (Tom.) la Vita di Cefare Borgia, Tit.———1671
        95 Le Vifioni Politiche Sopra gli Intereffi piu Recond. di Tutti Principi, e
        Republiche della Chriftianita ——— Germ. 1671
        96 Pallavicino (Fer.) le Bellezze dell' Annina ~~~————Bol. 1640
        97 Affarino (Luca) Ragguagli del Regno di Cipro. Ven. 1654
                                                         98 L

98 La Retorica delle Puttane ———

99 Conclave nel quale fu detto Fabio Chiggi detto Aleſſandro 7.—1664

100 Pallavicino (di Fer.) Opere Scelte ———   ———*Vill.* 1666

101 Malcardi (di Agoſt.) diſcorſi morali ſu la Tavola di Cebete Tebano.
                                                        Ven. 1653

102 Del Berni, Caſa, Maura, Varchi, Dolce, &c. Rime Piacevoli.
                                                        Vic. 1609

103 Conclavi de Pontefici Romani ——— ———   ———1668

104 Malvezzi (Virg.) il Romulo, il Tarquinio Superbo, Davide perſe-
      guitato, il Ritratto del privato Politico Chriſtiano, ſucceſſi
      principali della Monarchia di Spagna——— ———*Gen.* 1647

105 Guicciardini (Lod.) l'Hore di Ricreatione——— ———*Par.* 1610

106 Del Padre Poalo Opere, in 5 Vol.——— ———*Ven.* 1677

107 H. Cardinaliſmo di Santa Chieſa, en 3 Vol.——— — ———1668

108 Marino (Del Cav.) la Lira Rune, en 2 Par. 1 Vol.——*Ven.* 1653

109 Peruccio (And.) l'Epaminonda Melodrama ——— — *Nap.* 1684

110 Il Sindicato di Alexandro 7mo. con il Suo Viaggio nell' altro
      mondo.   —1668

111 Lori (d'And.) Egloghe ——— ———   —*Vin.* 1554

112 Opinione del Padre Paolo Servita, Conſultor di Stato, &c. *Ven.* 1680

113 Guarini (Bat.) Opere Poetiche   —1600

114 Bembo (Piet.) Gli Aſolani, &c. ———   · 1585

115 Taſſo (Torq.) le Sette giornate del Mondo creato———1608

116 Della Caſa (Giov.) Rime & Proſe ———   ——— 1575

117 Camillo (Gio.) l'Opere, &c. ———   ———   *Vin.* 1579

118 Arioſto (Lod.) Rime & Satyre ———   ———   *Ven.* 1614

119 Calandra, Amor conſtante, & Aleſſandro, 3 Comedie — 1669.-70

120 Sannazaro (Giac.) Arcadia con la Vita dell' Autore & Annot. da
      Tom. Porcacchi, 240. ———   ———*Ven.*1672

121 Taſſo (Torq.) Aminta Favola Boſcareccia, 240.   ——— *Par.* 1678

122 ———Il Goffredo ovèro Gieruſaleme liberata, 2 Vol.———1678

123 Il Paſtor Fido Tragicomedia del Sig. Bat. Guarini, 240—*Amſt.*——

124 Boccalini (Traj.) Pietra del Paragone Politico, 240———*Coſ.*1653

Libri Hiſpanici in Folio.

1 Pero Mexia Hiſtoria Imperial y Ceſarea ———   *Anv.* 1561

Lib. Hiſpanic. in Quarto.

1 Iturgia Ingleſa ———   ———   ———*A. Triomb.* 1663

2 Guzman de Alfarache, prima y ſecunda Parte ———*Burg.* 1619

3 Trarado de Re Militare que paſto entre Semóres don Gonçalo Fer-
   nand. de Cordova, Duque de Seſta, &c.———   ———*Bruſ.* 1590

4 Gracian (de Lorenzo) Obras, in 2 Vol. nitid compact. — *Mad.* 1664

5 Nunnez (Hern.) Refranes o Proverbois en Romance—*Mad.* 1619
   y la filoſofia vulgar de Juan de Mal Lara—Imperfect.——

NOTES[*]

[*] The *Bibliotheca Hookiana sive Catalogus Diverforum Librorum,* reproduced in its entirety beginning on page 143, is referred to in the following chapter notes as *Bib. H.*

Notes

CHAPTER 1. ROBERT HOOKE, F.R.S.

1. Henry Oldenburg to Adam Boreel, 13 December 1660 in *The Correspondence of Henry Oldenburg,* 10 vols., ed. and trans. A. Rupert Hall and Marie Boas Hall (Madison: The University of Wisconsin Press, 1985), no. 228. (Since this work is such a prime source for this study, it will be henceforth designated as Oldenburg, *Correspondence*).

2. Thomas Sprat, *The History of the Royal Society of London, for the Improving of Natural Knowledge* (London: Knapton, 1722), pp. 61f.

3. Samuel Sorbière, *Relation D'Un Voyage en Angleterre* (Cologne: Michel, 1666), p. 69.

4. Oldenburg to Sorbière, January 1663, in Oldenburg, *Correspondence,* no. 304.

5. Oldenburg to Martin Lister, 18/20 January 1670/71, in Oldenburg, *Correspondence,* no. 1601.

6. Samuel Colepresse to Oldenburg, February 1667/68, in Oldenburg, *Correspondence,* no. 769.

7. Oldenburg to Richard Norwood, February 1667/68 and Governor John Winthrop to Oldenburg, in Oldenburg, *Correspondence,* nos. 775, 1005.

8. Oldenburg to Sir John Dodington, 15 July 1670, in Oldenburg, *Correspondence,* no. 1487.

9. Philipp Jacob Sachs à Lewenheimb to Oldenburg, 1 October 1670, in Oldenburg, *Correspondence,* no. 1530; Martha Ornstein, *The Role of Scientific Societies in the Seventeenth Century* (London: Archon Books, 1963), p. 170.

10. John Beale to Oldenburg, 8 July 1671, in Oldenburg, *Correspondence,* no. 1743.

225

11. Among the most valuable sources for this study are the three extant diaries of Hooke: *The Diary of Robert Hooke, M.A., M.D., F.R.S. 1672-1680*, eds. Henry W. Robinson and Walter Adams (London: Taylor and Francis, 1853), p. 185 (to be henceforth cited as H. *Diary A*); *The Diary of Robert Hooke November 1688 to March 1690* (to be henceforth listed as H. *Diary B*); *The Diary [of Robert Hooke], December 1692 to 8 August 1693* (to be henceforth listed as H. *Diary C*). These last two diaries are reprinted in R.T. Gunther, *Early Science in Oxford*, 15 vols. (Oxford for the Author, 1930).

12. *The Posthumous Works of Robert Hooke*, Pub. Richard Waller (London: Smith & Walford, 1705), ii (henceforth designated as Waller).

13. John Aubrey, *Brief Lives*, 2 vols., ed. A. Clark (Oxford: Clarendon Press, 1898), p. 164.

14. Sir Geoffrey Keynes, *A Bibliography of Dr. Robert Hooke* (Oxford: Clarendon Press, 1960), no.2.

15. Thomas Birch, *The History of the Royal Society of London* (New York: Johnson, 1968), xcii.

16. Oldenburg to Boyle, 10 November 1664, in Oldenburg, *Correspondence*, no. 351; Margaret Espinasse, *Robert Hooke* (Berkeley: University of California Press, 1956), pp. 44, 45, 83.

17. *The Diary of Samuel Pepys*, 8 vols. in three, ed. by Henry B. Wheatley (London: Bell & Sons, 1928), IV, pp. 315, 316.

18. Oldenburg to Spinoza, 28 April 1665, in Oldenburg, *Correspondence*, no. 371.

19. Peter Nelson to Oldenburg, 22 August 1668, in Oldenburg, *Correspondence*, no. 946.

20. Henri Justel to Oldenburg, 20 October 1668, in Oldenburg, *Correspondence*, no. 978.

21. - 22. H. *Diary A*, pp. 310, 312; 163, 192, 292.

23. Oldenburg to Boyle, 27 January 1665/1666; Johann Hevelius to Oldenburg, 3 June 1668; Gaston-Ignace Pardies to Oldenburg, 5 January 1671/1672; Sir Robert Moray to Oldenburg, 16 November 1665; in Oldenburg, *Correspondence*, nos. 487, 878, 1859, 610.

24. - 32. H. *Diary A*, pp. 91, 138, 139, 479; 5, 113, 135; 8, 9, 60, 204; 54, 379; 96, 65, 137; H. *Diary C*, p. 180; H. *Diary A*, pp. 29; 53; 295; 146, 337, 403, 437.

33. Oldenburg to Boyle, 16 October 1666, in Oldenburg, *Correspondence,* no. 437.
34. H. *Diary A,* pp. 65, 96, 130, 331; John Crowne, *Juliana* (London: Cadman & Birch, 1671), in *Short Title Catalogue of Books Printed in England, Scotland . . . 1641-1700.* Comp. by Donald G. Wing (New York: Columbia University Press, 1945-1951), C7393 (henceforth designated as Wing); John Bulwar, *Pathomyotomia* (London: Moseley, 1649), Wing B5468; H. *Diary C,* p. 224.
35. Oldenburg to Beckman, 30 March 1668, in Oldenburg, *Correspondence,* no 822; Waller, xxvii.

CHAPTER 2. JOHN MARTYN, "PRINTER TO THE ROYAL SOCIETY"

1. The date of Martyn's birth is based upon his date of apprenticeship, 1634, which he entered approximately at the age of fifteen; see "Apprentices Register Books, July 29, 1605-27 June 1666," Ms. Stationers Hall, London. Permission granted for its use by the late R.T. Rivington, Esq., Clerk of Stationers Company.
2. For Allestry, see Henry R. Plomer, *A Dictionary of the Booksellers and Printers who were at Work in England, Scotland . . . from 1641 to 1667* (London: Bibliographical Society, 1901), p. 33; Oldenburg to Boyle, 19 December 1665, in Oldenburg, *Correspondence,* no. 473.
3. It is of interest to note that many of the Martyn and Allestry publications are to be found in the *Bibliotheca Hookiana,* the auction catalogue of Hooke's library which was sold at public sale 29 April 1703. The Auction Catalogue will be referred to as the *Bib.H.* with reference to division, format, and catalogue number. Hooke, *Micrographia,* 2 eds. in Wing M2620 and M2621 and *Bib.H.,* English Books in Quires, folio, 3; Malpighi, *Anatome plantarum* and *Dissertatio de bombyce* in Wing M345 and M349 and in *Bib.H.,* Foreign Books, Libri in Albiis, folio, 8 and Libri Latini, 4to, 200; Holder: H. *Diary A,* p. 173.
4. Birch, *The History of the Royal Society of London,* I, 321.
5. The firm printed three editions of Evelyn's *Sylva;* see Wing E3516-3518.

6. Birch, op. cit., 323.
7. Birch, op. cit., 378.
8. *The Record of the Royal Society of London* (London 1940), pp. 298ff.
9. Charleton, Wing C3688; Sprat, Wing S5032; Wilkins, Wing W2196; Horrocks, Wing H2868; Wallis, Wing W574; Willughby, Wing 2880; Birch, op.cit., 346.
10. Henry R. Plomer, *A Dictionary of the Booksellers and Printers who were at Work in England, Scotland . . . from 1641 to 1667,* pp. 158, 221, 83, 136.
11. See Note 5; 2 editions of Graunt; 3 of Willughby, *Ornithologia;* 2 of Lobo and 2 of Hooke, *Micrographia.*
12. John Beale to Oldenburg, 15 March 1669/70, in Oldenburg, *Correspondence,* no. 561.
13. Edward Arber, *The Term Catalogues 1668-1709,* 3 vols. (London: Privately Printed, 1903-1906), I, pp. 229, 205.
14. Treated in detail in Chapter 6.
15. Walter G. Bell, *The Great Fire of London in 1666* (London: Lane, 1970), pp. 139, 226; *The Diary of Samuel Pepys,* II, p. 301; *The Diary of John Evelyn,* ed. E.S. de Beer (London: Oxford University Press, 1959), p. 498.
16. Pepys, *Diary,* II, p. 310.
17. *The Diary of John Evelyn to which are added a Selection from the Familiar Letters* (London: Dickinson & Son, 1829), III, p. 346; Pepys, *Diary,* II, p. 310.
18. The *Riolan Catalogue* is extremely rare. It is a small quarto divided into two parts: I, 92pp; II, 36pp. There is an incomplete copy in the British Library. Information was originally given the author, courtesy of F. Geoffrey Rendall, Esq., Keeper of Printed Books, British Library.
19. See *Philosophical Transactions,* 25 March 1675, no. 112 and 26 July 1675, no. 116 for these Martyn Want Lists.
20. H. *Diary A,* pp. 353, 412, 431.
21. Pepys, *Diary,* II, p. 766; Georges Fournier, *L'Hydrographie* (Paris 1643); possibly Alvaro Semmedo, *History of China* (London 1655); Athanasius Kircher, *Musurgia Universalis* (Rome 1650); Gautier de la Costes, *Calprenede* (Paris 1644).
22. Keynes, *A Bibliography of . . . Hooke,* nos. 6, 7, 16, 19, 20.

NOTES

23. - 24. H. *Diary A*, pp. 73, 138, 139, 144, 336; for Plot and *Journal des Sçavans*, see *Bib. H.*, English Books in Quires, folio, 4-6; Libri in Albiis, 4to, 18.

25. H. *Diary A*, pp. 5, 365, 419, 267, 151, 283, 302, 225, 190; Regnier de Graaf, *De mulierum generatione inservientibus* (Leyden 1672), *Bib. H.*, Libri Latini, 8vo, 206-207; Briggs, *Ophthalmographia* (Cambridge 1676); Digby, *Receipts* (London 1670) and *Closet* (London 1671), Wing D1425, Wing D1428; Harvey, *The Family Physician* (London 1674), Wing H1064; Hagedorn, *De Catchetu, seu Terra Japonica* (Jena 1679); Borelli, *De motu animalium* (Rome 1680), *Bib. H.*, Libri in Albiis, 4to, 10; Grew, *History of Vegetables* (London 1674), *Bib. H.*, English Books, 8vo, 247; Lister, *De araneis & cochleis* (London 1678), *Bib. H.*, Libri Latini, 4to, 255; Plot, *The Natural History of Oxfordshire* (Oxford 1676), *Bib. H.*, English Books in Quires, folio, 4; Willughby, *Ornithologia* (London 1678), *Bib. H.*, English Books, folio, 87; Gerard, *The herbal* (London 1597), *A Short-Title Catalogue of Books printed in England, Scotland . . . 1475-1640*, eds. A.W. Pollard and G.R. Redgrave, (London: The Bibliographical Society, 1946), 11750 (henceforth designated as *STC*).

26. H. *Diary A*, pp. 151; 253; 256f; 13, 135; Baudrant, *Lexicon geographicum* (Isenach 1677), *Bib. H.*, Libri Latini, folio, 22; Zeiller, *Topographia Gallia* (Frankfurt 1675), 3 vols., *Bib. H.*, Libri Latini, folio, 32; Browne, *Travels in Hungary* (London 1673), *Bib. H.*, English Books, folio, 47; Tavernier, *Six Voyages through Turkey* (London 1681), *Bib. H.*, English Books, folio, 47; De Bry, *Collections* (Frankfurt A/M 1590-1634).

27. H. *Diary A.*, pp. 135, 146, 267, 233, 417, 91, 115, 16, 356, 253; Du Laurens, *Specimina mathematica* (Paris 1667), *Bib. H.*, Libri Latini, 4to, 352; *Archimede Redivivo* (Palermo 1644), *Bib. H.*, Libri Latini, 4to, 349; Schott, *Technica Curiosa* (Nuremberg 1644), *Bib. H.*, Libri Latini, 4to, 361; Mercator, *Institutiones astronomicae* (London 1676), *Bib. H.*, Libri Latini, 8vo, 370; Grimaldi, *De Lumiere* (Bologna 1661); Menzel, *Lapis Bononiensis* (Bielefeld 1675), *Bib. H.*, Libri Latini, 12mo, 219; Wedel, *De sale volatili,* (Frankfurt A/M 1672), *Bib. H.*, Libri Latini, 12mo, 206; Johnson, *Lexicon Chymicum* (London 1660), *Bib. H.*, Libri Latini, 8vo, 316; Le

NOTES

Febure, *Compleat Body of Chymistry* (London 1664), *Bib. H.,*
English Books, 4to, 92; Cesalpini, *De metallicis libri tres*
(Rome 1596), *Bib. H.,* Libri Latini, 4to, 245; Freart de
Chambray, *Parallel of Antient Architecture* (London 1664),
Bib. H., English Books, folio, 109.

28. - 32. Oldenburg to Lister, 4 February 1671/72; Duhamel to
Oldenburg, 19 and 21 April 1673; for Newton's editions of
Varenius, see *The Correspondence of Sir Isaac Newton,* 3 vols.,
ed. H.W. Turnbull (Cambridge 1959), I, 215; Vogel to
Oldenburg; Oldenburg to Sachs à Lewenheimb, 24 December
1671, in Oldenburg, *Correspondence,* nos. 1622, 2211, 2103,
2211, 1444, 1845.

33. Oldenburg to Leibniz, 24 April 1671, in Oldenburg,
Correspondence, no. 1685; Blunt, *Glossographia* (London
1670); Boyle, *Tractatus ... mira aeris rarefractio detecta*
(London 1670); Boyle, *Tractatus cosmicis qualitatibus*
(Amsterdam & Hamburg 1671); Glanville, *Plus ultra* (London
1668); *Mercurius Librarius, or a Catalogue of Books, 1668-
1670.*

34. Sachs à Leewenheimb to Oldenburg, 29 Oct. 1671 in Oldenburg, *Correspondence,* no. 1809.

35. Oldenburg to Leibnitz, 24 April 1671 in Oldenburg,
Correspondence, no. 1685.

36. H. *Diary A,* pp. 440, 448.

CHAPTER 3. MOSES PITT, PUBLISHER AND
PURVEYOR OF MATHEMATICAL TEXTS

1. John Dunton, *The Life and Errors,* 2 vols. (New York:
Franklin, 1968), I, p. 223; Collins to Wallis, n.d., in Stephen J.
Rigaud, *Correspondence of Scientific Men in the Seventeenth
Century,* 2 vols. (Oxford: Oxford University Press, 1851), II,
468.

2. Henry R. Plomer, *A Dictionary of the Printers and Booksellers
who were at Work in England, Scotland ... from 1668 to 1725*
(Oxford: Oxford University Press, 1922), p. 258.

3. Collins to Wallis, 2 February 1666/67, in Rigaud,
Correspondence, II, p. 470; Briggs, *Arithmetica* (London 1624);
Barrow, *Euclidis data* (Cambridge 1657).

4. Collins to Wallis, 2 February 1666/67, in Rigaud, *Correspondence,* II, p. 470.
5. Collins to Gregory, 25 March 1671, in Rigaud, *Correspondence,* II, p. 231.
6. For Scott, see Leona Rostenberg, *Literary, Political, Scientific, Religious, and Legal Publishing, Printing and Bookselling in England, 1551-1700: Twelve Studies,* 2 vols. (New York: Franklin, 1965), II, pp. 281-283; Scott, *Catalogus librorum ex variis Europae partibus advectorum* (London: Scott, 1674); Collins to Beale, 20 August 1672; Collins to Gregory, 25 March 1671, in Rigaud, *Correspondence,* II, p. 217 and I, p. 195.
7. Rostenberg, *Literary, Political, Scientific . . . Publishing . . . in England,* II, p. 290.
8. Wallis to Collins, 11 January 1669/1670, in Rigaud, *Correspondence,* II, p. 519; Plomer, *A Dictionary of Booksellers and Printers who were at Work in England, Scotland . . . 1641 to 1667* (London: Bibliographical Society, 1901), p. 83; Rahn, *Introduction to Algebra* (London: Pitt, 1668); H. *Diary C,* p. 224, *Bib. H.,* English Books, 4to, 108.
9. Collins to Vernon, 14 December 1671, in Rigaud, *Correspondence,* I, p. 176.
10. Wallis to Collins, 13 March 1668/69; Collins to Baker, 24 April 1667, in Rigaud, *Correspondence,* I, p. 176, II, p. 32.
11. Arber, *The Term Catalogues,* I, p. 49; Collins to Wallis, n.d., in Rigaud, *Correspondence,* II, p. 468.
12. Wallis to Oldenburg, 14 August 1670 in Oldenburg, *Correspondence,* no. 1500.
13. For works of Wallis, see Wing W580, W567; Arber, op. cit., p. 312; Brancker to Collins, 10 May 1671, in Rigaud, *Correspondence,* I, p. 167.
14. H. *Diary C,* p. 101; Dary, *Bib. H.,* English Books, 8vo, 299; Horrocks: Wing H2869; Ptolemy: *Bib. H.,* Libri in Albiis, 4to, 19; Steno: *Bib. H.,* English Books, 8vo, 198; *Discourse: Bib. H.,* English Books, 8vo, 36; *Philosophical Transactions: Bib. H.,* English Books in Quires, 4to, 2.
15. Wing M2783; Oldenburg to Lister, 23 December 1671, in Oldenburg, *Correspondence,* no. 1850.
16. Fulton, *Bibliography of the Honourable Robert Boyle,* 96, 97, 105, 106, 107, 119.

17. - 18. Wing P2585; Arber, op. cit., I, p. 38; Wing B699, B6257; M1434; C240; B1010; S6117; B2043; B2044; B2042; F2161; G536; S4246; Arber, op. cit., I, pp. 66, 186.
19. H. *Diary A*, p. 30; Stevin: *Bib. H.*, Libri Latini, folio, 260-262; Cardan: *Bib. H.*, Libri Latini, folio, 90; Liebault: *Bib. H.*, Libri Latini, 8vo, 297; Quercetanus (Du Cerceau): *Bib. H.*, Libri Latini, 8vo, 318; Du Choul: *Bib. H.*, Libri Latini, 8vo, 442; Bellonius: *Bib. H.*, Appendix, Libri Gallici, 4to, 5.
20. H. *Diary A*, pp. 45, 139; Torricelli: *Bib. H.*, Libri Latini, 4to, 399; Grandami: *Bib. H.*, Libri Latini, 4to, 587; Boyle: *Bib. H.*, English Books, 8vo, 214; Leonardo da Vinci: *Bib. H.*, Libri Latini, folio, 297; Boeckler: *Bib. H.*, Libri Latini, folio, 299; Diophantus: *Bib. H.*, Libri Latini, 4to, 401; Snell: *Bib. H.*, Libri Latini, 4to, 440; *Northwest Fox: Bib. H.*, English Books, 4to, 28; Regiomontanus: *Bib. H.*, Libri Latini, folio, 208; Kepler: *Bib. H.*, Libri Latini, 4to, 482; Riccioli: *Bib. H.*, Libri Latini, folio, 55; Herrera: *Bib. H.*, Libri Latini, folio, 24.
21. John Lawler, *Book Auctions in Seventeenth Century England* (London: Stock, 1898), pp. 121, 127f, 215; H. *Diary A*, p. 390; Accademia del Cimento: *Bib. H.*, Libri Latini, folio, 151; Vieta: *Bib. H.*, Libri Latini, folio, 174 and 4to, 547; Bassantin: *Bib. H.*, Libri Latini, folio, 211 and 16mo, 33; Scheffer: *Bib. H.*, English Books, folio, 16; Boccone: *Bib. H.*, Libri Latini, 8vo., 240.
22. H. *Diary A*, pp. 379, 371, 374; Arber, op. cit., I, p. 135; Jansson: *Bib. H.*, Libri Latini, folio, 13; Mercator: *Bib. H.*, Libri Latini, folio, 12; Ogilby: *Bib. H.*, English Books, folio, 140-146; Ortelius: *Bib. H.*, English Books, folio, 53; Zeiller: *Bib. H.*, Libri Latini, folio, 32; Saxton: *Bib. H.*, English Books, folio, 21, 20, 54.
23. Arber, op. cit., I, p. 135; Pitt, *The English Atlas*, Vol. 1, 2 and 3, see *Bib. H.*, English Books, folio, 52.
24. Moses Pitt, *The Cry of the Oppressed* (London: Pitt, 1691); R.V. Tooley, *Maps and Map-Makers* (London: Batsford, 1978), p. 53; John Johnson and Strickland Gibson, *Print and Privilege at Oxford in the Year 1700* (Oxford: Oxford University Press, 1946), p. 379.
25. Arber, op. cit., I, p. 379.
26. H. *Diary A*, p. 381; *The Correspondence of Sir Isaac Newton*, II, p. 264.

NOTES

27 - 32. H. *Diary A,* pp. 183, 349, 377, 353, 360, 369, 370, 371, 373; 374, 377, 422, 70, 408, 426, 427, 434, 444, 388, 380, 383, 85, 134, 342, 389, 377, 43, 388, 379; 38, 422, 430, 440; 441, 458, 88, 90, 119; 62, 117; Plomer, *Dictionary . . . 1668-1725,* p. 276; [Pitt], *Catalogus librorum in omni facultate et lingua rariorum nuperimme in Anglia post novissimum bellum;* Arber, op. cit., I, p. 189; [Pitt], *Catalogus Librorum in Regionibus Transmarinis super editorum.*
33. Johnson and Gibson, *Print and Privilege,* p. 76.
34. Nicolas Barker, *The Oxford University Press and the Spread of Learning* (Oxford: The Clarendon Press, 1978), p. 24.
35. Pitt, *The Cry of the Oppressed; Bibles:* Wing B2682, B2314, B3666, B3664.
36. Dugdale: Wing D4393; Maimonides: Wing M2852, M2854.
37. Tavernier: Wing T251, *Bib. H.,* English Books, folio, 47; Petty: Wing P1928; *Acta Eruditorum: Bib. H.,* Libri in Albiis, 4to, 12.
38. Lawler, *Book Auctions,* p. 219.
39. Pitt: Wing P2405, P2301.

CHAPTER 4. WILLIAM COOPER, ALCHEMICAL SPECIALIST

1. H. *Diary A,* p. 119.
2. Cooper, *The Philosophical Epitaph,* see Wing C6062; Plomer, *Dictionary . . . 1668-1725;* for Starkey and Philalethes, see Denis I. Duveen, *Bibliotheca Alchemica et Chemica* (London: Weil, 1949), p. 470; John Ferguson, *Bibliotheca Chemica* (Glasgow: Maclehose & Sons, 1906), 2 vols., II, p. 192.
3. William Cooper, *A Catalogue of Chymicall Books,* (London 1675).
4. For Helvetius, Philaletha, Houpreght, *Collectanea* and Geber, see Ferguson I, p. 383; II, p. 193; I, p.87; I, p. 169; Wing J55.
5. Lynn Thorndike, *A History of Magic and Experimental Science* (New York: Columbia University Press, 1959), VII, p. 153; Evelyn, *Diary,* pp. 298, 362, 691; Oldenburg to Boyle, 23 November 1659 in Oldenburg, *Correspondence,* no. 173.
6. Espinasse, *Robert Hooke,* p. 118.

7. F. Oswell to Oldenburg, 11 January 1672/73 in Oldenburg, *Correspondence,* no. 2132; for the writings of Starkey, see Wing S5271, S5273-S5276, S5281, S5286-S5288.
8. For the writings of Houpreght, Digby, *Collectanea,* Geber, Helmont, Glauber, Houghton, Platt, *Antient Laws* and Halley, see Wing H2941, D1422, C5103, J55, H1392, G845, H2933, P2412, A3069, H1805, H1806.
9. Arber, *The Term Catalogues,* I, 164; II, 138; Wing M2190.
10. Wing C6001 and Arber, *The Term Catalogues,* I, 218.
11. For the writings of Alexander of Piedmont, Agrippa, Ashmole, Bacon, Basil Valentine, Beguin, Bolnest, Boulton, and Croll, see *STC,* nos. 293-312; Wing A789, A3987; *STC* 1182; Ferguson I, 77f; Wing B1703; Ferguson I, 114; Wing B3489, C7022.
12. For the writings of Culpepper, Digby, Fludd, Heydon, and Mathews, see Wing C7549; D1435, D1437; F1391; H1677, H1676; Ferguson, *Bibliotheca Chemica,* II, p. 82.
13. For the writings of Paracelsus, Vaughan, Poleman, Sendivogius, Starkey, Ripley, the *Storehouse, Secrets* (by Eirenaeus Philaletha), *Four Patents,* Helmonts and Flammel, see Wing B3538, V143-V144, V146, V151, V153, V156; P2748; S1506; S5271-S5290A; Ferguson, *Bibliotheca Chemica,* II, pp. 267ff; *Storehouse: STC* 21057; Ferguson II, 192; *Four Patents,* not found; Wing E1390-E1402; *STC* 11027.
14. Fulton, *A Bibliography of... Boyle,* nos. 13, 33, 25, 72, 57, 70, 96, 77, 105.
15. For the writings of Barba, Pettus, Love, and Paracelsus, see Wing B678; P1908; L3246; B3543; Cooper also published the balneological treatises of Borlase, Jorden, Wittie, see Wing B3769, J1075, W3231; the medical texts of Acton, Maynwaring and others, see Wing A450, M512, 1510.
16. Wing H2491, E45; *STC* 25067A.
17. H. *Diary A,* p. 419; Fromond: *Bib. H.,* Libri Latini, 4to, 499; English Books, 8vo, 86; Libri Latini, 8vo, 431. For Cooper's role as an auctioneer, see Chapter 6.

CHAPTER 5. BOOK STALLS OF DUCK LANE AND MOORFIELDS

1. Dunton, *The Life and Errors,* I, p. 236; Pepys, *Diary,* VII, p. 378; H. *Diary A,* p. 199.
2. Dunton, op. cit., pp. 258, 229, 217, 292.
3. Plomer, *A Dictionary* . . . *1641 to 1667,* pp. 51, 179, 176.
4. Dunton, op. cit., pp. 235-236; Plomer, *Dictionary* . . . *1641 to 1667,* p. 263.
5. John Collins to Francis Vernon, n.d., in Rigaud, *Correspondence,* I, p. 115; Dunton, op. cit., p. 258; Plomer, *Dictionary* . . . *1668 to 1725,* p. 11.
6. Dunton, op. cit., pp. 209, 221, 235-236; Lawler, *Book Auctions in England,* p. 70.
7. Pepys, *Diary,* VIII, p. 312; Athanasius Kircher, *Musurgia Universalis* (Rome 1650), 2 vols.; Michel de Montaigne, *Essayes* (London 1603, 1613, 1632); Marin Mersenne, *L'Harmonie Universelle* (Paris 1636-1637); René Descartes, *Excellent Compendium of Musick* (London 1653).
8. *STC* 24873-24880; Pepys, *Diary,* VII, pp. 372, 378, 381 and VIII, 65, 73, 121.
9. Keynes, *Bibliography of Hooke,* no. 2; D.F. McKenzie, *Stationers' Company Apprentices 1605-1640* (Charlottesville, Virginia: Bibliographical Society of the University of Virginia, 1961), p. 404; Plomer, *Dictionary* . . . *1641 to 1667,* p. 179; *The Obituary of Richard Smyth, Secondary of the Poultry Compter,* ed. Sir Henry Ellis (London: Camden Society, 1849), p. 79.
10. Wing W811, C4550, G1912, H1053, M1501, M2517; M2136.
11. John Wallis to Oldenburg, 30 April 1664, in Oldenburg, *Correspondence,* no. 314; Ulug Begh: Wing U23 and *Bib. H.,* Libri Latini, 4to, 298, 299.
12. Gregory: Wing G1909; Collins to Gregory, n.d., in Rigaud, *Correspondence,* II, no. 412.
13. Oldenburg to Boyle, 18 April 1665 in Oldenburg, *Correspondence,* no. 412; Athanasius Kircher, *Mundus subterraneus* (Amsterdam 1655), *Scrutinium* (Rome 1658), *Bib. H.,* Libri Latini, folio, 46; Wing S517; Oldenburg to Boyle, 10 October 1665, in Oldenburg, *Correspondence,* no. 430; *Bib.H.,* English Books, folio, 98.

NOTES

14. Boyle to Oldenburg, 9 December 1665, in Oldenburg, *Correspondence,* no. 469; Oldenburg to Boyle, 19 December 1665, in Oldenburg, *Correspondence,* no. 473.
15. H. *Diary A,* p. 264.
16. Dunton, op. cit., I, p. 221.
17. Smith: Wing S4906; Hale's writings: Wing H244, H238, H252, H258; *Tryal:* Wing T2240.
18. H. *Diary A,* p. 15; Pepys, *Diary,* VII, p. 61; For Latin and English editions of Descartes's *Epistles,* see *Bib. H.,* Libri Latini, 4to, 102 and English Books, 4to, 125; Leotaud: *Bib. H.,* Libri Latini, 8vo., 235; Fioravanti: Wing F952, F953.
19. H. *Diary A,* passim; Dunton, op. cit., pp. 211-212; for works by Leybourne, see *Bib. H.,* English Books, folio, 97 and Appendix, English Miscellanies, folio, 47.
20. Darling: Wing D261, D262; Coley: Wing C5099; Palladio: Wing P206, P207; Hodder: Wing H2287, H2288; L'Ecluse: *Bib. H.,* Libri Latini, folio, 118, 119; Bellonius: *Bib. H.,* Appendix, Libri Gallici, 4to, 5; Cardan: *Bib. H.,* Libri Latini, folio and 8vo., 236, 358; for Hunt, see H. *Diary A,* passim.
21. H. *Diary A,* p. 170; Leona Rostenberg, *English Publishers in the Graphic Arts 1599-1700* (New York: Franklin, 1963), p. 76; for Duerer, see *Bib. H.,* Appendix, Libri Miscellanei, folio, 17.
22. H. *Diary A,* p. 176; Bacon: *Bib. H.,* Libri Latini, 8vo, 199, 200; Hood: *Bib.H.,* English Books, 4to, 113; Finé: *Bib.H.,* Libri Latini, 4to, 522; Dela Main: *Bib. H.,* (possibly) English Books, 4to, 125; Street and Childrey: Wing S2406, A1403; Digges: *STC* 6871; *Londons Flames:* Wing L2928; Hood: *STC* 13695; Wright: *STC* 26021; Heydon: *STC* 13266.
23. H. *Diary A,* p. 283; *Bib. H.,* Libri Latini, folio, 185, 186; Snell: *Bib. H.,* Libri Latini, 4to, 609; Schotten: *Bib. H.,* Libri Latini, 4to, 405; R.S., *Bib. H.,* English Books, 8vo, 288; Shakerley: *Bib. H.,* English Books, 8vo, 291.
24. Debes: H. *Diary A,* 392; 111; *Bib. H.,* English Books, 12mo, 47; Oughtred: Collins to Vernon, n.d., in Rigaud, *Correspondence,* I, p. 151, *Bib. H.,* Libri Latini, 8vo, 339, English Books, 4to, 125; Alhazen: *Bib. H.,* Libri Latini, folio, 270; Napier: H. *Diary A,* p. 111, *Bib. H.,* Libri Latini, 4to, 383, 384.
25. Cock: *Bib. H.,* English Books, 12mo, 59; Digges: H. *Diary A,* 183; *STC* 6371; Pellisson: *Bib. H.,* 8vo, 32; Billy: *Bib. H.,* Libri

Latini, 4to, 387; Pitiscus: *Bib. H.,* English Books, 123; Aldrovandi: H. *Diary A,* p. 199.

26. R.J. Mitchell, *A History of London Life* (London: Longmans, Green, 1958), p. 120; Pepys, *Diary,* I, p. 52; II, p. 56; V, p. 384; IV, p. 228; V, pp. 57, 401.

27. Evelyn, *Diary,* p. 648.

28. Hooke's numerous visits to Moorfields are particularly noted in his later diaries, H. *Diary B* and H. *Diary C,* November 1688 to March 1690 and December 1692 to August 1693; for the fate of Boyle's library, see Fulton, *A Bibliography of . . . Boyle,* p.v.

29. Platt: *Bib. H.,* English Books, 4to, 72; Dunton, *op. cit.,* p. 235.

30. Rostenberg, *English Publishers in the Graphic Arts,* pp. 56-60; H. *Diary A,* p. 184.

31. Francini: *Bib. H.,* English Books, folio, 113.

32. Le Muet: H. *Diary A,* p. 129; *Bib. H.,* Libri in Albiis, folio, 7; Vingboon, 2.

33. H. *Diary A,* p. 185; *Bib. H.,* Libri Latini, folio, 288-299; English Books, 4to, 137.

34. Dary: *Bib. H.,* English Books, 8vo, 299; Wing D278; Leybourne: *Bib. H.,* English Books, 4to, 135; Clark: Wing C4558; Crowne: Wing C7393.

35. Leybourne: Wing L1935; Walgrave: Arber, *The Term Catalogues,* I, p. 301; Twysden: Wing T3548; Partridge: Wing P631.

36. H. *Diary B,* p. 90; Besson: *Bib. H.,* Libri Latini, folio, 286.

37. Bouvelles: *Bib. H.,* Libri Latini, 8vo, 362; Psellus: *Bib. H.,* Libri Latini, 12mo, 243; Rahn: *Bib. H.,* English Books, 4to, 108; Froidmont: *Bib. H.,* Libri Latini, 4to, 110; Welper: *Bib. H.,* Libri Latini, 8vo, 306; Cardan: *Bib. H.,* Libri Latini, 8vo, 291; Pico: *Bib. H.,* Libri Latini, folio, 137.

38. H. *Diary C,* p. 224.

39. The *Bib. H.* cites medical treatises by Cardan: Libri Latini, 8vo, 290; folio, 136; 4to, 183; Fragoso: *Bib. H.,* Libri Latini, 8vo, 226; Hughes: *Bib. H.,* English Books, 12mo, 82.

40. H. *Diary C,* p. 219; Gorges: *Bib. H.,* English Books, 4to, 32; Hartlib: Wing H1000.

41. Plomer, *Dictionary . . . 1668 to 1725,* p. 191; Dunton, op. cit., I, p. 256.

42. Rostenberg, *Literary, Political . . . Printing and Bookselling in England*, I, p. 158, II, p. 305.
43. Duries: *Bib. H.*, English Books, 12mo, 44.
44. Malpighi: Wing M342B, 343, 344; Dionysius Perigetes: Wing D1522; H. *Diary A*, pp. 168, 199.
45. H. *Diary A*, pp. 51, 72, 75; Tycho: *Bib. H.*, Libri Latini, folio, 221.
46. Mersenne: *Bib. H.*, Libri Latini, folio, 246; Scheiner: *Bib. H.*, Libri Latini, folio, 195; Laet: *Bib. H.*, Libri Latini, 8vo, 323; Gunther: *Bib. H.*, Libri Latini, 8vo, 234; Archimedes: *Bib. H.*, Libri Latini, folio, 279; Anderson: Wing A3106.
47. H. *Diary A*, pp. 78, 188; Charamont: *Bib. H.*, Libri Latini, 4to, 435, 560.
48. H. *Diary A*, p. 199.
49. Kepler, *Selenographia:* H. *Diary A*, p. 212; *De Novis Stellis: Bib. H.*, Libri Latini, 4to, 486; Snell: *Bib. H.*, Libri Latini, 4to, 610.
50. H. *Diary A*, pp. 106, 147, 153, 324, 456; H. *Diary C*, p. 107; Speidell: *Bib. H.*, English Books, 4to, 116; Dee, Euclid: *Bib. H.*, English Books, folio, 94; Briggs: *STC* 3740; Schoner: *Bib. H.*, Libri Latini, folio, 277.
51. Plomer, *Dictionary . . . 1641 to 1667*, p. 143; H. *Diary A*, p. 181; H. *Diary C*, p. 181; Scot: *Bib. H.*, English Books, 4to, 59; Newton: *Bib. H.*, English Books, 4to, 134; Perkins: Wing P1559; Maynwaring: Wing M551.

CHAPTER 6. BOOK AUCTIONS AND AUCTIONEERS

1. Seaman Sale: Wing S2173; Lawler, *Book Auctions in Seventeenth Century England*, xxiii, 3ff. Since Lawler will be one of the principal sources for this chapter, it will henceforth be cited only as Lawler.
2. H. *Diary A*, 155; for Hooke's "List of Catalogues of Book Sales Held between August 1686 and August 1689," see Gunther, *Early Science in Oxford*, X.
3. Lawler, p. 10; Plomer, *Dictionary . . . 1641 to 1667*, p. 33.
4. Lawler, pp. 2f.
5. Eliot Bible: *Bib. H.*, Libri Latini, 4to, 311.
6. - 10. Lawler, pp. 7-10, 20-24; Wing K422, G942, P167, C1785.

11. Plomer, *Dictionary* . . . *1668 to 1725*, p. 99; Sir Robert Moray to Oldenburg, 11 October 1665, Boyle to Oldenburg, ca. 18 October 1665, R. Davies to Oldenburg, 11 December 1665, in Oldenburg, *Correspondence*, nos. 432, 441, 471.

12. Wing D426-D428.

13. - 15. Lawler, pp. 13-15, 26-28.

16. H. *Diary A*, pp. 412, 420; Kircher: *Bib. H.*, Libri Latini, folio, 46; Fromond: *Bib. H.*, Libri Latini, 4to, 110; Caneparius: *Bib. H.*, Libri Latini, 4to, 284.

17. Lawler, p. 45.

18. Plomer, *Dictionary* . . . *1668 to 1725*, p. 217; Lawler, p. 99.

19. Seaman: Wing S2179; Thompson: Wing T1031.

20. Lawler, xxx; James H. Hanford, *A Milton Handbook* (New York: Crofts, 1936), pp. 47, 57f (quotes Richardson but makes no reference to Millington).

21. Dunton, *Life and Errors*, I, p. 235.

22. Hooke, "List of Catalogues of Book Sales Held between August 1686 and August 1689."

23. Dunton, op. cit., I, p. 235.

24. Quoted in Lawler, p. xxxi; H. *Diary A*, p. 390.

25. - 34. Lawler, pp. 87, 46, 99; 52, 97, 62, 69, 88, 99, 110, 105.

35. Hooke, "List of Catalogues of Book Sales Held between August 1686 and August 1689;" Lawler, pp. xxxiii, 107.

36. H. *Diary B*, p. 251; H. *Diary C*, 107, 112, 116, 163, 169; Glisson (2 works): *Bib. H.*, Libri Latini, 4to, 193, 194; Vitruvius (High Dutch): *Bib. H.*, Libri Latini, folio, 293; Linschoten: *Bib. H.*, Libri Latini, folio; Denis: *Bib. H.*, Libri Latini, 12mo, 30; Marsham: *Bib. H.*, 4to, 31.

37. H. *Diary B*, p. 109.

38. Dunton, op. cit., I, p. 210; Holwell: Wing H2521; Kendal: Wing K281A; Everard: Wing E3543; Baudier: Wing B1165; Newton: Wing N1074.

39. Hooke, "List of Catalogues of Book Sales Held between August 1686 and August 1689."

40. H. *Diary B*, pp. 91, 92, 104, 105, 107, 108, 110, 122, 129, 142, 147; Dee, *Monas: Bib. H.*, Libri Latini, 8vo, 106; Hippocrates, *Aphorisms: Bib. H.*, 12mo, 158-160; Simon: *Bib. H.*, English Books, 4to, 1; Delle Valle: *Bib. H.*, Libri Latini, 12mo, 34 and English Books, folio, 40; Golius: H. *Diary B*, p. 147.

41. H. *Diary C,* pp. 239, 240, 251; Plomer, *Dictionary . . . 1668 to 1725,* p. 160.
42. H. *Diary C,* p. 251; Martinus, *China: Bib. H.,* Libri Latini, 8vo, 47; Gesner: *Bib. H.,* Libri Latini, folio, 145; Zwinger: *Bib. H.,* Libri Latini, folio, 36 and 4to, 168; Pitiscus: *Bib. H.,* English Books, 4to, 123; Bullialdus: *Bib. H.,* Libri Latini, folio, 183 and 4to, 573.
43. Plomer, *Dictionary . . . 1668 to 1725,* p. 298; Lawler, p. 170.
44. Herñandes: *Bib. H.,* Libri Latini, folio, 117; Cornutus: *Bib. H.,* Libri Latini, 4to, 224; Porta: *Bib. H.,* Appendix, Libri Miscellanei, 4to, 34; Zahn: *Bib. H.,* Libri Latini, folio, 273; H. *Diary B,* pp. 112, 116, 117, 119, 121, 122, 126, 127.
45. H. *Diary B,* p. 164.
46. Plomer, *Dictionary . . . 1668 to 1725,* pp. 58, 257, 269; Hooke, "List of Catalogues of Book Sales Held between August 1686 and August 1689."

CHAPTER 7. DOMESTIC CIRCULATION -
EXPORTATION AND IMPORTATION OF
FOREIGN BOOKS

The majority of the notes in this chapter are based on the Oldenburg *Correspondence.* Only the numbers of the letters are cited below for that source.

1. Oldenburg to Boyle, October 1661, no. 241; H. *Diary A,* pp. 90, 127, 132, 170.
2. Wallis to Oldenburg, 23 April 1668; 12 May 1666; 11 August 1666; 18 August 1666; 12 February 1666/67, nos. 512, 521, 557, 561, 609; Collins to Pell, 4 December (n.y.), in Rigaud, *Correspondence,* I, p. 119.
3. Henry Powle to Oldenburg, September 1666; Richard Reed to Oldenburg, 10 February 1667/68 and 21 February 1669/70; Lister to Oldenburg, 16 January 1670/71; Oldenburg to Lister, 16 January 1673/74, nos. 57, 774, 1400, 2429; H. *Diary B,* p. 134.
4. Oldenburg to Boyle, 13 October 1664, no. 336.
5. Boyle to Oldenburg, 23 December 1665, no. 474.
6. Sir Robert Moray to Oldenburg, 19 October 1665, no. 438.

7. David Lidman, *Treasury of Stamps* (New York: Abrams, 1975), p. 42.
8. Justel to Oldenburg, 16 May 1666, no. 526.
9. Oldenburg to Boyle, 10 December 1667; Oldenburg to Sluse, 16 July 1669, nos. 720, 245.
10. Oldenburg to Sluse, 19 June 1668; Sluse to Oldenburg, 14 October 1668, nos. 891, 1977.
11. Collins to Oldenburg, 15 March 1669/70, no. 1424.
12. Collins to Oldenburg, ca. 10 March 1670/71, no. 1449.
13. Oldenburg to Boyle, 24 September 1667 and 31 October 1667; Oldenburg to Pierre Carcavy, 2 January 1667/68; Justel to Oldenburg, 12 February 1667/68, nos. 735, 744, 778.
14. Justel to Oldenburg, 20 May 1668, no. 865.
15. Oldenburg to Huygens, 15 June 1668 and 5 July 1668; Justel to Oldenburg, February 1667/68; Matthias Paisen to Oldenburg, July 1670; Malpighi to Oldenburg, 10 November 1670 and 15 July 1670, nos. 1215, 1230, 768, 1490, 1547, 1488.
16. Pierre Petit to Oldenburg, 3 October 1660, no. 225.
17. Justel to Oldenburg, 20 March 1666/67 and 23 January 1668/69; Sir John Dodington to Oldenburg, 13 February 1670/71, nos. 622, 1084, 1591.
18. Pardies to Oldenburg, 8 June 1672, no. 1988.
19. Oldenburg to Hevelius, 18 March 1671/72; Henshaw to Oldenburg, 12 December 1672, nos. 1924, 2105.
20. Justel to Oldenburg, 15 July 1668, no. 919.
21. Pardies to Oldenburg, 10 October 1671, no. 1988.
22. Oldenburg to Paisen, 18 October 1669, no. 305.
23. Winthrop to Oldenburg, November 1668; Oldenburg to Winthrop, 11 April 1671, nos. 1005, 1675.
24. Oldenburg to Jacob Sachs à Lewenheimb, 22 December 1671; Martin Vogel to Oldenburg, 13 August 1672, nos. 1845, 2048.
25. Oldenburg to Leibniz, 24 April 1671, no. 1685.
26. Moray to Oldenburg, 10 October 1665, no. 431.
27. Oldenburg to Malpighi, 4 August 1669; Collins to Oldenburg, ca. 12 September 1669, nos. 1265, 1283.
28. Malpighi to Oldenburg, 15 April 1670, no. 1450.
29. Rostenberg, *Literary, Political, Scientific, Religious and Legal Publishing, Printing and Bookselling in England, 1551-1700*, II, pp. 281ff.
30. H. *Diary B*, pp. 116, 249.

31. H. *Diary B,* pp. 84, 151, 161, 189; Leclerc: *Bib. H.,* Libri Latini, 12mo, 120; *Journal des Sçavans: Bib. H.,* 12mo, 115.
32. Darrell: Wing D270; Tachard: H. *Diary B,* p. 86; Baillet: *Bib. H.,* Libri Latini, 8vo, 116.
33. H. *Diary C,* pp. 242, 243, 259, 265; Davity: *Bib. H.,* Libri Latini, 12mo, 38.
34. Boyle to Oldenburg, 15 December 1665; Oldenburg to Boyle, 30 December 1665, nos. 474, 476.
35. Boyle to Oldenburg, 29 August 1665; Oldenburg to Boyle, 16 January 1665/66, nos. 401, 482.
36. Justel to Oldenburg, September 1668; Sluse to Oldenburg, 25 February 1668/69, nos. 956, 1119.
37. Rostenberg, op. cit., II, p. 310.
38. Magalotti to Oldenburg, 16 June 1668; Vogel to Oldenburg, 8 January 1669/70 and 28 February 1672/73; Paisen to Oldenburg, ca. 10 January 1668/69, nos. 887, 1361, 2170, 1071.
39. Paisen to Oldenburg, 27 November 1669, no. 1329.
40. Winthrop to Oldenburg, 12 November 1668, no. 1005.
41. Oldenburg to Spinoza, 28 April 1665 and September 1665, nos. 371, 406; Duhamel to Oldenburg, 29 November 1672, no. 2103.
42. Rostenberg, op. cit., II, p. 281.
43. Oldenburg to Auzout, 2 January 1668/69, no. 1061.
44. Oldenburg to Boyle, 18 September 1665, no. 412.
45. Rigaud, *Correspondence,* I, p. 186.
46. Oldenburg to Sluse, 16 July 1669 and 14 September 1669, nos. 1245, 1284.
47. Oldenburg to Sluse, 28 April 1671, no. 1687.
48. Malpighi to Oldenburg, 15 April 1670, no. 1450.
49. Oldenburg to Boyle, 29 January 1665/66 and 2 October 1666, nos. 487, 572.
50. Collins to Vernon, 11 March 1672 in Rigaud, *Correspondence,* I, p. 186.
51. Oldenburg to Sir John Finch, 10 April 1666, no. 507.
52. Oldenburg to Boyle, 27 January 1665/66 and 24 December 1667, nos. 492, 735.
53. Witsen to Oldenburg, 10 December 1671; Le Boe Sylvius to Oldenburg, 13 May 1671, nos. 1671, 1698.
54. Winthrop to Oldenburg, 25 September 1672, no. 2071.
55. *Correspondence of Sir Isaac Newton,* III, p. 171.

CHAPTER 8. *THE PHILOSOPHICAL TRANSACTIONS*

Many of the notes in this chapter are based on the Oldenburg *Correspondence.* Only the numbers of the letters are cited below for that source.

1. Birch, *The History of the Royal Society of London,* p. 321.
2. Oldenburg to Boyle, 2 September 1667 and 9 December 1666, nos. 662, 473.
3. *Philosophical Transactions,* 3 July 1665, no. 5.
4. Moray to Oldenburg, 11 October 1665 and 30 October 1665; Boyle to Oldenburg, 28 October 1665, nos. 432, 442, 441.
5. Nos. 442, 441.
6. *Philosophical Transactions,* 6 December 1665, no. 6.
7. Oldenburg to Boyle, 9 December 1665, no. 473.
8. Boyle to Oldenburg, 23 December 1665, no. 474.
9. Oldenburg to Boyle, 30 December 1665 and 24 March 1665, nos. 476, 501.
10. Rostenberg, *Literary, Political, Scientific, Religious, and Legal Publishing, Printing, and Bookselling in England, 1551-1700,* II, p. 4.
11. Oldenburg to Boyle, 10 September 1666, no. 566.
12. Oldenburg to Boyle, 18 September 1668 and 23 October 1666, nos. 568, 579.
13. Oldenburg to Boyle, 25 November 1666, 12 September 1667, 24 September 1667, 17 December 1667, nos. 584, 662, 664, 728.
14. Nos. 662, 664, 728.
15. Beale to Oldenburg, 27 June 1668, no. 893.
16. Oldenburg to Boyle, 5 November 1664, no. 348.
17. Oldenburg to Sir Henry Howard, 27 July 1666, no. 552.
18. Oldenburg to Boyle, 3 December 1667, 17 December 1667, 24 December 1667, nos. 712, 728, 735.
19. Oldenburg to Ercole Zani, 21 January 1669/70; Boyle to Oldenburg, 3 April 1668; Sir John Dodington to Oldenburg, 8 March 1671/72, nos. 1373, 830, 1919.
20. Boyle to Oldenburg, 19 March 1665/66, no. 500.
21. Vogel to Oldenburg, February 1670/71, no. 1638.
22. John Sterpin to Oldenburg, 24 February 1670/71, no. 1638.

23. Oldenburg to Sterpin, 17 April 1671; Hevelius to Oldenburg, 19 November 1668; Denis to Oldenburg, August 1672, nos. 1677, 1015, 2051.
24. Christopher Sand to Oldenburg, 24 January 1672/73 and 28 February 1672/73, nos. 2135, 2171.
25. Nicolaus ab Hoboken to Oldenburg, 29 July 1672, no. 2040.
26. Dodington to Oldenburg, 12 April 1673, no. 1953.
27. Winthrop to Oldenburg, 12 November 1668, no. 1005.
28. Oldenburg to Hevelius, 2 August 1669; Huygens to Oldenburg, 30 March 1672, nos. 1262, 1944.
29. H. *Diary A,* pp. 26, 34, 49, 67, 141, 322; Dodington to Oldenburg, 12 April 1672, no. 1953.

CHAPTER 9. THE COLLECTOR

1. - 3. H. *Diary A,* pp. 70, 111, 318, 449, 453; 276, 278; 125, 168, 275, 313; 263. 8 October 1676: " Sent for by Dr. Diodati from Paris severall books mentioned in Journall des Scavans."
4. Naudé: *Bib. H.,* English Books, 4to, 183; Durie: *Bib H.,* English Books, 12mo, 44; Labbé: *Bib. H.,* Libri Miscellanei, 8vo and 12mo, 49; Lomeier: *Bib. H.,* Libri Miscellanei, 8vo and 12mo, 77; Gallois: *Bib. H.,* Libri Gallici, 8vo and 12mo, 53; *Elzevier Catalogue: Bib. H.,* Libri Latini, 12mo, 82; Simon: H. *Diary B,* p. 192; Van der Linden: *Bib. H.,* Libri Latini, 8vo, 203 and Libri in Albiis, 4to, 30.
5. Borel: *Bib. H.,* Libri Latini, 12mo, 80; *Bibliotheca Oizeliana: Bib. H.,* Libri Latini, 8vo, 104; Sorel: *Bib. H.,* Libri Gallici, 8vo and 12mo, 52; Hyde: *Bib. H.,* Libri Latini, 4to, 614; Sion College Library: *Bib. H.,* Libri Latini, 4to, 613; Grew: *Bib. H.,* English Books, folio, 80; Beughem: *Bib. H.,* Libri in Albiis, 12mo, 6, (the collection also included 3 additional bibliographical tools by Beughem: *Apparatus ad histor. Lit., Bibliographia medica, La France scavante,* Libri in Albiis, 12mo, 5; Libri Latini, 12mo, 81; Libri Latini, 12mo, 122); H. *Diary A,* pp. 88-89.
6. La Caille: H. *Diary B,* p. 175; Almeloveen: *Bib. H.,* Libri Miscellanei, 8vo and 12mo, p. 76; Moxon: H. *Diary A,* p. 339; *Bib. H.,* English Books, 4to, 143.
7. H. *Diary B,* pp. 17, 103, 115, 121, 147.

8. H. *Diary A*, pp. 116, 275.
9. H. *Diary B*, p. 127; Vitruvius: H. *Diary A*, p. 154; Marot: *Bib. H.*, Libri Latini, 4to, 137; Evelyn: *Bib. H.*, English Miscellanies, 8vo. and 12mo, 18.
10. H. *Diary A*, pp. 270, 371, 428; Oughtred: *Bib. H.*, Libri in Albiis, 8vo., 25; Kircher: *Bib. H.*, Libri Latini, folio, 41.
11. - 12. H. *Diary A*, 412, 8; H. *Diary B*, 131, 114, 20, 172; H. *Diary C*, 212, 225; Hevelius: *Bib. H.*, Libri Latini, folio, 202; Della Valle: *Bib. H.*, English Books, folio, 40; Zahn: *Bib. H.*, Libri Latini, folio, 273.
13. H. *Diary A*, pp. 15, 17, 188, 214, 240, 242, 269, 294, 296, 310, 364, 392; H. *Diary C*, p. 242.
14. H. *Diary A*, 396, 71, 251.
15. - 16. H. *Diary A*, pp. 9, 16, 51, 56, 69, 165, 119, 325, 353; Alpinus: *Bib. H.*, Libri Latini, 4to, 221; Le Febure: *Bib. H.*, English Books, 4to, 92; Streete: *Bib. H.*, English Books, 4to, 120, 126; Foster: *Bib. H.*, English Books, 4to, 126; H. *Diary A*, pp. 34, 69, 245, 258, 340, 105, 139, 382.
17. H. *Diary B*, pp. 754, 203; Boyle: *Bib. H.*, English Books, 8vo, 201; Petty: *Bib. H.*, English Books, 12mo, 60; Yonge: *Bib. H.*, English Books, 8vo, 284; Boccone: *Bib. H.*, Libri Latini, 8vo, 240.
18. H. *Diary A*, pp. 312, 60, 317.
19. H. *Diary C*, p. 193. For information about the presentation of the copy of Willis to Bishop Tillotson, the author is highly indebted to the late Jacob Zeitlin of Los Angeles, California.
20. - 23. H. *Diary A*, pp. 288, 313, 447; 10, 41, 51, 11, 45; 365, 138, 29; 357, 151, 441, 352, 46, 176, 160, 278, 355; H. *Diary B*, pp. 119, 147, 6; H. *Diary C*, pp. 387, 296.

CHAPTER 10. ANALYSIS OF THE LIBRARY

1. Copy of *Bibliotheca Hookiana* consulted, courtesy of the British Library.
2. H. *Diary A*, p. 340 and *Bib. H.*, Libri Latini, 8vo, 11.
3. Andreae: *Bib. H.*, Libri Latini, folio, 85; Albumasar: *Bib. H.*, Libri Latini, 4to, 410; Caxton: *Bib. H.*, English Miscellanies, folio, 10; Firmicius: *Bib. H.*, Libri Latini, folio, 204; Frederick R. Goff, *Incunabula in American Libraries* (New York:

Bibliographical Society of America, 1964), nos. A-580, A-359, M-884, F-191.

4. - 6. H. *Diary A,* 175, 179, 278; 5, 348, 308, 416; H. *Diary B,* 92, 119; H. *Diary C,* 232; Waller, ii; Espinasse, *Hooke,* p. 152; De Graaf: *Bib. H.,* Libri Latini, 8vo, 206; *Woemans Boke: Bib. H.,* English Books, 4to, 84; Fernel: *Bib. H.,* Libri Latini, 8vo, 435; Hippocrates: *Bib. H.,* Libri Latini, folio, 106 and 12mo, 158-160; Paracelsus: *Bib. H.,* Libri Latini, folio, 139; Vesalius: *Bib. H.,* Libri Latini, folio, 99 and 12mo, 175; Stensen: *Bib. H.,* Libri Latini, 12mo, 161; Wecker: *Bib. H.,* Libri Latini, 12mo, 197.

7. H. *Diary B,* p. 112; Briggs: *Bib. H.,* Libri Latini, 8vo, 207; Glisson: *Bib. H.,* Libri Latini, 4to, 193 and 12mo, 170; Harvey: *Bib. H.,* Libri Latini, 12mo, 164, 165; Boyle: *Bib. H.,* English Books, 12mo, 84, 8vo, 212, 213, 218, 223, 225 and Libri Latini, 4to, 98; Highmore: *Bib. H.,* Libri Latini, 12mo, 201 and English Books, 8vo, 249; Sydenham: *Bib. H.,* Libri Latini, 8vo, 289; Thruston: *Bib. H.,* Libri Latini, 8vo, 274; Venner: *Bib. H.,* English Books, 4to, 88; Willis: *Bib. H.,* Libri Latini, 4to, 195, 196 and 8vo, 212, 12mo, 210; Schroder: *Bib. H.,* Libri Latini, 4to, 250; *Pharmacopeiae Londini: Bib. H.,* Libri Latini, folio, 102; Willis: *Bib. H.,* Libri Latini, 12mo, 211; H. *Diary B,* pp. 17, 103, 115, 121.

8. Keynes, *Bibliography of . . . Hooke,* nos. 6-7; Hooke: *Bib. H.,* English Books in Quires, folio, 3; Leeuwenhoek: H. *Diary C,* p. 244; Remmelin: *Bib. H.,* Libri Latini, folio, 102; Stackmaier: *Bib. H.,* Libri Latini, 12mo, 162.

9. Waller, iii; H. *Diary A,* pp. 240, 271, 313.

10. H. *Diary A,* p. 70: "Bought of Mr. Aubery Euclid Works Greek and Latin 10sh;" p. 147: "At Wins. Bought of him J. Dees Euclid for which I am to pay him 5sh;" p. 359: "At Auction bought Clavius Euclid 4s.6d.;" p. 388: "At Pitts auction bought Melder Euclid 19d.;" H. *Diary B,* p. 105: "Bought of Hussy Holland Euclid 3d.;" Euclid: *Bib. H.,* Libri Latini, 4to, 463; 12mo, 483; folio, 341; English Books, folio, 94; Newton: *Bib. H.,* Libri Latini, 4to, 542; Hobbes: *Bib. H.,* Libri Latini, 4to, 394, 585; English Books, 8vo, 322; Horrocks: *Bib. H.,* Libri Latini, 4to, 418; Barrow: *Bib. H.,* Libri Latini, 4to, 403 and 8vo, 416; Napier: *Bib. H.,* Libri Latini, 12mo, 229, 4to, 383, 384; English Books, 8vo, 89.

11. H. *Diary A*, p. 29: "Bought Copernicus Tower Hill 2sh.;" p. 45: "With Mr. Blackburne I bought Galileo Dialogue of Motion 3s.6d.;" p. 75: "Bought of Littleberry Ticho Brahe 10sh.;" Copernicus: *Bib. H.*, Libri Latini, folio, 219; Brahe: *Bib. H.*, Libri Latini, folio, 221; Galileo: *Bib. H.*, Libri Latini, 4to, 473, 474, 588; Hevelius: *Bib. H.*, Libri Latini, folio, 197-202; Libri in Albiis, folio, 10-13; Kepler: *Bib. H.*, Libri Latini, folio, 214-215; 4to, 483-489; 8vo, 375-376; Libri Miscellanei, 4to, 28; Peurbach: *Bib. H.*, Libri Latini, 8vo, 387; Ptolemy: *Bib. H.*, Libri Latini, folio, 206, 207; 4to, 343, 344; 8vo, 390; Libri in Albiis, 8vo, 21; Regiomontanus: *Bib. H.*, Libri Latini, 4to, 457, 494; Schoner: *Bib. H.*, Libri Latini, 4to, 449; Streete: *Bib. H.*, English Books, 4to, 120; Wing: *Bib. H.*, English Books, 8vo, 304; Wittie: *Bib. H.*, English Books, 8vo, 275.

12. Bacon: *Bib. H.*, Libri Latini, 8vo, 199; English Books, 12mo, 80; Boyle: *Bib. H.*, English Books, 8vo, 211; Barra: *Bib. H.*, Libri Latini, 12mo, 135; Bartolinus: *Bib. H.*, Libri Latini, 4to, 190; Fromond: *Bib. H.*, Libri Latini, 4to, 110; Perrault: *Bib. H.*, Libri Latini, 12mo, 57.

13. Hall: *Bib. H.*, Libri in Albiis, 4to, 46; Foster: *Bib. H.*, English Books, 4to, 131; Clavius: *Bib. H.*, Libri Latini, folio, 278; Finé: *Bib. H.*, Libri Latini, 4to, 522.

14. H. *Diary A*, p. 176; Gadbury: *Bib. H.*, English Books, 4to, 122; Hecker: *Bib. H.*, Libri Latini, 4to, 450; Kepler: *Bib. H.*, Libri Latini, 4to, 490.

15. Gilbert: *Bib. H.*, Libri Latini, folio, 81 and 4to, 583; Keill: *Bib. H.*, Libri Latini, 8vo, 475; Borelli: *Bib. H.*, Libri Latini, 4to, 277, 549; Cabei: *Bib. H.*, Libri Latini, folio, 80; Gassendi: *Bib. H.*, Libri Latini, 8vo, 195; Grandami: *Bib. H.*, Libri Latini, 4to, 587; Guericke: *Bib. H.*, Libri Latini, folio, 154; Grimaldi: *Bib. H.*, Libri Latini, 4to, 290; Kircher: *Bib. H.*, Libri Latini, folio, 44, 45; Marchetti: *Bib. H.*, Libri Latini, 4to, 548; Pardies: *Bib. H.*, Libri Latini, 12mo, 240; Viviani: *Bib. H.*, Libri Latini, 4to, 59; Pascal: *Bib. H.*, Libri Latini, 12mo, 137; Boyle: *Bib. H.*, English Books, 8vo, 204, 206, 207, 214-216, 220, 221, 226; Libri in Albiis, 8vo, 12.

16. Barrow: *Bib. H.*, Libri Latini, 4to, 498; Gregory: *Bib. H.*, Libri in Albiis, 8vo, 28; Ango: *Bib. H.*, Libri Latini, 8vo, 256; Albohazen Haly: *Bib. H.*, Libri Latini, folio, 270; Euclid: *Bib. H.*, Libri Latini, 4to, 336; Porta: *Bib. H.*, Libri Latini, 4to, 503.

17. More: *Bib.H.*, Libri Latini, 4to, 533; Galileo: *Bib. H.*, Libri Latini, 8vo, 415; La Hire: *Bib. H.*, Libri Latini, 12mo, 255; Wallis: *Bib. H.*, Libri Latini, 4to, 527, 369; Hall: *Bib. H.*, English Books, 12mo, 62; Besson: *Bib. H.*, Libri Latini, folio, 286; Boeckler: *Bib. H.*, Libri Latini, folio, 299; Neri: *Bib. H.*, Libri Latini, 4to, 84; Schott: *Bib. H.*, Libri Latini, 4to, 364, 361.

18. Hunt: *Bib. H.*, English Books, 8vo, 289; Newton: *Bib. H.*, English Books, 4to, 134 and 8vo, 301; Primate: *Bib. H.*, English Books, 8vo, 308; Leybourne: *Bib. H.*, English Books, 4to, 135 and English Miscellanies, folio, 47.

19. Bacon: *Bib. H.*, Libri Latini, 12mo, 214; Badcocke: *Bib. H.*, English Books, 8vo, 165; Digby: *Bib. H.*, English Books, 8vo, 279; Agrippa: *Bib. H.*, Libri Latini, 4to, 306; Barba: *Bib. H.*, English Books, 8vo, 257; Croll: *Bib. H.*, Libri Latini, 4to, 240; Fludd: *Bib. H.*, Libri Latini, folio, 303, 305 and 4to, 590; Geber: *Bib. H.*, Libri Latini, 4to, 230; Lull: *Bib. H.*, Libri Latini, 8vo, 324, 325, 448; Menzel: *Bib. H.*, Libri Latini, 12mo, 219; Wedel: *Bib. H.*, Libri Latini, 12mo, 206; Boyle: *Bib. H.*, English Books, 8vo, 201, 205.

20. More: *Bib. H.*, English Books, 8vo, 10; Naudé: *Bib. H.*, English Books, 8vo, 30, 184; Scot: *Bib. H.*, English Books, 4to, 59; Trithemius: *Bib. H.*, Libri Latini, 4to, 15; Cardan: *Bib. H.*, Libri Latini, 4to, 181; Fontenelle: *Bib. H.*, English Books, 8vo, 36; Lavater: *Bib. H.*, Libri Latini, 4to, 302; Porta: *Bib. H.*, Libri Miscellanei, 8vo, 139.

21. H. *Diary B*, p. 119; Belon: *Bib. H.*, Libri Gallici, 4to, 5 and Libri Latini, 8vo, 229; Bonani: *Bib. H.*, Libri Latini, 4to, 213; Godaert: *Bib. H.*, English Books, 4to, 89; Lister: *Bib. H.*, Libri Latini, 4to, 215, 255; Pitsfield: *Bib. H.*, English Books, folio, 86; Willughby: *Bib. H.*, English Books, folio, 87.

22. H. *Diary A*, pp. 19, 125, 137, 146; Evelyn: *Bib. H.*, English Books, folio, 129 and 8vo, 260; Sloane: *Bib. H.*, English Books, folio, 221; Cornutus: *Bib. H.*, Libri Latini, 4to, 224; Hernandes: *Bib. H.*, Libri Latini, folio, 117; L'Ecluse: *Bib. H.*, Libri Latini, folio, 118.

23. H. *Diary A*, pp. 7, 26, 34, 49, 67, 79, 141, 261, 272, 278, 284, 311, 322, 325; H. *Diary B*, p. 154; H. *Diary C*, p. 200; *Philosophical Transactions: Bib. H.*, English Books in Quires, 4to, 2.

24. H. *Diary A,* pp. 160, 168, 189, 278, 325, 364, 370, 407; H. *Diary B,* p. 122; H. *Diary C,* pp. 211, 222, 240; *Journal des Sçavans: Bib. H.,* Libri Latini, 12mo, 115 and Libri in Albiis, 4to, 18.

25. Blegny: *Bib. H.,* Libri Latini, 12mo, 19; Bayle: *Bib. H.,* Libri Latini, 12mo, 12.

26. H. *Diary B,* pp. 184, 161; *Bibliotheque Universelle* (ed. by Leclerc): *Bib. H.,* Libri Latini, 12mo, 120.

27. H. *Diary B,* pp. 96, 102; H. *Diary C,* pp. 210, 239; Martha Ornstein, *The Role of Scientific Societies in the Seventeenth Century* (London: Archon Books, 1963), pp. 203f.; *Acta Eruditorum: Bib. H.,* Libri Latini, 4to, 130 and Libri in Albiis, 4to, 12.

28. H. *Diary A,* p. 388; *Saggi di Naturali Esperienze: Bib. H.,* Libri Latini, folio, 151 and English Books, 4to, 74.

29. *Acta ... Hafniensis: Bib. H.,* Libri Latini, 4to, 187-190.

30. Duhamel: *Bib. H.,* Libri Latini, 4to, 26, 122; Pellisson: *Bib. H.,* English Books, 8vo, 32; Sturm: *Bib. H.,* Libri Latini, 4to, 105 and Libri in Albiis, 4to, 57.

31. H. *Diary A,* pp. 67, 137, 141, 101, 154, 245, 251, 291; Bacon: *Bib. H.,* Libri Latini, 4to, 506; Evelyn (trans. of Freard de Chambray): *Bib. H.,* English Books, folio, 109; Boyle: *Bib. H.,* English Books, 8vo, 210; Dugdale: *Bib. H.,* English Books, folio, 30; Sanderson: *Bib. H.,* English Books, folio, 106; Bosse: *Bib. H.,* Libri Latini, 8vo, 441, 444; Leonardo da Vinci: *Bib. H.,* Libri Latini, folio, 297; Marot: *Bib. H.,* Libri Latini, 4to, 131; Vitruvius: *Bib. H.,* Libri Latini, folio, 292-294; Vasari: *Bib. H.,* Libri Italici, 4to, 9, 10.

32. H. *Diary A,* p. 294.

33. Butler: *Bib. H.,* English Books, 4to, 140; Holder: *Bib. H.,* English Books, 8vo, 228; Lock: *Bib. H.,* English Books, 4to, 49; Simpson: *Bib. H.,* English Books, 8vo, 329; Descartes: *Bib. H.,* Libri Latini, 4to, 102.

34. Keynes, *Bibliography of ... Hooke,* no. 16.

35. H. *Diary A,* p. 65.

36. H. *Diary B,* p. 75; H. *Diary C,* p. 210; Burnet: *Bib. H.,* English Books, folio, 133; Evelyn: *Bib. H.,* English Books, 8vo, 197; Plot: *Bib. H.,* English Books in Quires, folio, 4-6; Whiston: *Bib. H.,* English Books, 8vo, 200; Woodward: *Bib. H.,* English Books, 8vo, 199; Ittig: *Bib. H.,* Libri Latini, 8vo, 185;

Bushnell, Maynwaring, and Perkins: H. *Diary A*, p. 181; Blagrave: *Bib. H.*, English Books, 4to, 132; Evelyn: *Bib. H.*, English Books, 8vo, 153; Molloy: *Bib. H.*, English Books, 8vo, 93; Besson: *Bib. H.*, Libri Latini, 4to, 608; Galileo: *Bib. H.*, Libri Latini, 4to, 392.

37. Brome: H. *Diary A*, p. 212; Moxon: H. *Diary A*, p. 276.
38. Carpenter: *Bib. H.*, English Books, 4to, 40; Gordon: *Bib. H.*, English Books, 8vo, 23; Gore: *Bib. H.*, Libri Latini, 8vo, 78; Baudrant: *Bib. H.*, Libri Latini, folio, 22; Labbé: *Bib. H.*, Libri in Albiis, 8vo, 3; Pomponius Mela: *Bib. H.*, Libri Latini, 4to, 85 and 12mo, 14; English Books, 4to, 4; Hues: *Bib. H.*, Libri Latini, 8vo, 381; Sanson: *Bib. H.*, Libri in Albiis, 8vo, 12; Varenius: *Bib. H.*, Libri Latini, 12mo, 15; English Books, folio, 8.
39. Maps and Atlases: H. *Diary A*, pp. 9, 35, 135, 143, 307, 453; Zeiller: *Bib. H.*, Libri Latini, folio, 32; Ogilby, *Atlas Chinensis: Bib. H.*, English Books, folio, 144; *Atlas Japannensis: Bib. H.*, Libri Latini, folio, 145; *Asia: Bib. H.*, English Books, folio, 141; *Africa: Bib. H.*, English Books, folio, 140; *America: Bib. H.*, English Books, folio, 142; *Britannia: Bib. H.*, English Books, folio, 146.
40. Adams: *Bib. H.*, English Books, folio, 22; Jansson: *Bib. H.*, Libri Latini, folio, 13; Goos: *Bib. H.*, English Books, 4to, 55; Martini: *Bib. H.*, Libri Latini, folio, 14 and 8vo, 47; Seller: *Bib. H.*, English Books, folio, 54.
41. Drake et al.: *Bib. H.*, Libri Latini, 4to, 273; Hakluyt: *Bib. H.*, English Books, folio, 50; Mocquet: *Bib. H.*, Libri Latini, 8vo, 42; Ray: *Bib. H.*, English Books, 8vo, 77.
42. Stow: *Bib. H.*, Libri Latini, 8vo, 53; English Books, 4to, 42; Martin: *Bib. H.*, English Books, 8vo, 80; Wallace: *Bib. H.*, English Books, 8vo, 70.
43. Ray: *Bib. H.*, English Books, 12mo, 47; Guicciardini: *Bib. H.*, Libri Latini, folio, 33; Versailles: *Bib. H.*, English Books, 12mo, 14; Brunel: *Bib. H.*, Libri Miscellanei, folio, 25; Fiston: *Bib. H.*, English Books, 4to, 41; Lassels: *Bib. H.*, Libri Miscellanei, folio, 34 and Libri Gallici, 8vo, 27.
44. Debes: *Bib. H.*, English Books, 12mo, 47; Olaus Magnus: *Bib. H.*, Libri Latini, folio, 58 and 12mo, 21; Scheffer: *Bib. H.*, English Books, folio, 16; Pighius: *Bib. H.*, Libri Latini, 8vo, 51;

Collins: *Bib. H.*, English Books, 8vo, 73; Chevalier: *Bib. H.*, English Books, 8vo, 48.

45. Sandys: *Bib. H.*, English Books, folio, 41; Rycaut: *Bib. H.*, English Books, folio, 32; Withers: *Bib. H.*, English Books, 8vo, 71; Thevenot: *Bib. H.*, Libri Latini, 4to, 274; Nicolay: *Bib. H.*, Libri Latini, 4to, 272; Coronelli: *Bib. H.*, Libri Latini, 4to, 60.

46. Fryer: *Bib. H.*, English Books, folio, 45 and English Books in Quires, folio, 1; Knox: *Bib. H.*, English Books, folio, 34; English Books in Quires, folio, 2; English Miscellanies, folio, 6.

47. Herbert: *Bib. H.*, English Books, folio, 43; *Adventures: Bib. H.*, English Books, 8vo, 63; Jobson: *Bib. H.*, English Books, 4to, 29; Greaves: *Bib. H.*, English Books, 8vo, 89; Wansleb: *Bib. H.*, English Books, 8vo, 72; Lobo: *Bib. H.*, English Books, 8vo, 46; Benjamin of Tudela: *Bib. H.*, Libri Latini, 8vo, 41 and Libri Miscellanei, 8vo, 162.

48. Mendoza: *Bib. H.*, English Books, 4to, 36; Samedo: *Bib. H.*, English Books, folio, 14; Le Comte: *Bib. H.*, English Books, 8vo, 84; Kircher: *Bib. H.*, Libri Latini, folio, 41, 42; Varenius: *Bib. H.*, English Books, 8vo, 67; La Loubere: *Bib. H.*, English Books, folio, 38; Tachard: H. *Diary B*, pp. 86, 90.

49. Hawkins: *Bib. H.*, English Books, folio, 49; Narborough: *Bib. H.*, English Books, 8vo, 79; Queiros: *Bib. H.*, English Books, 4to, 25.

50. H. *Diary A*, p. 416; H. *Diary B*, p. 78; H. *Diary C*, pp. 195, 201.

51. Grynaeus: *Bib. H.*, Libri Latini, folio, 25; Peter Martyr: *Bib. H.*, Libri Latini, 8vo, 32; Laet: *Bib. H.*, Libri Latini, folio, 26; Esquemeling: *Bib. H.*, English Books, 4to, 38; Libri in Albiis, 4to, 32.

52. Morton: *Bib. H.*, English Books, 4to, 29; Josselyn: *Bib. H.*, English Books, 8vo, 83, 250; Gorges: *Bib. H.*, English Books, 4to, 32; Eliot, *New Testament: Bib. H.*, Libri Latini, 4to, 311; Charles Evans, *American Bibliography*, 15 vols., (New York: Smith-American Antiquarian Society, 1941-1962), I, p. 64; Eliot, *Indian Grammar: Bib. H.*, Libri Latini, 4to, 311; Evans, op. cit., I, 106.

53. Smith: *Bib. H.*, English Books, folio, 37; Williams: *Bib. H.*, English Books, 4to, 30.

54. Thevet: *Bib. H.*, Libri Latini, 4to, 28; Creux: *Bib. H.*, Libri Latini, 4to, 268; Lescarbot: *Bib. H.*, English Books, 4to, 26;

Hennepin, *Louisianie: Bib. H.,* Libri in Albiis, 12mo, 3; Hennepin, *Voyages: Bib. H.,* English Books, 8vo, 82.
55. Speake: *Bib. H.,* English Books, 8vo, 66; Hickeringill: *Bib. H.,* English Books, 12mo, 12; Rochfort: *Bib. H.,* Libri Latini, 4to, 270; Gage: *Bib. H.,* English Books, 8vo and 12mo, 8.
56. Zarate: *Bib. H.,* English Books, 4to, 27; Pagan: *Bib. H.,* English Books, 8vo, 69; Herñandes: *Bib. H.,* Libri Latini, folio, 117.

Index

Academic journals, books on, 131-133

Alchemy, books on, 24, 25, 29, 42-48, 129-130

Allestry, James, 13, 14, 15, 17, 18, 54, 89, 90, 99, 102, 103

Amsterdam, Holland, 1, 3, 53, 85, 88, 104

Art, books on, 133

Ashmole, Elias, 42, 46; *Theatrum Chymicum*, 42

Aubrey, John, 10, 44

Auctions, xvi, 66-81; principal auction sales: *Bibliotheca Hookiana* (April 1703), xii, xiv, xv, 64, 123, 141-224; Maitland Sales (1689-1690), 79-80; Seaman Sale (1676), 66-68; for principal auctioneers (Cooper, Hussey, Millington, Walford) see under individual names

Barret, Philip, 8, 9, 113

Barrow, Isaac, 2, 88; *Lectiones geometricae*, 3; Euclid, ed., 34; *Lectiones opticae*, 85

Beale, John, 3, 16, 19, 28

Bibles, Psalters, Prayer Books, 39

Bibliography, study of, 115

Bibliotheca Hookiana, xii, xiv, xv, 64, 123, 141-224

Botany and Horticulture, books on, 130-131

Boyle, The Hon. Robert, xiii, xvi, 2, 3, 4, 6, 23, 24, 31, 44, 47, 53, 59, 60, 62, 70, 82, 83, 84, 89, 91-92, 93, 94, 101, 102, 103, 106, 120

Brahe, Tycho, xvi, 53

Brancker, Thomas, 28, 30; *Table of numbers less than one hundred thousand,* 31

Carcavy, Pierre de, 85, 86

Carrier Service, 82-84, 101; Bartlet, 83, 84; Burnhill, 83; Loft, 83; Mills, 83; Moor, 83; Pell, 83

Cartography and Travel, books on, 28, 133-134, 135, 136-39

Charles II, King of England, 2, 4, 84, 90

Collegium Naturae Curiosorum, 3, 89

Collins, John, 23, 26, 27, 28, 30, 53, 83, 85, 94, 95, 96, 109-110

Cooper, William, xvi, 42-48, 66, 67, 68, 69, 70, 72, 82, 94; *Catalogue of chymicall books,* 42, 43, 44, 45, 46, 67; *Philosophical epitaph,* 42, 44

Daems (or Dames), Henry, 85, 95

Danzig, Germany (now Poland), 82, 104

Davis, Richard, 31, 53, 54, 70, 71, 100, 101, 102

Descartes, René, xvi, 27, 95, 133; *Compendium of musick,* 51, 55; *Epistles,* 55

Digby, Sir Kenelm, 43, 46

Diplomatic corps, 85, 87, 88, 91, 95

Dodington, Sir John, 3, 87, 106, 109, 110

Duck Lane, xii, xv, 49-58; 65, 66, 82, 113; booksellers of: Anderson, 50; Axe, Thomas, 50; Boddington, Nicholas, 50; Coniers, Joshua, 50, 57; Hubbald, Frank,

253